Social Security Systems
in Latin America

Francisco E. Barreto de Oliveira
Editor
IPEA, Brazil

**Published by the Inter-American Development Bank
Distributed by The Johns Hopkins University Press**

Washington, D.C.
1994

The views and opinions expressed in this publication are those of the authors and do not necessarily reflect the official position of the Inter-American Development Bank.

Social Security Systems in Latin America

© Copyright 1994 by the Inter-American Development Bank

1300 New York Avenue, N.W.
Washington, D.C. 20577

Distributed by
The Johns Hopkins University Press
2715 North Charles Street
Baltimore, MD 21218-4319

Library of Congress Catalog Card Number: 94-73306
ISBN: 0-940602-91-1

AUTHORS

Acedo, Clementina
Sociologist, Visiting Fellow, Instituto de Estudios Superiores de Administración (IESA), Venezuela

Beltrão, Kaizô I.
Engineer, Graduate Studies Advisor, Escola Nacional de Ciências Estatísticas/ Instituto Brasileiro de Geografia e Estatística (ENCE/IBGE), and Consultant, Instituto de Pesquisa Econômica Aplicada (IPEA), Brazil

Bour, Juan Luis
Chief Economist, Fundación de Investigaciones Económicas Latinoamericanas (FIEL), Argentina

Cristini, Marcela
Senior Economist, FIEL, Argentina

Delgado, José
Economist, FIEL, Argentina

Márquez, Gustavo
Economist, Associate Professor, IESA, Venezuela

Medici, André Cezar
Social Policies Coordinator and Consultant, Instituto de Estudos do Setor Público/ Fundação do Desenvolvimento Administrativo (IESP/FUNDAP), Brazil

Mujica Riveros, Patricio
Economist, Visiting Professor and Researcher of Economics, School of Economics and Administration, Universidad de Chile

Oliveira, Francisco E. B. de
Engineer, Researcher, Consultant and Coordinator of Social Security Project, IPEA, Brazil

Panadeiros, Mónica
Senior Economist, FIEL, Argentina

Susmel, Nuria
Economist, FIEL, Argentina

FOREWORD

This is the eleventh book of a series published under the Centers for Research in Applied Economics Project sponsored by the Inter-American Development Bank. In keeping with the centers' objective of addressing the major economic and social problems affecting Latin America and the Caribbean, this volume presents social security research in Argentina, Brazil, Chile, and Venezuela.

Latin America and the Caribbean have been Western Hemisphere and Third World leaders in developing social security. In fact, some countries of the region have offered benefit programs to civil servants, the military, and workers in strategic industrial sectors since the end of the last century.

Social security systems today boast relatively broad coverage and offer a long list of benefits. But the region faces many challenges, forcing policymakers to find alternative solutions and possible areas for reform. Insufficient funding and a lack of incentive to improve quality and efficiency often cause social security programs to fall short of their proposed missions. Large deficits, low contribution rates, widespread tax evasion, and increasing insolvency exacerbate the problem. Targeting those segments of the population most urgently in need of social assistance also presents a challenge.

As elsewhere, most social security systems in Latin America have grown out of decisions by influential groups who resist any change that might threaten their privileges. Reforms bear fruit only in the medium and long terms, and further government action and more consensus among targeted populations are needed. This book proposes reforms to help save the region's social security systems.

Flexibility, coverage, and stability over time are essential to successful systems. Social insurance providers should consider participants' socioeconomic status and offer a variety of plans. The aged, poor, and marginalized constitute a high-risk group that necessitates a health insurance scheme that redistributes costs. Communities should agree on efficient and just minimum levels of health care. Competition among public and private health service providers is vital.

Experience in the region shows that giving communities direct control over program resources and results increases program efficiency and that careful targeting of the population improves the efficiency of any social assistance program. All reform efforts must increase public awareness by clearly stating who wins and who loses under any proposed system.

Nohra Rey de Marulanda
Manager
Integration and Regional Programs Department

CONTENTS

CHAPTER ONE

Social Security in Argentina, Brazil, Chile, and Venezuela

Francisco E. Barreto de Oliveira

Any comparative study of several different countries, especially of social services, is beset with difficulties. First, the very concept of social security must be defined. Second, a taxonomy must be developed to permit a consistent, uniform analysis of diagnostic and policy options. Finally and perhaps most importantly, even within a single region countries can have such different social, economic and cultural characteristics that any comparison becomes purely illustrative.

Given these limitations, this book does not undertake a comparative analysis of the existing or proposed systems in each of the countries examined. At most, it aims to present within a general and simplified analytical framework a number of social security problems common to more than one country and specific to each system in other respects. Social security is understood to comprise the full range of social insurance, health and social welfare programs, regardless of their political, administrative, institutional, or economic-financial structure.

Synopsis of the Social Security Systems

Demographic Characteristics

Table 1.1 presents an overview of several demographic variables that are important in the design and function of social security systems.

The total populations of the countries studied differ considerably. Chile, the least populated country, has a population less than 10 percent that of Brazil, which has the largest population. Even between the populations of Argentina and Venezuela and between the latter and Chile, the differences are substantial (64 percent and 49 percent more, respectively).

The size of each population obviously produces different social security systems. Other important factors include the economically active population, which

Table 1.1. Selected Demographic Characteristics, 1990

	Argentina	Brazil	Chile	Venezuela
Total population[1]	32.3	150.4	13.2	19.7
Urban population (%)	86.0	75.0	86.0	84.0
EAP[2]	12.3	63.0	4.9	7.1
Percentage of population over 65 yrs. old	9.1	4.4	5.9	3.5
TFR[3]	2.8	3.2	2.5	3.6
Infant mortality[4]	29.0	57.0	17.0	34.0
Life expectancy (in years)				
Men	68	63	69	70
Women	78	69	76	77

Source: World Bank, World Development Report, 1992.
Notes: [1] Millions of residents.
[2] Economically active population in millions.
[3] Total fertility rate = children per woman of child-bearing age.
[4] Per 1,000 live births.

represents roughly 37 percent of the total population of each country (except in Brazil, where it is a little more than 40 percent); the wide variation in the proportion of population over 65 years old, primarily between Argentina (9.1 percent) and Venezuela (3.5 percent); and the high rate of infant mortality in Brazil, which is more than three times higher than in Chile, which has the lowest rate of the four countries (17 percent).

Socioeconomic Factors

Table 1.2 presents a number of socioeconomic features, which, because they reflect on the age and health of the populations under study, are potentially relevant to the study of the social security systems.

Brazil not only has a larger economy than the other countries, but it also has the largest volume of exports, although they represent scarcely 7.5 percent of gross domestic product (GDP), unlike the other countries studied. In the other countries, exports are concentrated in a smaller number of products, especially in Chile and Venezuela. In 1990, Chilean exports of copper and its derivatives represented 47 percent of the total, while in Venezuela oil exports accounted for 72 percent of the total.

Per capita income in the four countries is quite similar. It is analyzed along with other socioeconomic indicators such as income distribution, which appears to be better in Venezuela and worse in Argentina, Chile and Brazil, in that order. The 1980 Gini coefficient for Chile was not available when this study was prepared, but in three of the countries at least, income distribution worsened in the 1980-89 period.

Finally, Brazil's low literacy rate and its high average rate of annual infla-

Table 1.2. Socioeconomic Characteristics, 1990

	Argentina	Brazil	Chile	Venezuela
Gross domestic product (GDP)				
(Billions of US$)	93.3	414.1	27.8	48.3
Per capita income (US$)	2,370	2,680	1,940	2,560
Gini coefficient[1]				
1980	0.41	0.59	—	0.43
1989	0.48	0.63	0.57	0.44
Open unemployment (% of EAP)[2]	7.4	4.3	6.5	10.5
EAP wage spread (% by quintile)[3]				
1st quintile	—	2.34	—	4.70
2nd quintile	—	5.70	—	9.20
3th quintile	—	10.70	—	14.00
4th quintile	—	18.60	—	21.50
5th quintile	—	62.60	—	50.60
Literacy rate				
(% of population over 15 years of age)	95	81	93	88
Exports/GDP (%)	13.2	7.5	30.9	35.7
Balance of payments	1,789	-395	-2,983	9,221
Average rate of inflation (1980-90)	395.2	284.3	20.5	19.3

Source: World Bank, 1992.
Notes: [1] Pscheropoulos, 1992.
[2] Economically active population.
[3] The first quintile represents the lowest-income group; the fifth, the highest.

tion place it in a very unfortunate position. Inflation was largely responsible for the disruption of its economy and the concentration of income in the 1980s.

Social Insurance Systems

Table 1.3 presents a summary of the social security systems.

Note the low level of coverage in Venezuela, associated with the high ratio of contributors to passive subscribers typical of a new system (the first law dates from 1966). The new Chilean system, reformed in 1980, is the only one that includes a capitalization system with contributions made exclusively by workers and administered by private entities. The total public deficit of the social insurance system is calculated as the sum (minus nonsubscriber contributions) of the following items: payments to ex-beneficiaries of the old system (i.e., settling the accounts of those entering the new system), benefits paid to nonsubscribers (i.e., those opting to maintain their coverage under the old system), the minimal benefits supplement, and acknowledgment bonds.

Health Care Systems

Unlike the pension system, which in Chile is administered entirely by the private sector, the public sector permanently administers at least part of the health

Table 1.3. Social Insurance Systems, 1992

	Argentina	Brazil	Chile	Venezuela
Spending Indicators				
% of GDP	8.0	4.0	—	0.1
Public social insurance deficit	1.5	—	4.5	—
Coverage (% of EAP)[1]	48.0	71.0	65.0	35.0
Solvency Indicators				
Contributors/Inactive	1.5	2.5	—	17.0
Contributors/Affiliates	—	—	0.6	—
Financial System	Distrib.	Distrib.	Capitaliz.	Distrib.
Wage Contributions				S,O,D[2]
Employee	10.0	9,0	S/O/ 10.0	1.9
(% of total)	(31.0)	(27.1)	D 1.5	(29.0)
Employer	16.0	20.0	—	4.6
(% of total)	(49.0)	(54.3)	—	(71.0)
State	—	—	—	—
(% of total)	(20.0)	(10.2)	—	—
Others	—	—	—	—
(% of total)	—	(8.4)	—	—
Administration	Public	Public	Private	Private

Source: Bour, 1993; Márquez and Acedo, 1993; Mujica Riveros, 1993; and Oliveira et al, 1993.
Notes: [1] Economically active population.
[2] S = Survivor, O=Old-Age, and D=Disability.

Table 1.4. Health Care Systems, 1992

	Argentina	Brazil	Chile	Venezuela
Description of the system	• Public • Social projects (unions)	• Public • Institutional • Private (accredited)	• Public (FONASA) Institutional Elective • Private (ISAPRES)	• Public Social Ins. • Public Ministry of Health
Expenses as % of GDP	2.0 (public) 3.3 (soc. projec.)	2.3 (Co-payment not included)	3.0	1.0
Contributions				
Employee, wage-based	8.0	30% of the	7.0	2.10
Employer, wage-based	6.0	health care	—	5.15
State	Supplement	amount	—	—
Administration	• Public • Unions	Public International: Private Outpatient: Public	Mixed	Public
Co-payment	Social Proj.: Yes Public: No	No	Yes	No

Source: Author's elaboration.

Table 1.5. Social Welfare System Assistance Programs, 1992

	Argentina	Brazil	Chile	Venezuela
Types of assistance	• Family • Financial • Benefits • Marriage benefit • Funeral assistance (FGTS) • Maternity wage • Unemployment insurance • (FGTS)	• Life pension allowances • Unemployment compensation assistance • Unemployment insurance	• Family • Old-age • Disability • Maternity • Family assistance assistance • Unemployment insurance	• Maternity allowances • Welfare pensions • Funeral • Family wage
Financing	Specific contributions	Specific contributions Social Ins. contributions	Specific contributions	Specific contributions Social Ins. contributions

Source: Author's calculations.

care system in the four countries. Table 1.4 summarizes the four health care systems.

Social Welfare Systems

Table 1.5 presents a general analysis of each country's welfare program, including a summary of the types of social assistance offered and the means of financing used to pay for the programs.

Diagnosis

This chapter aims to provide a brief diagnosis of the major problems, both common and specific, that the countries have experienced in their social security, health care and social welfare systems.

Although a problem is common to more than one country, its relative importance in their decision-making processes might be entirely different. Social and political factors specific to each country lead to different perceptions of variables contributing to social security problems and, therefore, to very different courses of action. Every effort was made to consider the diagnosis presented in the study of each country, but there is always the risk that the summary's essential simplifications and reductions will give insufficient weight to some variable. In much the same way, problems considered specific to each country are sometimes encountered in others as well.

Table 1.6. Social Insurance Diagnosis

Common problems	Argentina	Brazil	Chile	Venezuela
Falling contributor/ beneficiary ratio	1.33[1]	1.5[1]	—	5.0[1]
Growing insolvency	yes	yes	—	yes
Contribution evasion	yes	yes	—	—
Climbing rates	yes	yes	—	yes
Lack of transparency	yes	yes	yes	yes
Incomplete informal sector coverage	yes	yes	yes	yes

Specific problems	Argentina	Brazil	Chile	Venezuela
	Nonprovision of benefits. Demand for benefits not tied to contributions levels (wages). High level of included wages.	Years of service not equitable. Shared costs social insurance/welfare. High replacement (benef./health). Lack of an adjustment clause.	Growth of demand exceeds growth in the number of active and eligible participants.	General structure of the organization. Poor investment structure. Use of funds for medical care.

Source: Author's calculations.
Notes: [1] Estimated ratios for the year 2015.
[2] Estimated ratios for the year 2030.

Diagnosis of the Social Security Systems

Table 1.6 presents a diagnostic summary of the social insurance systems, indicating the common and specific problems of each country.

A reduction in the contributors/beneficiaries ratio has a direct impact on the system's ability to finance its operations on a fee-for-service basis (hereafter referred to as pay-as-you-go financing). The Venezuelan system reduced the ratio the most, cutting active contributors from 17 to 5 for each beneficiary.

Insolvency is a growing problem in all the countries except Chile, which has a capitalization system with predefined contributions. Evasion of contribution payments is a limited problem in Argentina and Brazil. This is not the case for complexity (*i.e.,* the public's difficulty with the system in terms of its organization and operation) and the difficulty of extending coverage to the informal sectors, which are common to all four countries.

Health Care Systems

Table 1.7 presents a summary of the major problems, both common and specific, of the four health care systems.

Table 1.7. Health Care Diagnosis

Common problems	Argentina	Brazil	Chile	Venezuela
Lack of transparency	yes	yes	yes	yes
Incompetent management	yes	yes	yes	yes
Poor quality services	yes	yes	yes	yes
Deficit	yes	—	no	yes
Inappropriate quality and efficiency incentives	yes	yes	yes	yes
Specific problems	Social projects: Lack of competition among insurers (unions). Climbing rates.	Inadequate social control.	Public: Inadequate infrastructure investments. Inflexible health plans. Private: Lack of equity in benefit distribution. Discrimination against high-risk groups. Deficiencies.	

Source: Author's calculations.

Welfare Systems

Lack of focus is common to the social welfare systems of the four countries. Even in countries where welfare benefits are distributed to a well-defined and relatively well-controlled public as in Brazil and Chile, segments of the poor population are inadequately served while other low-priority groups receive benefits to which they are not entitled. This is due to the lack of mechanisms for monitoring, exercising social control and evaluating the effectiveness of the welfare programs.

Although there are no quantitative data for welfare programs that encourage the distribution of in-kind goods and services, there is a strong impression that these programs are subject to even greater abuses than those that provide cash benefits.[1]

---

[1] The National Milk Program *(Programa Nacional de Leche)* and various "coupon" systems (repairs, food, transportation, etc.) in Brazil have proven ineffective. The welfare programs organized by the LBA *(Legião Brasileira de Assistência)* were even investigated by Congress and the Federal Police.

Table 1.8. References for Social Insurance Reform Proposals

Pillar	Administrator	Obligatory	Benefit	System
1st	Public	Yes	Minimal Defined	Distribution
2nd	Public	Yes	Proportional to	
	Private	No	contributions	Indiv. capitaliz.
			Defined cont.	Collect. capitaliz.
			Defined benef.	
3rd	Private	No	—	Capitalization

Source: Author's calculations.

Reform Proposals

Social Insurance

Although the details of the reform proposals differ, a set of conceptual references common to all can be clearly identified. These references are diagrammed in Table 1.8.

The basic framework for all the systems rests on three pillars. The first is a compulsory public system with predefined benefits and a guaranteed minimum value, which functions as a pay-as-you-go system.

The second pillar is a system that can be either publicly or privately administered, compulsory or not, that provides benefits in proportion to contributions. If the contributions are predefined, this second pillar necessarily functions as an individual capitalization system, but if the benefits are predefined, the rational alternative is a collective capitalization system.

Taking this model as a reference, it is easy to show that the degree of "mutual interest" of social insurance, defined by the level of the transfers between and within generations, is indicated by the dividing line between the two components. The higher the ceiling of the public system, the more "integral" the first pillar tends to be.

Note that the word "integral" is used here in the sense that the system operates in such a way that various income transfers are effected between different groups of society. There is no guarantee that these transfers will be in the right direction; far from it. The existence of a greater degree of theoretical mutual interest means that, in practice, the system is not extremely unfair: many times, a high incidence of evasion combined with political pressures from powerful groups results in a shrinking number of contributors paying for the privileges of a few.

According to this same line of reasoning, mutual interest does not ensure efficiency. On the contrary, in the economic climate of the developing nations, it is an acknowledged fact that the lack of a clear connection between the value of

Table 1.9. Social Insurance: Project Variables and Restrictions

Reform design variables	Reform restrictions	
Ownership right	Transition	• Recognition of rights
Long-term tability		• Fiscal impact
Equity		• Initial equilibrium
Intergenerational		• Long-term equilibrium
Intragenerational	Political resistance	
Coverage		
Flexibility		

Source: Author's calculations.

the contribution and the value of the benefit is one of the basic motivations for evasion. Thus, in the interest of efficiency, the trend identified in all of the studies is to reduce the first pillar—compulsory, public and integral—as much as possible, leaving more room for the second. The third pillar is basically a private, optional system with a capitalization arrangement.

Even the "Chilean model," which at first glance seems to be an exception, fits this three-pillar framework. The first pillar is the guarantee of minimum benefits for the elderly and the necessary insurance in cases of disability. The second pillar—the system of Pension Fund Administrators (AFPs, *Administradoras de Fondos de Pensión*)—is private and features an individual capitalization system with predefined contributions. The third pillar is typically represented by the complementary, private and optional system of voluntary savings that each participant can capitalize in his own individual account.

The proposals of Argentina and Brazil also fit this model: basic social insurance with a single benefit (Argentina) and with limits up to the equivalent of three "minimum incomes" for old-age and disability benefits. The basic difference is in the second pillar; in Argentina, a compulsory system based on the Chilean model is proposed, while in Brazil the proposed system is private, complementary and completely optional. Apart from the distinctive characteristics of each proposal, there are also several variables and restrictions applicable to social insurance reform, which are discussed below and summarized in Table 1.9. Several variables are considered essential for planning social insurance reforms.

Right of Ownership. Any reform must make clear what the ownership rights of current and future participants are. In other words, in the case of individual capitalization, it must be clearly understood that the funds accrued are unquestionably the property of the participant.

Although at first glance this concept would appear to be self-evident, the inferences to be drawn from it are varied and complex. It must be made clear, for example, that individual assets will to some extent be vulnerable to any type of direct or explicit seizure and no less to inflation. The "price" to be paid for the assets must be made clear, as well as the minimum rates of return. Finally, it must be well understood that the redistribution objectives of certain political sectors are and will remain secondary to the accumulation of reserves.

Even in the basic system of public social insurance, the term "right of ownership" means that the rules of play must be clear and well understood by the public and they must be adhered to despite political pressure. Only in this way can the public systems attract a large segment of the public and have the desired mutual interest, not in terms of theoretical transfers but in terms of a practical economic reality. Moreover, the broad, unrestricted guarantee of the right of ownership is the foundation upon which the second and third pillars of a social insurance system rest; without it, these pillars would simply crumble through lack of credibility.

Long-term Stability. A social insurance system must include self-financing mechanisms to maintain long-term economic and financial equilibrium without accruing liabilities.

This equilibrium is essential for long-term contracts, whether in a pay-as-you-go or a capitalization system. In the former, in which the benefits are generally predefined, all participants must understand the trend of necessary contribution rates based on long-term actuarial projections that are constantly adjusted. Obviously, these rates must be adjusted to each society's ability to pay.

In capitalization systems, especially in those with predefined contributions, the rates used must be compatible with the probable rate of return of long-term investments in the economy. When used to simulate the accumulation of reserves and to calculate probable future benefits, a rate that is too high can prove disappointing and yield benefits considerably less satisfactory than projected.[2]

On the other hand, extremely low rates used in designing social insurance systems with capitalization can require extremely large contributions, which discourages affiliation with the system.

Equity. The glaring social inequities characteristic of Latin American societies are also reflected in the social insurance systems. In fact, it is often the case that those who need protection the least get the most from the system, while those who pay a great deal receive very little.

These distortions clearly represent the interests of socioeconomic groups with disproportionate political power. Consequently, equity both between and within generations is crucial to the reform of social insurance systems if greater social justice is an objective.

---

[2] The projected value of the benefits of a capitalized system tends to be fairly sensitive to variations in the rate of capitalization.

Scope. One of the main problems that arise in the reform of a social insurance system is undoubtedly that of expanding its coverage. Many Latin American countries have fairly old, relatively generous systems covering only the so-called formal segment of the work force. It has even been suggested that the very existence of social insurance programs, with contributions deducted from the worker's pay, is one of the primary reasons for the informalization of the labor market.

In any case, designing full-coverage systems is perhaps the chief technical problem. One possible solution is to offer fairly modest—and, therefore, low-cost—benefit plans, with clearly defined ownership rights and with the advantages of affiliation made very clear to participants.

Chile's experience shows that affiliation incentives must also be financial and that marketing is essential for expanding coverage.[3]

Flexibility. As with any "product," social insurance must also suit the consumers who form its market. Given the economic and social disparities that exist in most Latin American countries, the greatest possible flexibility in benefit plans, costs, and operating procedures is vital. In other words, once the bases of social security are established, each "consumer" must be allowed to choose the social insurance option that is right for him instead of being forced to accept a package that is often inconsistent with his financial means or his preferences.

This principle is not only firmly rooted in welfare theory but can also greatly facilitate "marketing" the system to customers who are not yet covered.

Restrictions

Just as there are basic variables for reform planning, there is also a series of restrictions common to new social insurance systems.

Transition. Perhaps the most serious impediment to the reform of social insurance systems in Latin America is the acknowledgment of rights. In fact, nearly all of the social insurance systems provide for some type of subscriber rights at the time of transition: for those who are already receiving a benefit, this right is unquestionably the continuation of their benefits.[4] For those who are still working, there is also a right to some form of compensation, and only the method of calculating it varies.

Generally, for those still employed, the proposals have in common some form of "acknowledgment bond" equal to the current value of contributions to

---

[3] Marketing in the technical sense of product design, consumer information, sales strategy, and so on.
[4] Clearly, these are lifetime benefits such as old-age and time-of-service pensions. Temporary benefits—to which the beneficiary must have his rights acknowledged until such time as they are terminated—are therefore not included.

date, the value of the benefits to which the subscriber is entitled, or perhaps only a part of those values. This "bond" can take the form of a lump-sum payment or an annuity, depending on which is politically or economically more appropriate.

Acknowledging rights calls attention to the transition's fiscal impact. Obviously, to avoid disequilibrium in the public sector accounts, the need to finance all of the beneficiaries of the old system and the bonds of the new system must be taken into account, both at the start of the transition and so long as there is anyone entitled to benefits or bonds under the old system.

Regardless of the reform proposed, no new charges will be generated for the old system; these liabilities, typical of a pay-as-you-go system, already existed with or without reform. What is often erroneously termed a "social insurance deficit" is, in fact, a means of reflecting this liability in the accounting.

Reforms generally do not have any type of "instantaneous impact" on public finances. What actually happens is a reordering of the financing sources at the "instant" of the change. Potential economic and financial effects occur only with the passage of time, as the number of beneficiaries from the old system decreases and they are replaced by subscribers subject to the new rules.

There are basically two options for financing the transition: through the fiscal budget (*i.e.,* freeing up government assets by privatizing state enterprises) or through some type of joint contribution arrangement whereby contributors to the new system continue financing the old beneficiaries during the transition period. Various combinations of these options, which are nonexclusive, offer a wide range of possible solutions.

In the first option, typical of the Chilean experience, throughout the transition the need exists to generate a fiscal surplus. The Brazilian proposal calls for a combination of freeing up government assets to finance acknowledgment bonds and a joint contribution from new contributors, which decreases with time, to finance the old beneficiaries.

In any case, it is extremely important that the transition occur without upsetting the equilibrium of public finances. Otherwise (and especially if the new system includes partial or total capitalization), it is entirely possible that the government might appropriate social security funds to finance its deficit.

Political Resistance. Most of the social security systems of Latin America are the product not of advance planning but rather of a sequence of political events. The most powerful social groups tend to obtain all sorts of advantages and privileges, and it is not unusual for this to happen at the expense of a large majority of citizens with less political power and, more important, less public visibility. The same forces that work to obtain the privileges also exert enormous political resistance against any type of change not designed to enhance those privileges.

In addition, changes in social insurance tend to produce economic—and possibly political—results only in the medium and the long term. Conversely, the damage that these changes can cause politically and in elections is immedi-

Table 1.10. Health Care Project Variables

• Financing of high-risk groups The elderly, the poor, etc. (group insurance) • Financing of individual insurance Contribution/benefit ratio	• Subsidized demand or subsidized supply • Market regulation Insurers Providers of services

Source: Author's calculations.

ately apparent. While most politicians agree theoretically and generally that changes in the social security system are necessary, few are actually prepared to lend objective support to any reform that runs counter to the established interests.

How can this "political paradox" be overcome? Obviously, there is no definitive answer to this question. Experience shows that the best way to minimize political resistance to social insurance reform is to include it in a more comprehensive package of economic and social reforms. Perhaps only in this way can the negotiations of the political process be raised to a higher plane, thus preventing the adulteration and dilution of technically coherent proposals.

Health Care

Defining a common framework for the various health care proposals for each individual country, as for social insurance, was not possible. But some aspects are crucial to the planning of all such reforms.

Table 1.10 summarizes the major variables used in planning the new health care system. These variables are explored below.

Financing High-risk Groups. Health care for high-risk segments of the population—such as the elderly, the poor and anyone not covered by the system—is problematic for all of the countries studied. Individual insurance coverage is not viable because it would entail high costs because of the degree of risk associated with population segments utterly unable to pay such costs. Some type of collective insurance that redistributes costs so that society in general assumes responsibility for paying, albeit partially, for the health care of these most vulnerable groups is therefore necessary.

Contribution/Benefit Ratio. The question of contributions versus benefits is critical, not only for the planning of social insurance reforms but health care programs. In fact, what is at stake is the concept of mutual interest. In other words, in a totally integral health-care system, there is no correlation between contributions and user benefits. The existing public systems in much of Latin America are of this type.

At the opposite extreme, a health-care system can maintain a strict proportion between what the user contributes and the services he receives. Although in this type of system there may be some form of reciprocity, it is definitely not a integral system in the sense of promoting redistribution. Chile's private social insurance health-care system (ISAPRES, *Instituto de Salud Previsional*) is of this type.

There is a trade-off between mutual interest and efficiency. Thus, as the degree of mutual interest of a health-care system increases, so does the tendency to pay a price in terms of loss of economic efficiency, and vice versa.

The above statement is the result of an empirical observation of how the health-care systems actually operate. To the extent that benefits are unrelated to contributions, the right of ownership is diluted, and an element fundamental to the functioning of the system is lost: user control. Moreover, a nonintegral system can create egregiously unfair situations, but it may be viable for certain social groups.

A proper balance between mutual interest and efficiency seems to be critical in planning the reform of health-care services. It also seems clear that the basic social system must include a minimum health care system, which should also be collective and integral, and supplemented with mechanisms to ensure an appropriate proportion between contributions and benefits.

Subsidized Demand or Subsidized Supply. Given that a certain degree of mutual interest is necessary in the design of health-care systems, which necessarily leads to cross subsidies, a critical question arises: subsidize demand or subsidize supply?

The proposals of Argentina and Brazil fall within demand subsidy. A system of "vouchers" available to all, the value of which is proportional to the actuarial health risk of each individual and that is financed with general resources, would provide coverage for the entire population of the country.[5] Provided with these vouchers, users would join a Health Maintenance Organization (HMO, *Entidad Mantenedora de Salud*), which in exchange for a fixed, per capita amount equal to the value of the individual voucher would agree to provide basic and comprehensive health care to the individual. In theory, the incentive for efficiency would come from the competition between HMOs since the system allows the insured not only to choose freely between the various organizations but also to change HMOs if not satisfied after a minimum period of membership. Moreover, since a given number of users produce a given income—equal to the sum of the vouchers and, therefore, independent of the

---

[5] This description more closely approximates Brazil's proposal for health care reform, although several of the basic points also apply to Argentina's proposal.

quantity and quality of services provided—the HMOs would tend to reduce their costs. Finally, this reduction in costs, which in principle could affect the quality and quantity of services provided, would be counterbalanced by the competition between HMOs.

Equally important to the voucher-and-HMO system, health care providers could reorganize themselves into HMOs, whereupon their incomes would no longer depend on budget allocations. Like other HMOs, their incomes would consist of all the "vouchers" they are able to collect in the market. In this way, competition to provide better services would be fostered between strictly private organizations and public entities functioning within a totally autonomous system.

In Chile, the system is more like health insurance since the benefits are, to some extent, proportional to the contributions (premiums). There is also an entire series of exclusions, which may explain the limited coverage of the system. One possible option might be to create some form of cross subsidy, but apparently this is not being considered in Chile at the moment.

Most of the countries of the region adopted supply subsidy in establishing public, universal health-care systems. In fact, these subsidies, normally granted case-by-case, are replete with deficiencies and distortions. There are no market incentives for efficiency since costs and production are controlled by the bureaucracy, and access to the network of services depends on intricate political processes that usually favor the upper classes.

Market Regulation. Most of the existing systems, and especially the proposed reforms, provide for the participation of a normally broad spectrum of economic, public and private agents. Given the intrinsic nature of the product—health—and the "imperfections" of the market, the problem of regulation and control becomes extremely important. To ensure efficiency, this regulation of "insurers" and health-care providers must maintain a balance between the need to protect the individual and freedom of choice in the market.

Although the countries studied have varying degrees of government control and intervention in the health care field that necessitate fairly dissimilar solutions, the regulatory process must take up the slack left by the economic incentives. Mechanisms must be in place to prevent private agents from "socializing" losses in the event of omission (*i.e.,* the transfer of potential losses to the government). Alternatives such as reinsurance, little known in Latin America, could be considered.

Social Welfare

There seem to be only two basic variables in the design of welfare reforms: social control and focusing.

Social Control

Society can exercise control directly over the results and over the resources allocated to welfare programs. The various country experiences examined indicate that community participation in planning, executing and monitoring programs tends to raise substantially the levels of efficiency and effectiveness.

Social control, as a replacement for or supplement to bureaucratic and administrative controls, appears to have a marked inhibitive effect on abuses and fraud, further discouraging the frequent tendency of program beneficiaries to remain too long on the welfare rolls.

Focusing

Focusing welfare programs is not only a criterion for rationing resources but also, and primarily, a means of achieving greater efficiency. Focusing resources on actions that benefit genuine high-priority groups avoids the dispersion of efforts that has done so much to undermine these programs in Latin America. Given the comparatively greater need of the groups assisted, the results also tend to be more substantial in relative terms.

Conclusions

Each of the four country studies presents the social security problem reasonably. And the proposed reforms in each country appear to be coherent in concept and capable of solving the major problems identified in the diagnostic phase.

The questions, then, are essentially political: How can politicians be convinced to support changes that, although they will result in greater well-being and equity in the medium and the long terms, might cause enormous damage politically in the short term? How can the powerful, active pressure of the established interests of a privileged minority be resisted and the needs of the underprivileged, underrepresented majority be served?

Obviously, there are no easy or immediate answers to these questions. There are preconditions, however, without which the chances of success of any reform are substantially reduced.

First, accurate and objective information must be prepared and disseminated concerning who wins and who loses, how much is lost, and how much is gained under the current system and under each of the proposed options. Heightening public awareness is thus an essential, preparatory stage of any change. Second, a plan for "reforming" the existing system must be developed and carried out. Better mechanisms to detect evasion and fraud—including the improvement and reorganization of the information, audit, and other systems—are the most important objectives of this stage. Public participation and control must also be improved.

Meanwhile, the scope of reform must be properly limited to avoid creating in the public mind the illusion that these measures will solve all of the problems identified. This is a fairly serious risk, especially in view of the political resistance to change, and it can become a significant obstacle when essential structural reforms are introduced.

As in the diagnostic stage, the structural reform stage must include a full-scale campaign to educate the public in general and political leaders in particular about the economic, financial, and operational viability of the proposals, as well as about the respective equity questions. As mentioned above, guaranteeing existing rights is essential for the political success of profound changes in the social security regulations.

As the proposals move through the legislative process, the integrity and coherence of each proposal must be protected, preventing their being broken up into meaningless fragments. Small concessions can often distort the initial proposal, paving the way for rapid and uncontrollable disintegration.

Finally, social security reforms, because of their economic, political and social importance, must necessarily be part of a broader set of reforms, with a clear explanation of the objectives and goals to be attained.

Far-reaching measures presuppose the political power of whoever proposes them: most often, it is the political power of the government. Consequently, one of the essential conditions of social security reform is the existence of a coherent government plan that enjoys broad public and political support. Any reform effort that does not satisfy these conditions tends at the very least to be ineffective and, at worst, to result in a social security system that is less viable and more inequitable than the one it replaced.

Bibliography

Bour, J.L. 1993. *Sistemas de seguridad social en la región: Problemas y alternativas de solución. Argentina.* Working Paper No. 148. Washington, D.C.: Inter-American Development Bank.

ECLA. 1991. *Anuario estadístico de América Latina y el Caribe.* Santiago de Chile: ECLA.

Márquez, G., and C. Acedo. 1993. *El sistema de seguros sociales en Venezuela: Problemas y alternativas de solución.* Working Paper No. 151. Washington, D.C.: Inter-American Development Bank.

Mujica Riveros, P. 1993. *Sistemas de seguridad social: La experiencia chilena.* Working Paper No. 149. Washington, D.C.: Inter-American Development Bank.

Oliveira, F.E.B. *et al.* 1993. *Brazilian Social Security System: Problems and Alternatives.* Working Paper No. 163. Washington, D.C.: Inter-American Development Bank.

Pscheropoulos, G. *et al.* 1992. *Pobreza y distribución del ingreso en América Latina: La historia de los años ochenta.* Regional Studies on Latin America No. 27. Washington, D.C.: BIRF.

———. 1993. *Poverty and Income Distribution in Latin America: The Story of the 1980s.* Washington, D.C.: World Bank.

United Nations Development Programme. 1991. *Human Development Report, 1991.* New York: Oxford University Press.

World Bank. 1992. *World Development Report 1992.* Washington, D.C.: World Bank.

CHAPTER TWO

Establishing Equity in Argentina

Juan Luis Bour, Marcela Cristini, Nuria Susmel,
José Delgado, and Mónica Panadeiros

Argentina's economic decline in the eighties revealed the structural problems of its social security system. This system was established early in Argentina and achieved full coverage during the Second World War. The various subsystems were administered by the state (retirement pay and pensions, family allowances, passive subscriber health benefits) and by unions (health coverage). The system was organized around principles of social solidarity and income redistribution (pay-as-you-go social insurance system, uniform health coverage financed with contributions proportional to income).

Government noncompliance (failure to make employer contributions to the retirement system, virtual seizure of the funds of the retirement system and flagrant violation of legal guarantees for mobility of allowances) and incompetence in the social service organizations led to general disillusionment among beneficiaries and a high incidence of social contribution evasion, as this chapter indicates. These structural problems worsened over time as coverage of the various subsystems (including deterioration of the active/passive ratio, increase in the costs of medicine, erosion of real wages, among others) expanded.

This study determined that the long-term financial stability of the social insurance system would have required reserves totaling nearly $134 billion (approximately 65 percent of gross domestic product—GDP). But the system actually has no reserves and cannot finance even its current expenditures. Contribution evasion rates climbed to 48 percent in 1992, the active/passive ratio was 1.49, and the years of contributions required to ensure actuarial balance between income and expenditures was a third higher than the number specified by law.

For family allowances, the intended redistribution among various income levels was ineffective and led to high administrative costs.

In health care, the system promoted transfers between workers in the same union and was hampered by incompetent service provision. The redistribution of health care expenses for passive subscribers included beneficiaries who received up to four times the national average wage.

As part of the sweeping economic reform introduced in 1989, all of these systems were reexamined with a eye to their reorganization. In cases such as health care, unemployment, and work-related accidents, changes have already been made. But in other areas such as family allowances and the social insurance system, the only progress has been in reorganizing management.

Reforms in progress tend to target organizations that offer individual capitalization and insurance programs without neglecting the needs of the low-income sectors. Our policy recommendations are based on evaluation of these reforms.

Some systems stress reorganization more than others. The new retirement system has some specific problems with incentives for participating, which limits its impact on evasion. Moreover, large segments of the population are still without coverage, and the short-term financial stability of the system is questionable. A 7-10 percent hike in taxes may be necessary.

Health care subscribers should be allowed to choose among the various providers, the government should define a plan for minimum coverage, and a maximum price should be established. A redistribution fund should be established to provide health care for those at the greatest risk and with the lowest incomes.

The current system of family allowances, which is too costly, should be scrapped in favor of a human resources training program based on a single education allowance. Finally, the coverage for unemployment and work-related accidents should be reoriented toward individual insurance for workers and companies.

National Social Insurance System (Retirements and Pensions)

In 1904, with the passage of Law No. 4349 creating the first national social insurance fund, a system of retirements and pensions was gradually established, financed primarily with payroll deductions and based on the capitalization of contributions, with funds invested in public debt securities. Lack of sufficient fiscal discipline led to over-investment in securities. In 1946, these securities (which constituted the reserves of the various funds) were redeemed and replaced with social insurance bonds. These bonds were not redeemed, compromising the growth of the system and its medium- and long-term viability.

In response to the crisis, Laws No. 18037 and No. 18038 of 1968 abolished the former capitalization system and established a pay-as-you-go system, thus breaking the connection between the contributions made by individuals during their active years and the benefits collected during retirement. Income from contributions was used to cover expenditures, and the active subscribers were responsible for supporting the passive subscribers. Altough legislated by these laws, the pay-as-you-go system had actually been functioning since the early 1960s. The accrual process had become ineffective in the late fifties. From then on the income of the funds was insufficient to cover outflows, so Treasury funds had to be used to cover the growing deficits.

Law No. 18037 established the social insurance system for salaried employees, and Law No. 18038, for self-employed workers. Together with their various amendments, they governed the social insurance system of Argentina until early 1993.[1] In addition to the general system, there are others especially for those who perform specific tasks for the government. These are known as special or "privileged" systems since they provide better benefits than the general system.

Salaried employees must contribute 10 percent of their wages to the social insurance system, and employers must contribute 16 percent. Self-employed workers must contribute 26 percent, calculated on the basis of seven predefined contribution categories, which are assigned to individuals according to the type of work they do and their years of experience.

The current social insurance system provides: regular retirement, old-age retirement, disability retirement and pensions.

To be eligible for ordinary retirement, male employees must be 60 years old and female employees 55. They must also have 30 years of service and must have made contributions for at least 20 of those years. Those over the retirement age compensate for deficiencies in years of service at the rate of two years of excess age for every year of service short of the retirement minimum. Employees of both sexes are eligible for old-age retirement at 65 years of age and with 10 years of service.

Table 2.1 shows how social insurance benefits are calculated and how little correlation there is between contributions made and benefits obtained. Benefits depend essentially on the best wages paid in the final years of an individual's active life, with a proportional and adjustable guarantee of the wage paid at the time of retirement.

The right to a pension is based on the death of a retiree or an active subscriber or one eligible for retirement. This right benefits widows, widowers, common-law spouses, minor children in the subscriber's care up to 18 years of age (21 if in school and any age if disabled) and dependent parents.

With 30 years of employment and at least 15 years of contributions, self-employed men are eligible for regular retirement at 65 years of age, and

---

[1] Provincial systems and alternative funds (usually belonging to professionals) coexist with the national social insurance system. A retirement reciprocity system has functioned since 1946, enabling individuals to transfer from one system to another without losing their contributions.

Table 2.1. Employee Social Insurance Benefits

Retirement Allowance	Pension Allowance
The retirement wage is calculated initially as the average of the adjusted wages collected during the three best years, whether continuous or not, included in the period of 10 immediately preceding retirement. The following percentages are applied to these wages:	
Ordinary and disability retirement	
70%, if, at retirement, the affiliate is no more than two years over the minimum age.	75% of the allowance
78%, if, at retirement, the affiliate is more than three years over the minimum age.	
80%, if, at retirement, the affiliate is more than four years over the minimum age.	
82%, if, at retirement, the affiliate is more than five years over the minimum age.	
Old-age retirement	
60% of the retirement wage.	75% of the allowance

Source: FIEL, based on legislation in effect as of December 1992.

women, at 60. Those over the retirement age can make up for insufficient years of employment in the same way as salaried employees. Self-employed workers are eligible for old-age retirement at 70 years with 10 years of service. The retirement allowance is calculated on the basis of the weighted average of the categories in which the individual made contributions, the weighting factor being the years of contribution in each of these categories. Seventy percent to 82 percent is applied to this amount as in the system for salaried employees. The survivor's pension in this case is also 70 percent of the allowance to which the subscriber was or would have been entitled.

In addition to retirements and pensions, the national social insurance system provides the following benefits:

- disability pensions, granted to disabled indigents not eligible for a disability retirement;
- burial allowance, equal to three "minimum incomes" (i.e., three months' wages calculated at the minimum wage rate effective at the time of the subscriber's death); and,
- special pensions, granted by legislative decree and financed with general revenue funds.

Since 1986, many laws have been passed to improve the financing of the national social insurance system. Some of them generated funds from sources outside the system (fuel and energy taxes, VAT, for example) to increase revenues, while the aim of others was to limit the expenditure thereof. Even so, the current crisis in Argentina's social insurance system could not be avoided.

Table 2.2. Wage-Price Comparison, 1985-92
(Base 1985 = 100)

Year	INGR (Average)	IPC (Average)	INGR/ IPC
1985	100.00	100.00	100.00
1986	1,018.37	1,462.45	69.63
1987	2,081.91	3,383.17	61.54
1988	9,455.27	14,987.08	63.09
1989	240,735.24	476,497.75	50.52
1990	628,552.89	11,502,481.99	54.60
1991	15,927,358.33	31,249,229.28	50.97
1992	20,720,752.39	39,029,967.79	53.09

Source: FIEL, based on data from the Secretariat of Social Security, 1992b.
Note: INGR is the general wage level index, and IPC is the consumer price index.

The Current Situation

The social insurance crisis in Argentina originated in the trend of the basic variables of the pay-as-you-go system, the choices made in managing it, the growing instability of the economy in the late 1980s, the high levels of evasion of social insurance contributions and the gradual aging of the population. This economic instability and the runaway inflation of 1989 and 1990 affected the real level of the system's benefits, as indicated in Table 2.2, which shows the lag in the general wage index used to determine the adjustability of the benefits based on the consumer price index. Once the initial benefit is calculated, it is adjusted on the basis of the variations in this wage index, with the result that the benefits paid lose their initial correlation to the wage received in the subscribers' last position.

Table 2.3 shows the substantial deterioration of the average wage-allowance ratio between 1978 and 1989.

Table 2.4 shows the trend of the number of beneficiaries per social insurance fund and the trend of average benefits, as well as the decline of their purchasing power.

In September 1992, the Social Security Secretariat tied the retirement and pension index (wage index) to the general price index of March 31, 1991, which was more significant in the case of the benefits granted by the Industry, Trade and Civil Activities Fund and the State Fund. In these cases, the year's average benefits rose sharply compared with those of the preceding year, and even the figures for December were higher than the annual average. This increase, however, was insignificant in the case of the benefits granted by the Self-Employed Fund.

The mobility applied to the social insurance benefits affected their structures disproportionately. Beneficiaries of the Self-Employed Fund, for example,

Table 2.3. Wage-Allowance Ratio, 1978-89
(Percentages)

	Wage/allowance ratio[1]	Average retirement/ average wage[2]
December 1978	70	73
December 1979	56	87
December 1980	51	66
December 1981	50	71
December 1982	43	62
December 1983	37	62
December 1984	25	49
December 1985	26	n.a.
1985 average	24	67
1986 average	21	45
1987 average	23	48
1988 average	22	51
1989 average	60	n.a.

Source: FIEL, based on data from the Secretariat of Social Security, 1992b.
Notes: [1] Only for allowances larger than the minimum.
[2] All figures are annual averages.

accumulated benefits at minimum levels for the entire social insurance system. This was not true of the benefits granted by the State Fund, which were favored in many cases by a mobility linked to the wage paid in the equivalent active position. Despite the substantial adjustment of its benefits in September 1992, nearly 30 percent of the Industry, Trade and Civil Activities Fund retirement and pension benefits remained at the system's minimum until December of that year (see Tables 2.5 and 2.6).

The level of evasion clearly reflects the lack of incentives to contribute to the system. Table 2.7 estimates the degree of evasion in the social insurance system since 1992, taking into account the official estimates of the economically active population and the performance of the system's budget that year.

In a pay-as-you-go system, the contributions of active workers support the passive subscribers, according to an arrangement whereby intergenerational transfers finance the benefits. The contributors/beneficiaries ratio is thus extremely important. Increased unemployment affects it negatively, as do evasion and the aging of the population. In Argentina (where the birth and mortality rates are modest compared with other Latin American countries), the percentage of individuals over 65 years of age in the total population rose from 5 percent in 1950 to 9.8 percent in 1990.

These factors have contributed to the reduction of the contributors/beneficiaries ratio to levels that threaten the medium- and long-term financial equilibrium of the social insurance system. In mid-December 1992, this ratio was 1.86

Table 2.4. Beneficiaries and Real Average Benefits, 1985-92
(1985 average = 100)

Year	Retirees (average)	Pensioners (average)	Retirement average	Pension average
1985	832,486	433,450	100	100
1986	850,857	446,399	93	95
1987	857,037	456,477	86	85
1988	867,040	470,785	88	83
1989	872,114	481,896	80	77
1990	894,652	499,803	70	68
1991	918,292	512,803	68	65
1992	944,110	528,508	73	70
Dec. 1992	958,962	539,552	90	83
State Fund				
1985	369,499	232,156	100	100
1986	371,061	234,832	92	94
1987	368,354	236,119	90	83
1988	371,847	241,643	91	80
1989	375,646	246,757	84	77
1990	383,657	253,692	77	76
1991	395,646	258,793	84	76
1992	416,197	265,385	93	80
Dec. 1992	426,572	269,269	114	90
Self-Employed Fund				
1985	571,352	272,098	100	100
1986	598,379	284,465	96	97
1987	620,939	296,659	70	70
1988	636,539	311,932	67	59
1989	652,022	327,993	61	57
1990	682,223	346,840	66	66
1991	709,272	361,655	63	63
1992	712,237	372,829	59	60
Dec. 1992	708,691	376,173	56	56
System Total				
1985	1,773,337	937,705	100	100
1986	1,820,297	965,696	94	95
1987	1,856,330	989,224	82	80
1988	1,875,425	1,024,361	83	75
1989	1,899,782	1,056,645	75	71
1990	1,960,532	1,100,335	70	69
1991	2,023,210	1,133,251	70	67
1992	2,072,554	1,166,721	73	69
Dec. 1992	2,094,215	1,184,994	86	77

Source: FIEL, based on data from the Secretariat of Social Security, 1992b.

Table 2.5. Distribution of Retirements by Monthly Allowance Bracket, Close of Fourth Quarter, 1992

Allowance Brackets (*In pesos*)		Number of cases		Percentage of total payments
		Absolute	Percentage	
Industry, Trade and Civil Activities				
150.00 -	150.00	516,997	53.9	28.8
150.01 -	180.00	24,044	2.5	1.5
180.01 -	260.00	57,406	6.0	4.9
260.01 -	400.00	215,302	22.5	23.6
400.01 -	650.00	80,965	8.4	15.1
650.01 -	1,000.00	37,247	3.9	11.0
1,000.01 -	2,000.00	25,732	2.7	13.6
2,000.01 and above		1,269	0.1	1.5
	Total	958,962	100.0	100.0
State and Public Services				
150.00 -	150.00	26,277	6.2	2.2
150.01 -	180.00	15,720	3.7	1.4
180.01 -	260.00	90,212	21.1	11.3
260.01 -	400.00	146,270	24.3	25.1
400.01 -	650.00	83,868	19.7	23.3
650.01 -	1,000.00	40,976	9.6	18.0
1,000.01 -	2,000.00	21,080	4.9	15.5
2,000.01 and above		2,169	0.5	3.2
	Total	426,572	100.0	100.0
Self-employed				
150.00 -	150.00	691,649	97.6	95.9
150.01 -	180.00	13,348	1.9	2.2
180.01 -	260.00	2,647	0.4	0.5
260.01 -	400.00	313	0.0	0.0
400.01 -	650.00	50	0.0	0.0
650.01 -	1,000.00	43	0.0	0.0
1,000.01 -	2,000.00	444	0.1	0.4
2,000.01 and above		188	0.0	1.0
	Total	708,682	100.0	100.0
System Total				
150.00 -	150.00	1,234,923	59.0	33.3
150.01 -	180.00	53,112	2.5	1.6
180.01 -	260.00	150,265	7.2	6.1
260.01 -	400.00	361,885	17.3	19.5
400.01 -	650.00	164,883	7.8	14.8
650.01 -	1,000.00	78,266	3.7	11.1
1,000.01 -	2,000.00	47,256	2.3	11.7
2,000.01 and above		3,626	0.2	1.9
	Total	2,094,216	100.0	100.0

Source: FIEL, based on data from the Secretariat of Social Security and the Administration of the Secretariat of Social Security, 1992b.

Table 2.6. Distribution of Pensions by Monthly Allowance Bracket at Year-end 1992

Benefit Brackets (in pesos)			Number of cases		Percentage of total payments
			Absolute	Percentage	
Industry, Trade and Civil Activities					
150.00	-	150.00	257,134	47.7	29.9
150.01	-	180.00	9,594	1.8	1.3
180.01	-	260.00	180,548	33.5	35.1
260.01	-	400.00	51,250	9.5	12.6
400.01	-	650.00	28,899	5.4	11.5
650.01	-	1,000.00	7,410	1.4	4.7
1,000.01	-	2,000.00	4,717	0.9	4.9
	Total		539,552	100.0	100.0
State and Public Services					
150.00	-	150.00	25,800	9.6	5.1
150.01	-	180.00	12,387	4.6	2.7
180.01	-	260.00	147,548	54.8	42.5
260.01	-	400.00	51,147	19.0	21.3
400.01	-	650.00	24,156	9.0	16.4
650.01	-	1,000.00	5,001	1.9	5.5
1,000.01	-	2,000.00	3,230	1.2	6.5
	Total		269,269	100.0	100.0
Self-Employed					
150.00	-	150.00	368,483	98.0	97.0
150.01	-	180.00	7,057	1.9	2.2
180.01	-	260.00	292	0.1	0.1
260.01	-	400.00	115	0.0	0.1
400.01	-	650.00	33	0.0	0.0
650.01	-	1,000.00	47	0.0	0.0
1,000.01	-	2,000.00	146	0.0	0.6
	Total		376,173	100.0	100.0
System Total					
150.00	-	150.00	651,417	55.0	37.5
150.01	-	180.00	29,038	2.5	1.9
180.01	-	260.00	328,388	27.7	29.5
260.01	-	400.00	102,512	8.7	12.4
400.01	-	650.00	53,088	4.5	10.4
650.01	-	1,000.00	12,458	1.1	3.9
1,000.01	-	2,000.00	8,093	0.7	4.4
	Total		1,184,994	100.0	100.0

Source: FIEL, based on data from the Secretariat of Social Security and the Administration of the Secretariat of Social Security, 1992 a,b.

Table 2.7. Economically Active Population (EAP) Contributing to the National Social Security System, 1992

	Total	Forced to contribute	Number of contributors	Evasion (%)
Total EAP	12,527,949	9,372,448	4,890,082	47.83
Employees	4,745,138	4,745,138	3,824,224	19.41
Rural and domestic	1,392,224	1,392,224	270,383	80.58
Armed forces and security	143,667	0	—	—
Administrations and municipalities	1,252,692	0	—	—
Self-employed	3,441,801	3,235,086	795,465	75.41
Under 16 years of age	228,420	—	—	—
Unemployed	914,712	—	—	—
Free labor	409,295	—	—	—

Source: Author's calculations based on data from the Secretariat of Social Security.

for salaried employees, 0.73 for self-employed workers and 1.49 for the social insurance system as a whole (in 1980 this systemwide ratio was 1.82).

In response to demographic trends, the rates of contribution to the system were modified. The successive adjustments of both personal and employer contributions follow no recognizable pattern, due in large measure to the short-term approach of the decision-making process.

Despite these modifications, the self-employed system has had sizable deficits for years. Between 1985 and 1989 this system's self-financing capabilities covered only 15 percent of its expenditures.

The system for salaried employees finances some of the deficits of the self-employed system, which causes distortions in distribution to also be observable in the privileged systems. Although these systems account for only a very small percentage of the system's total affiliates, their exclusion from the general system opposes the principles of solidarity, equality and equitable distribution. In fact, in June 1990, these beneficiaries represented barely 2 percent of the total passive subscribers and generated no more than 3 percent of the benefit costs, but their average benefit was 54 percent higher than for salaried employees.

Disablity has contributed increasingly to the financial deficit of the system and should be examined more closely. Disabled beneficiaries quit working at ages below the legal minimums and, consequently, generate benefits that remain in the system for a comparatively longer period of time. The actuarial debt to these beneficiaries, therefore, is considerably larger than what the system assumes when a regular retirement is granted. No financial provision is made to offset the greater long-term deficit caused by disability benefits.

Over the years, disability benefits as a percentage of the total benefits paid varied between 6 percent and 10 percent, depending on the organizations and funds granting the benefit. These percentages changed substantially in 1980 and climbed to levels much higher than the international average. In the Self-Employed Fund, for 1990 approximately 26 percent of all retirements were because of disability. In the State Fund, the figure was 18 percent, and in the Industry and Trade Fund, 17 percent.

The problem is especially acute in some provinces. For the Self-Employed Fund, the largest numbers appear in Santiago del Estero (67 percent), Misiones (59 percent), San Juan (58 percent) and Corrientes (50 percent), all of which were calculated on the basis of total retirements. The figures for the State Fund are less alarming, although still high, such as those for Formosa (36 percent), Corrientes (35 percent) and San Juan (33 percent). A similar situation exists for the Industry and Trade Fund in provinces such as Formosa, Misiones and San Juan. The excessively liberal granting of this benefit is evidenced by the fact that in the 1981-89 period, a number of audits were performed involving approximately 2,700 beneficiaries of disability retirements, and 26 percent of the benefits were revoked.

Government-proposed Reform

To combat growing decline, the government presented a proposal to reform the national social insurance system, leading to the creation of the new Integrated Retirement and Pension System (SIJP, *Sistema Integrado de Jubilaciones y Pensiones*). This system is divided into three parts: a publicly administered pay-as-you-go system that pays a uniform benefit at the time of retirement, a privately administered mandatory capitalization system, and an optional capitalization system, to which individuals can make voluntary social insurance contributions.

Foremost in the government proposal is that personal contributions of salaried employees and self-employed workers will be deposited in individual capitalization accounts, administered by private management organizations known as Retirement and Pension Fund Administrators (AFJP, *Administradoras de Fondos de Jubilaciones y Pensiones*). The personal contribution for salaried employees is 11 percent, and the employer contribution is 16 percent. Self-employed workers must contribute 27 percent in predefined categories. Individuals over 45 years of age when the reform enters into force (hereinafter referred to as active subscribers in transition) must also contribute an additional 2 percent to 3 percent, known as the compensatory premium.

The pay-as-you-go system grants a universal basic benefit (PBU, *prestación básica universal*), a compensatory benefit (PC, *prestación compensatoria*), and disability retirement for individuals over 45 years of age when the reform enters into force (hereinafter referred to as individuals in transition). The PBU will consist of a fixed amount for each retiree, depending entirely on the number of years contributions were made. To determine the PBU, the average mandatory social insurance contribution (AMPO, *aporte medio previsional obligatorio*) must be calculated, which is the quotient of the monthly average of personal contributions and the monthly average of affiliates. The PBU is equal to 1.5 AMPO for individuals who have contributed for 30 years, with the allowance increasing 2 percent for every additional year of service up to 45 years (to become eligible for the PBU, the beneficiary must be 65 years of age and have 30 years of service with contributions).

The PC is granted to active subscribers in transition when they become eligible for regular retirement and consists of 2 percent per year of contributions to the former social insurance system up to a maximum of 30 years, taking as a base the average wages of the individual's last 10 years of service.

Benefits of the pay-as-you-go system are financed with the employer contribution for salaried employees, with 16 of the 27 percentage points of the contribution of self-employed workers, with the proceeds of the compensatory premium rate, with the transfers from the AFJP of the funds of active subscribers in transition who become disabled, with the proceeds of the tax on real estate used in the productive process and other specially allocated tax resources and with general revenue funds.

A compensatory premium rate is applied, and funds accumulated by active subscribers in transition who become disabled are transferred to the pay-as-you-go system because the state assumes the risk of covering disability and the death of active subscribers 45 years of age or younger when the reform enters into force.

Given that the new law provides universal coverage, the PC will enable active individuals surprised by the change (active subscribers in transition) to obtain acknowledgment of the contributions they have made. This benefit seeks to place all those who contributed to the old system in an equitable position, taking into account the number of years actually contributed up to a maximum, which is added to the PBU. This practically guarantees those who are close to retirement an amount similar to the one they would have under the current legislation. The PBU is the integral element of the new system. It will be paid by the state and will be nearly the same for all individuals, thus constituting a method of income redistribution that will benefit those who, based on their contributions to the system, had the lowest wages or earnings.

For active subscribers in transition, requirements for benefits will be redefined. This redefinition will involve changing the retirement age, which will be gradually raised to 65 years of age for both men and women, and the method of calculating the social insurance benefit, using the average of the last 10 years' earnings as the retirement wage to estimate the benefit. The government agrees to pay the benefits to which passive subscribers in transition (current retirees and penioners) are legally entitled according to the legislation in force at the time of their retirement.

Once subscribers become eligible for the retirement benefit, the amount accumulated in their individual capitalization accounts (CCI, *Cuenta de*

Capitalización Individual) entitles them to a social insurance life annuity, to a timed withdrawal or to a proportional withdrawal.[2]

Capitalization also entitles the subscriber to early retirement or to deferred retirement. Individuals are entitled to early retirement if they have accumulated enough funds to entitle them to an annuity equal to or greater than 50 percent of the retirement base and more than twice the maximum PBU granted by the pay-as-you-go system.[3] In this case, the individual receives no income from the pay-as-you-go system after retiring until he satisfies the requirements established by it. In the case of deferred retirement, the individual can, with his employer's consent, postpone the collection of regular retirement pay, in which case he is not entitled to distribution until retirement and both the subscriber's and the employer's contributions continue, or choose regular retirement, in which case he is again not entitled to distribution until retirement and only the employer's contributions necessary for financing the public system continue.

Actuarial Balance

The actuarial balance measures the difference between the current actuarial value of the flow of revenue from personal and employer contributions collected on the wages of current active affiliates of the fund and the current actuarial value of future obligations to the future beneficiaries among the subscribers, plus the obligations to current passive subscribers. The actuarial deficit of a social insurance system therefore represents the current value of the funds needed but not available at the time of the determination to pay its future obligations to current active subscribers and to pay its obligations to current passive subscribers until the exhaustion of their respective benefits. Consequently, the actuarial balance measures the level of reserves that the system should have accumulated from the start of its operations to cover the obligations it assumed when each affiliate joined the system, until the actuarial determination is made.[4]

---

[2] In the first instance, the AFJP must transfer the entire amount in the CCI to a Retirement Insurance Company *(CSR, Compañía de Seguros de Retiro)*, which will guarantee the beneficiary a life annuity, transferable to a pensioner. Therefore, upon retirement, if the subscriber chooses a life annuity, the entire amount in his CCI is withdrawn from the AFJP. In the second case, the AFJP continues managing the individual's CCI, determining each year how much he can withdraw and receive on a monthly basis. The proportional withdrawal is for beneficiaries whose initial holding for timed withdrawal is less than 70 percent of the maximum PBU granted by the pay-as-you-go system. In this case, the individual is entitled to withdraw from the fund this 70 percent, the annuity being extinguished through depletion of the fund or upon the death of the beneficiary.

[3] The retirement base is defined as the average of the taxable monthly earnings or income declared in the five years preceding the month in which the subscriber chooses the retirement benefit.

[4] This definition of actuarial balance is the one given by Barral Souto, National Bank Retirement Fund *(Caja Nacional de Jubilaciones Bancarias)*: Law No. 11575. Technical Report and Actuarial Balance on December 31, 1933 (March 1, 1935), one of the founders of Argentina's actuarial school.

Table 2.8. Actuarial Balance of the National Social Insurance System, 1992
(Millions of 1992 pesos)

	Current actives			Total current[4]		
	Inflows[1]	Outflows[2]	Percent[3]	Retirements	Pensions	Actuarial balance
Employees	114,299.8	121,527.1	29.88	70,580.4	28,431.6	(106,239.3)
Self-employed	4,781.4	10,445.3	26.20	14,872.6	7,554.7	(28,091.3)
System total	119,081.3	131,972.5	—	85,453.0	35,986.4	(134,330.6)

Source: FIEL, 1992a.
Notes: [1] Revenue from contributions.
          [2] Benefit payments.
          [3] Disability and early death.
          [4] Retirees and pensioners.

Table 2.9. Actuarial Imbalance for Different Number of Contributing Years
(In pesos)

	Employees		Self-employed	
Contributing years	Total	Percentage of outflows	Total	Percentage of outflows
40	(19,779)	-115.80	(4,228)	-69.71
39	(18,965)	-107.60	(3,898)	-62.20
38	(18,109)	-99.53	(3,555)	-54.89
37	(17,209)	-91.61	(3,199)	-47.77
36	(16,264)	-83.83	(2,828)	-40.84
35	(15,270)	-76.19	(2,442)	-34.10
34	(14,222)	-68.67	(2,041)	-27.54
33	(13,123)	-61.31	(1,624)	-21.18
32	(11,970)	-54.09	(1,191)	-15.01
31	(10,762)	-47.04	(743)	-9.05
30	(9,496)	-40.13	(280)	-3.29
29	(8,168)	-33.37	197	2.24
28	(6,780)	-26.77	689	7.57
27	(5,331)	-20.35	1,196	12.70
26	(3,820)	-14.09	1,718	17.63
25	(2,248)	-8.02	2,256	22.38
24	(622)	-2.15	2,811	26.96
23	1,064	3.55	3,383	31.38
22	2,810	9.06	3,973	35.62
21	4,618	14.40	4,582	39.70
20	6,487	19.57	5,210	43.64
19	8,426	24.59	5,866	47.47
18	10,432	29.47	6,545	51.17
17	12,506	34.19	7,249	54.73
16	14,651	38.77	7,979	58.16
15	16,872	43.22	8,738	61.47

Source: FIEL, 1992a.
Note: A negative value indicates an actuarial surplus.

The results of the actuarial calculations for the National Social Insurance System are shown in Table 2.8.

As indicated, the system should have accumulated reserves of 134 billion 1992 pesos to cover all its long-term obligations to current beneficiaries and to the potential beneficiaries among the current active affiliates. The debt to current passive affiliates (if the real level of current benefits remains the same) is 121,000 billion pesos.

Assuming an average individual for each system, with an average employment and salary history, and comparing the size of the contributions this individual is expected to make with the retirement and pension expenses he is expected to generate in the future, it is possible to determine the minimum years of contribution necessary to keep this individual from becoming an actuarial burden to the system. Table 2.9 shows the actuarial deficit caused by individuals who contribute regularly for the number of years indicated. The table shows that the minimum number of years of contribution necessary to prevent an individual from causing an actuarial deficit is 23 years for a salaried employee and 29 years for a self-employed worker. These figures are much higher than the years of service with contributions required by law.

Projected Growth of the Pay-As-You-Go System

Based on the legal provisions concerning minimum retirement ages, the benefits to be provided by the system and the contribution required for eligibility, a projection of the current pay-as-you-go system was made for a period of 25 years starting in December 1992, the last month for which official figures were available. The mortality tables used for Argentina for the 1995-2000 period come from CELADE (*Centro Latinoamericano de Demografía*; Latin American Demographics Center) estimates, which provide shorter life expectancies than the GAM71s initially considered for making the projections. The disability tables are the standard tables used by claims experts in the private insurance sector, which were applied to all of the social insurance funds, despite the fact that the disability risk is different. The criteria described were used because no other reliable information was available. The ages at which subscribers enter the system as contributors are between 25 and 30 years for both sexes, and it is assumed that income by age group fits a Poisson probability distribution. For passive subscribers, the initial distributions by age and by sex come from official sources. For active subscribers, CELADE estimates of distribution by age and sex of the economically active population were again used. Finally, the contribution rate, average benefits and average wages were assumed to be constant.

Tables 2.10 and 2.11 show the results of the system projection for the next 25 years. The base year starts in December 1992, and the figures for active and passive individuals are the ones for the beginning of the period. Income and

Table 2.10. Projected Trend in Social Insurance Beneficiaries
(Thousands of individuals)

Year	Based on current actives (1)	(2)	(3)	Based on current inactives (2)	(3)	Current pensioners	Based on new affiliates 30-year projection (1)	(2)	(3)
Base	4,890	0	0	2,094	0	1,184	0	0	0
1	4,824	89	20	1,995	63	1,137	135	0	0
2	4,743	181	42	1,899	121	1,090	286	0.1	0.1
3	4,649	303	60	1,804	174	1,044	450	0.5	0.3
4	4,543	443	79	1,709	223	999	633	1	0.7
5	4,430	589	100	1,616	269	940	823	2	1
6	4,320	728	123	1,523	310	896	1,011	3	2
7	4,207	866	147	1,431	348	852	1,202	4	2
8	4,092	1,003	173	1,340	380	808	1,395	6	4
9	3,975	1,138	200	1,251	409	765	1,532	8	5
10	3,847	1,284	230	1,163	433	723	1,679	14	9
11	3,726	1,413	261	1,077	452	681	1,819	22	14
12	3,603	1,539	294	994	467	640	1,961	31	20
13	3,477	1,660	329	913	477	601	2,104	40	26
14	3,349	1,777	366	835	482	562	2,274	50	33
15	3,220	1,888	404	760	484	525	2,445	61	40
16	3,088	1,993	443	688	481	489	2,617	73	48
17	2,956	2,092	484	619	473	454	2,791	84	56
18	2,821	2,183	525	554	463	421	1,965	97	65
19	2,686	2,267	567	493	448	389	3,136	109	74
20	2,550	2,342	609	437	431	359	3,307	123	84
21	2,415	2,406	652	384	411	330	3,476	137	95
22	2,280	2,460	694	335	388	303	3,645	152	107
23	2,145	2,503	736	291	364	277	3,814	168	120
24	2,010	2,537	776	251	338	253	3,977	184	134

Source: FIEL, 1991b.
Notes: (1) Actives.
       (2) Retirees
       (3) Pensioners

expenditures, however, are estimated at December of each period. The active/passive ratio tends to remain on its downward course, and if the monetary variables remain constant, the financial deficit of the system tends to worsen. Starting with a social insurance deficit of 20 percent, measured on the basis of expenditures to pay benefits, in 10 years this deficit would climb to 25 percent and toward the end of the period would be above 30 percent. The social insurance deficit is defined as the deficit resulting exclusively from the difference between the income from employer and employee contributions and the payment of retirement benefits and pensions. This is why the deficit is not the same as the overall budget deficit of the social insurance system, which includes other financial flows administered by the system.

Table 2.11. Projected Trend of Social Insurance Funding

(In millions of pesos)

Year	Total population (in millions) (1)	(2)	(3)	A/I*	Inflows Employee	Employer	Outflows Retirement	Pensioner	Deficit Amount	Percentage
Base	4,890	2,094	1,184	1.49	3,270	5,232	7,233	3,430	2,161	20.27
1	4,959	2,085	1,221	1.49	3,321	5,314	7,222	3,527	2,113	19.65
2	5,030	2,081	1,254	1.50	3,373	5,397	7,281	3,612	2,121	19.47
3	5,100	2,108	1,280	1.50	3,427	5,484	7,423	3,685	2,197	19.77
4	5,177	2,154	1,303	1.49	3,484	5,574	7,613	3,737	2,291	20.18
5	5,254	2,207	1,311	1.49	3,541	5,666	7,812	3,779	2,384	20.57
6	5,331	2,254	1,332	1.48	3,598	5,757	8,008	3,838	2,491	21.02
7	5,409	2,302	1,350	1.48	3,656	5,849	8,209	3,892	2,596	21.45
8	5,488	2,350	1,366	1.47	3,694	5,911	8,413	3,942	2,750	22.25
9	5,508	2,398	1,381	1.45	3,708	5,933	8,647	3,988	2,994	23.69
10	5,527	2,463	1,396	1.43	3,721	5,954	8,891	4,032	3,248	25.13
11	5,546	2,514	1,410	1.41	3,734	5,975	9,100	4,073	3,464	26.29
12	5,564	2,564	1,423	1.39	3,746	5,995	9,307	4,110	3,676	27.39
13	5,582	2,614	1,434	1.37	3,767	6,027	9,510	4,144	3,860	28.26
14	5,624	2,663	1,445	1.36	3,797	6,075	9,707	4,173	4,007	28.87
15	5,665	2,710	1,454	1.36	3,827	6,123	9,894	4,200	4,143	29.39
16	5,706	2,754	1,462	1.35	3,856	6,170	10,070	4,222	4,265	29.84
17	5,747	2,796	1,479	1.34	3,885	6,217	10,234	4,242	4,373	30.21
18	5,787	2,835	1,475	1.34	3,913	6,261	10,386	4,259	4,471	30.52
19	5,822	2,871	1,480	1.33	3,938	6,301	10,522	4,273	4,555	30.78
20	5,857	2,902	1,485	1.33	3,963	6,341	10,637	4,286	4,618	30.94
21	5,891	2,928	1,490	1.33	3,988	6,381	10,730	4,297	4,658	30.99
22	5,925	2,948	1,494	1.33	4,012	6,419	10,803	4,306	4,677	30.95
23	5,959	2,963	1,498	1.33	4,034	6,455	10,854	4,315	4,679	30.84
24	5,988	2,973	1,502	1.33	4,053	6,484	10,890	4,327	4,679	30.75

Source: FIEL, 1991b.
Notes: (1) Actives.
        (2) Retirees.
        (3) Pensioners.
         * Actives/Inactives Ratio.

Financial and Actuarial Evaluation of the Reform

Based on the characteristics of the proposed reform of the national social insurance system, an evaluation was made of the flows of funds the system will generate in 25 years, assuming that it takes effect January 1, 1994. The same average wages and passive subscriber benefits and the same mortality and disability tables were used as for the projection of the current system. The demographic variables were taken from the projection of the current system, using the results for the first year. This method was chosen since it is assumed that the reform will enter into force one year later, at the start of the last projection mentioned. The annual

Table 2.12. Financial Trend of the Social Insurance System
(Millions of pesos)

| | Payments to current inactives | | | | Actives in transition | | | | |
| | Current retirees | | Current | | Employees | Premium | Disability | Benefits payments | |
Year	(1)	(2)	pensioners	Total	contrib.	rate	payments	Basic	Allowance
Base	7,343	0	3,548	10,890	5,374	287	0	0	0
1	7,004	167	3,405	10,577	5,338	279	14	29	70
2	6,673	321	3,267	10,261	5,291	269	29	70	171
3	6,345	463	3,131	9,939	5,235	257	42	122	298
4	6,020	596	2,995	9,611	5,169	244	55	189	449
5	5,697	718	2,822	9,238	5,098	230	66	244	610
6	5,377	830	2,690	8,898	5,023	215	75	306	780
7	5,060	932	2,559	8,552	4,943	200	83	368	958
8	4,747	1,023	2,430	8,201	4,859	184	89	431	1,144
9	4,438	1,103	2,302	7,844	4,770	168	93	493	1,338
10	4,136	1,170	2,176	7,482	4,677	152	95	556	1,539
11	3,839	1,226	2,052	7,118	4,579	135	95	618	1,745
12	3,550	1,269	1,931	6,751	4,478	118	93	679	1,957
13	3,268	1,301	1,812	6,383	4,372	101	88	741	2,175
14	2,997	1,320	1,697	6,015	4,262	83	81	801	2,398
15	2,735	1,328	1,586	5,650	4,168	66	71	861	2,625
16	2,484	1,325	1,478	5,287	4,030	49	58	921	2,847
17	2,244	1,310	1,374	4,929	3,909	32	42	982	3,063
18	2,017	1,285	1,274	4,577	3,783	16	22	1,043	3,271
19	1,803	1,251	1,179	4,234	3,654	0	0	1,103	3,472
20	1,602	1,208	1,088	3,899	3,523	0	0	1,163	3,660
21	1,415	1,157	1,022	3,575	3,388	0	0	1,221	3,836
22	1,242	1,098	920	3,262	3,252	0	0	1,278	3,999
23	1,084	1,934	843	2,962	3,112	0	0	1,333	4,147
24	940	965	770	2,677	2,971	0	0	1,386	4,281

Source: FIEL, 1991b.
Notes: (1) Retirees
(2) Pensioners

financial flows were evaluated at December of each year of the projection, assuming a real annual rate of 4 percent.[5]

It was assumed that the rate of the compensatory premium collected by the government as an additional contribution for individuals in transition is 3 percent of the wage and that the commissions collected by the AFJP account for 3 of the 11 percentage points contributed by active individuals, with said commission including the cost of disability and early death coverage. For pensions funds, it

[5] This means that the annual flows are not merely the sum of the monthly amounts (thus corresponding to the budget criterion used in the projection of the current system) but rather the updated total.

Table 2.13. Financial Trend of the Social Insurance System
(Capitalized flows in millions of pesos)

Year	Disability and death contrib. for actives in transition	Gross demand for public sector resources	Employer contrib. upon entry of actives	Net demand for public sector resources	Actives in transition		Entry of actives		Totals	
					Individual contrib.	AFJB balance	Individual contrib.	AFJB balance	Individual contrib.	AFJB balance
Base	0	5,229	0	5,229	2,687	2,687	0	0	2,687	2,687
1	96	5,142	138	5,004	2,669	5,453	69	69	2,738	5,522
2	195	5,109	285	4,824	2,646	8,286	143	214	2,788	8,500
3	297	5,123	448	4,674	2,618	11,172	224	447	2,842	11,619
4	400	5,176	621	4,555	2,585	14,098	311	776	2,895	14,874
5	503	5,201	806	4,395	2,549	17,064	403	1,210	2,953	18,274
6	604	5,275	988	4,287	2,512	20,062	494	1,753	3,006	21,815
7	704	5,357	1,176	4,182	2,472	23,084	588	2,411	3,060	25,495
8	801	5,445	1,301	4,145	2,430	26,120	650	3,157	3,080	29,277
9	895	5,539	1,425	4,114	2,385	29,160	712	3,996	3,098	33,156
10	984	5,638	1,552	4,085	2,339	32,194	776	4,932	3,115	37,126
11	1,068	5,739	1,682	4,057	2,290	35,213	841	5,972	3,131	41,183
12	1,145	5,844	1,815	4,029	2,239	38,202	908	7,117	3,147	45,319
13	1,214	5,952	1,979	3,973	2,186	41,150	990	8,391	3,176	49,541
14	1,274	6,063	2,148	3,915	2,131	44,041	1,073	9,801	3,205	53,842
15	1,324	6,175	2,320	3,855	2,074	46,862	1,160	11,353	3,234	58,215
16	1,362	6,280	2,495	3,786	2,015	49,596	1,247	13,054	3,263	62,650
17	1,387	6,378	2,672	3,706	1,955	52,226	1,336	14,912	3,291	67,138
18	1,397	6,467	2,848	3,620	1,892	54,732	1,424	16,933	3,316	71,665
19	1,391	6,547	3,025	3,521	1,827	57,094	1,513	19,123	3,340	76,217
20	1,367	6,569	3,205	3,364	1,762	59,307	1,602	21,490	3,364	80,796
21	1,342	6,588	3,386	3,201	1,694	61,351	1,693	24,043	3,388	85,394
22	1,315	6,604	3,569	3,034	1,626	63,205	1,785	26,789	3,411	89,994
23	1,286	6,617	3,749	2,868	1,556	64,846	1,875	29,735	3,431	94,581
24	1,255	6,628	3,922	2,706	1,486	66,249	1,961	32,886	3,447	99,136

Source: Author's calculations based on data from FIEL.

was assumed that all of the individuals chose to withdraw their funds upon retirement and to obtain a life annuity in the private insurance sector.

Tables 2.12 and 2.13 show the projection of the reformed system for the first 25 years of the transition to its final, long-term form. Of particular note are the trend of benefit payments to current passive subscribers and the income that the pay-as-you-go system will receive from current active subscribers by collecting the employer contribution, the compensatory premium, and transfers from the AFJP of funds accumulated by individuals in transition who become disabled. Also noteworthy are the expenditures of the pay-as-you-go system to pay the PBU, the PC and the benefits owed as a result of the disability and early death coverage of active subscribers in transition. Next, these flows are added to those generated upon the retirement of active subscribers, which gives the total net

Figure 2.1. Net Demand over 25 Years for Public Distribution System with PBU Equal to 40 Percent of the Average Wage
(In millions of 1992 pesos)

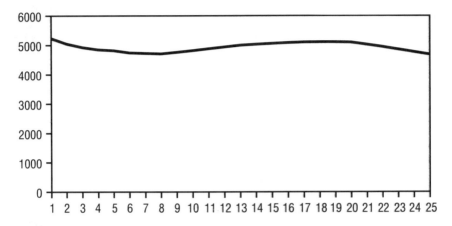

Source: Author's estimates.
Note: PBU stands for universal basic benefit.

demand for resources in the pay-as-you-go system administered by the public sector. The income of the AFJPs from commissions and the accumulation of pension funds will aid mandatory capitalization.

As indicated in the tables, the deficit of the pay-as-you-go system is decreasing and the current discounted value of the deficits in the projected period is 64.538 billion pesos. Moreover, the funds accumulated by the AFJPs total 2.687 billion pesos the first year, climbing to 33.156 billion pesos in 10 years, to 76.217 billion pesos in 20 years, and to 99.136 billion pesos in 25 years. Consequently, in 25 years, the government will be able to finance only 46 percent of the deficit of the pay-as-you-go system, placing up to 50 percent of government securities in the pension funds and leaving 34.919 billion pesos (at the current discounted value) as the balance to be covered using specially allocated tax revenues and general revenue funds.

To demonstrate the sensitivity of the results to changes in the universal basic benefit, which in the new system is equal to the current minimum benefit, the pay-as-you-go system deficit was again calculated, assuming that with this PBU it would be possible to obtain 40 percent of the national average wage instead of the 16.5 percent of the reform proposal (see Figure 2.1).[6]

---

6 This percentage was being discussed in Parliament in early 1993.

As a result of the changes, the public sector must now cover a deficit in the pay-as-you-go system it administers equal to 76.986 billion pesos at the current discounted value (for the flow of deficits in the first 25 years). Therefore, considering the placement of securities for 50 percent of the pension funds accumulated in 25 years in the AFJPs, it will be possible to cover only 39 percent of the discounted deficit of the pay-as-you-go system in this manner, leaving a balance of 47.322 billion pesos, which is 36 percent higher than the one obtained with a PBU equal to 16.5 percent of the national average wage.

Recommendations for Reform

In promoting equity and intergenerational mutal interest, the main attraction of the new system is the connection between the benefits and the contributions made during the subscriber's active years. Individuals with different years of contributions and similar wage histories during their last 10 working years cannot be eligible for the same benefit. This is a throwback to the concept of social insurance based on individual social insurance savings but without overlooking individuals with low incomes who, upon retirement, are not eligible for a minimum survivor's benefit. Therefore, the redistributive element is preserved, guaranteeing the PBU if the annuity to be capitalized is insignificant.

Other elements of the new legislation, however, require closer examination.

- In the reform proposal, the mobility of the benefits is linked to the trend of the average wage implicit in the collection. Although this guarantees an adjustment mechanism compatible with the financial capacity of the system, it can be affected by evasion, which is a chronic problem in the current social insurance system.
- By authorizing debt instruments representing up to 80 percent of the fund accumulated in the AFJPs, the government jeopardizes the long-term financial stability of the system and undermines the credibility of the reform.
- The adjustment of life annuities obtainable in the private insurance sector is unclear, which lessens the appeal of this option at retirement.
- No predetermined percentage of the personal contribution has to be earmarked for capitalization, there being no a priori limits other than the competition between AFJPs in setting commissions and the percentage of the wage designated to pay the cost of disability and early death coverage.
- The state guarantees the private insurance sector life annuities against bankruptcy or insolvency of the insurer, up to approximately 82.5 percent of the national average wage (implicit in the social insurance collection). This guarantee may harm individuals who have capitalized a larger amount because their salary is above average or those who have made larger contributions during their working lives.

- The new system does not explain the status of workers in rural areas who contribute to the system by agreement, and it is in these cases that informality and evasion are the most common.

Social Health Insurance

It was only in the early years of this century that the concept of health insurance took root in Argentina. After the Second World War, significant advances in industrial development, urbanization and unionization accelerated the growth of union-sponsored voluntary health insurance. During the Perón administration (1945-55), gradual progress was made toward mandatory social insurance as the state established specific social programs administered by unions, which initially benefited civil servants and gradually spread to other fields. Passage of Law No. 18610 in 1970 institutionalized and organized the social services system and made coverage for all salaried employees and their immediate families mandatory.[7] Administration of these entities was entrusted to professional associations. Minimum employer and employee contributions were established to finance the system, and welfare benefits could be provided directly or by contracting with public or private suppliers. The system was expanded in 1971 with the passage of Law No. 18980, which promoted the creation of social service organizations for management personnel not included in collective labor agreements. Law No. 19032 created the National Social Security Institute for Retirements and Pensions (INSSJyP, *Instituto Nacional de Seguridad Social para Jubilados y Pensionados*), which extended mandatory social insurance coverage to the retirees and pensioners of the national social insurance system and their immediate families. Although the rules governing the system were replaced, first in 1980 (Law No. 22269) and then in 1989 (Law No. 23660), the financial organization of the system has actually remained unchanged since the beginning, except for the necessary increases in employer and employee contributions.

Diagnosis of the Current Situation

The social services system currently governed by Law No. 23660 comprises just under 300 legally distinct entities, whose activities are regulated by the National Social Security Administration. The system benefits approximately 17.5 million individuals, or 55 percent of the country's total population. Adding to these so-

---

[7] Not included in this category are military personnel and civilian employees of the armed forces, the security forces, the federal police, employees of provincial and municipal governments, MCBA (Municipality of Buenos Aires) personnel and management personnel not included in collective labor agreements.

Table 2.14. Trend of the Beneficiary Population by Institutional Type, 1983-90

Institutional type	1983	1984	1986	1988	1990
Union	5,773,235	6,441,263	6,588,391	6,888,962	7,014,977
State	550,635	744,154	735,225	744,725	765,927
By agreement	221,341	235,360	239,462	234,810	233,471
Management personnel	722,231	827,223	903,217	936,495	979,109
Mixed administration	8,662,306	8,881,397	8,891,316	8,653,732	8,426,827
By membership	32,281	96,913	40,318	57,881	59,321
Law 21476	49,087	55,378	57,264	59,377	60,200
Privatization of enterprises	21,464	24,228	26,853	27,533	26,402
INOS/ANSSAL	16,032,580	17,305,918	17,482,046	17,603,515	17,566,234
Others[1]	—	5,051,160	5,704,200	6,372,500	—
Total	—	22,357,078	23,186,246	23,976,015	—

Source: FIEL data based on INOS.
Notes: [1] Provincial and municipal, Judicial Branch and National Congress, Armed Forces and Security Personnel.

cial service organizations those of the provinces and municipalities, those of the Judicial Branch and of the National Congress, and those for armed forces and security personnel—all governed by specific laws—the population with mandatory medical coverage is nearly 75 percent of all the country's residents (see Table 2.14).

Based on official information from the National Social Insurance Revenue Institute, it is estimated that the total income of the social service organizations governed by Law No. 23660 was approximately US$3.8 billion in 1992, or about 37 percent of the total spending on health care (combined expenditures of the public and private sectors), and 3 percent of GDP. The work of this sector is primarily that of providing insurance: its basic function is to administer the benefits to which the users are entitled and, with the funds collected, to pay for the medical services used. Generally speaking, it has developed no installed capacity nor does it have the professional bodies needed.

The organization of the system completely eliminates competition among the various entities since the beneficiaries cannot choose a health insurance provider but must affiliate with the institution associated with the union organization to which they belong. This means that the social service organizations have no economic incentive to provide high-quality services or to develop efficient management systems. This manner of organizing also causes great differences in size and great disparities in the administrative expenses of the various social service organizations. For a large number of beneficiaries, this results in duplicate coverage; since contributions to the system are based on wages, those individuals who have more than one job have more than one affiliation, as do households in which more than one member of the immediate family works.

To finance the system, the resources of each social service organization come from an employer contribution of 6 percent of the affiliate's pay and 3 percent contributed by the affiliate. Of this amount, the social service organization receives 90 percent, the remainder going to the National Social Insurance Administration (ANSSAL, *Administración Nacional del Seguro de Salud*) to build the Redistribution Fund. For social service organizations for management personnel, these percentages increase to 85 percent and 15 percent, respectively. The Redistribution Fund is used—after deducting ANSSAL operating expenses—to make grants, loans, and so on to the social service organizations that need them.

This financing arrangement creates countless cross subsidies among groups of beneficiaries that often yield unwanted results. In the first place, because there is no connection whatever between the actuarial cost of the medical care of each individual and his or her contribution to the system, resources from the population least at risk of disease transfer to the high-risk population. Moreover, since the services are the same for all affiliates at a given social service organization, regardless of their contributions, within each field of activity the individuals with the largest incomes subsidize those with the fewest resources. Similarly, smaller families subsidize larger families, since the contribution to the system—except in certain provincial social service organizations—is unrelated to the number of family members who are beneficiaries of the system.

As a result, strong incentives have been created to evade contributions to the system by understating income, and contributions decrease but the benefits remain the same. Moreover, since the principle of mutual interest is limited to each social service, horizontal inequity occurs since individuals in the same circumstances receive different benefits simply by virtue of their employment in different fields of activity. The Redistribution Fund is the only integral mechanism among social service organizations. This system of financing based on the payroll means that there is no connection at all between the resources of each organization and its projected expenses, which should be the case in any insurance organization. No mechanisms outside the system ensure its financial stability because the income of the social service organizations is linked to the growth of real wages and their expenses to the use of the services by the beneficiaries.

Although the flaws in the organization of the system were present from the start, the situation was complicated in the 1980s as higher administrative costs, increasingly expensive medical technology, and incentives to overuse health care services drove up expenses. A drop in wages and increased evasion reduced system resources.

As a result, the social service organizations experienced recurring financial deficits throughout the last decade. In an effort to reduce these enormous deficits, the social service organizations and the government implemented various policies, some of which significantly distorted the health care market. To begin with, when a social service organization has a financial problem, it asks ANSSAL for a grant. According to Law No. 23660, 70 percent of the Redistri-

Table 2.15. Average Monthly Contribution and Expenditure by Category of Beneficiary, 1992

(In U.S. dollars)

Category	Amount
Contribution per active regular beneficiary	34
Expenditure per beneficiary (excluding INSSJyP)	15
Expenditure per inactive beneficiary	37

Source: FIEL, 1991b.

bution Fund should automatically go to the organizations with the lowest income per beneficiary; the remainder is distributed as ANSSAL sees fit. ANSSAL, however, has a very difficult time gathering information since it has no reliable record of the flow of funds to the organizations it is supposed to supervise.[8] In the end, most of the Redistribution Fund is dispersed in a wholly arbitrary manner to cover deficits—the largest deficits do not always signify the smallest incomes—and in response to political pressure. The discretional use of these funds is significant, given the volume of resources involved and, therefore, the redistributive capacity of the system. In fact, taking the growth observed in the first half of 1992 as a base, this account grows annually by about US$250 million. If these funds were used to subsidize the social service organizations containing the 25 percent of the beneficiary population with the lowest incomes—not counting the passive population—an annual per capita subsidy of about US$70, which is 40 percent of the average per person expenditure of the system (see Table 2.15), would be enough.

In addition to asking ANSSAL for grants, social service organizations with financial difficulties delay paying suppliers for services rendered, sometimes for considerable periods of time, with the result that suppliers often decide to suspend medical care to the beneficiaries of such organizations.

In addition, the authority responsible for reducing the expenses of the system has traditionally controlled the prices of the services through the official price list (*Nomenclador Nacional*). Since the suppliers are an extremely diverse group (professionals, hospitals, pharmaceutical laboratories, etc.) and they are generally organized into professional associations, confederations and business associations, setting prices creates a distribution struggle. As a result of the pro-

---

[8] Furthermore, it is widely believed that the number of beneficiaries reported to ANSSAL by each social service organization is incorrect since not all of the names that should be are removed from the list, and when they are it is only after a considerable delay, so that the number of beneficiaries is falsely increased.

Table 2.16. Trend of Contributions to the System, 1970-92
(Percentages)

| | On wages | | | | On S.A.C.(c) | | | | |
| Effective date | Worker | | Employer | Total | Worker | | Employer | Total | Comments |
	(a)	(b)			(a)	(b)			
1970 (Law 18.610)	1	2	2	3 or 4	1	2	2	3 or 4	cap
1971 (Law 18.980)	1	2	2	3 or 4	3	3	3	6	cap
1974 (Dec. 189/74)	1	2	2	3 or 4	3	3	3	6	no cap
1974 (Dec. 1684/74)	1	2	2.5	3.5 or 4.5	3	3	3.5	6.5	no cap
1975 (Law 21.216)	2	3	4.5	6.5 or 7.5	3	3	3.5	6.5	no cap
1980 (Law 22.269)	3	3	4.5	7.5	3	3	4.5	7.5	no cap
1980 (Law 23.660)	3	3	6	9	3	3	6	9	no cap

Source: FIEL.
Notes: (a) Without primary group.
      (b) With primary group.
      (c) SAC: supplementary annual wage.

cess of economic deregulation initiated by the current administration, in late 1991 the government stopped controlling the prices of medical services. Since then, the social service organizations have been setting prices, often unilaterally and sometimes apparently through negotiating with the providers of services, but with results—owing once again to the beneficiaries' "captive" status—similar to those produced by the former policy of price controls. Neither pricing policy (unilateral setting of prices or negotiation) prevents suppliers from engaging in dishonest practices such as billing for services not provided, falsely increasing the number of services to compensate for the drop in price, collecting a separate, unauthorized fee from users and cutting back on the quality of service. When the financial crisis of the social service organizations became apparent and the various sectors involved applied pressure, it was decided repeatedly to raise the employer and employee contributions to the system (see Table 2.16).

In short, the social services system has serious flaws, which, although thrown into sharp relief by Argentina's economic decline in the 1980s, are largely the result of organizational deficiencies caused by inappropriate incentives.

Distributive Effects of the Social Services System

Because social health insurance is organized by field of activity in Argentina, the main redistributive impact of the system is produced within each social service organization. In fact, although all individuals contribute the same percentage of their wages to the social service organization for their professions, the social insurance coverage they receive in exchange is the same for all of the affiliates of a given organization, but there are vast differences between organizations. This feature of the system greatly complicates the task of measuring the redistributive impact since doing so requires identifying and comparing the various social services provided by each organization. Available information does not permit an analysis of this scope.

The social service organization for retirees and pensioners within the INSSJyP is a special case. This organization is funded mainly by 2 percent from social insurance income and 5 percent from the employer and employee contributions based on the wages of active workers. This financing arrangement has a redistributive effect among the beneficiaries of the system themselves since each of them contributes according to what he earns and all receive the same coverage. The arrangement also effects a transfer of resources from active to passive affiliates. This is the health insurance system with the largest number of beneficiaries in the country—approximately 3.3 million people, or nearly 20 percent of the population covered by Law No. 23660. Its annual budget is nearly US$1.5 billion. Of this total amount received from the INSSJyP each year, approximately US$200 million comes from the contributions of the beneficiaries of the system and US$1.3 billion from the contributions of active subscribers.

This volume of resources implies an average expenditure per covered individual of US$37 per month, which is the per capita average for the health insurance of the population of passive subscribers. Using this average—and assuming that all individuals have the same risk of disease—it is possible to calculate the gross benefit that each of them receives from the system. Part of this expenditure is financed by the beneficiaries themselves, who contribute 2 percent of their social insurance income for this purpose. This means that the monetary cost of the insurance carried by each individual varies according to the amount of social insurance income. Since the coverage is the same for everyone in this population group, the net benefits of the system are also a function of the income received. The calculations indicate (see Table 2.17) that for individuals whose monthly retirement income is under US$1,900, the contribution to the system is less than the benefit received, so that health insurance is a means of redistributing income in their favor.

The high level of the cut-off figure is particularly important, given that the average wage in Argentina is approximately US$500 per month. The effect was significant for beneficiaries who were receiving the minimum social insurance income in December 1992; the net transfer of resources represented more than 22 percent of this income. Above the $1,900 monthly figure, the opposite occurs and the net contributions to the system—less the benefits—become positive, representing more than 1 percent of the social insurance income in the highest categories. Thus, for most passive subscribers, health insurance has a positive redistributive impact, given that only 0.15 percent of individuals are in social insurance income categories above this level. Moreover, for all retirees and pension-

Table 2.17. Distributive Effects of Health Insurance: Retirees and Pensioners[1]

Monthly allowance ($)	No. of cases	Average monthly allowance	Monthly contrib.	Monthly benefit[2]	Net monthly benefit	Average net benefit (%)
To 150.50	1,886,340	149.79	3.00	37	34.00	22.70
150.51 to 160.00	16,972	155.21	3.10	37	33.90	21.84
160.01 to 179.49	32,707	170.25	3.40	37	33.60	19.73
179.50 to 180.50	32,471	170.00	3.60	37	33.40	18.56
180.51 to 200.00	78,946	193.05	3.86	37	33.14	17.17
200.01 to 224.49	40.832	212.11	4.24	37	32.76	15.44
224.50 to 225.50	90.319	225.00	4.50	37	32.50	14.44
225.51 to 240.00	52.154	232.87	4.66	37	32.34	13.89
240.01 to 260.00	216.404	253.28	5.07	37	31.93	12.61
260.01 to 280.00	189.084	263.58	4.27	37	31.73	12.04
280.01 to 291.99	37.869	286.19	5.72	37	31.28	10.93
292.00 to 293.00	11.656	292.51	5.85	37	31.15	10.65
293.01 to 300.00	22.047	296.73	5.93	37	31.07	10.47
300.01 to 350.00	115.148	323.58	6.47	37	30.53	9.43
350.01 to 400.00	88.595	374.16	7.48	37	29.52	7.89
450.01 to 450.00	65.502	423.91	8.48	37	28.52	6.73
450.01 to 500.00	50.523	474.05	9.48	37	27.52	5.81
500.01 to 550.00	40.264	523.69	10.47	37	26.53	5.07
550.01 to 572.19	15.826	560.98	11.22	37	25.78	4.60
572.20 to 573.20	638	572.70	11.45	37	25.55	4.46
573.21 to 602.19	17.026	587.47	11.75	37	25.25	4.30
602.20 to 603.20	583	602.56	12.05	37	24.95	4.14
603.21 to 650.00	23.581	625.92	12.52	37	24.48	3.91
650.01 to 700.00	21.447	674.12	13.48	37	23.52	3.49
700.01 to 763.09	22.143	730.00	14.61	37	22.39	3.06
763.10 to 764.10	375	763.61	15.27	37	21.73	2.85
764.11 to 793.09	8.292	778.55	15.57	37	21.43	2.75
793.10 to 794.10	520	793.60	15.87	37	21.13	2.66
794.11 to 800.00	1,552	797.11	15.94	37	21.06	2.64
800.01 to 1,000.00	40,425	886.83	17.74	37	19.26	2.17
1,000.00 to 1,200.00	20,772	1,090.59	21.81	37	15.19	1.39
1,200.00 to 1,424.19	14,766	1,312.45	26.25	37	10.75	0.82
1,424.20 to 1,425.20	530	1,424.36	28.49	37	8.51	0.60
1,425.21 to 1,600.00	5,649	1,507.86	30.16	37	6.84	0.45
1.600.01 to 1,898.59	6,786	1,733.08	34.66	37	2.34	0.13
1,898.60 to 1,899.70	6,328	1,899.12	37.98	37	-0.98	-0.05
1,899.71 to 2,000.00	470	1,946.91	38.94	37	-1.94	-0.10
2,000.01 to 2,200.00	796	2,098.78	41.98	37	-4.98	-0.24
2,200.01 to 2,400.00	612	2,297.54	45.95	37	-8.95	-0.39
2,400.01 to 2,600.00	964	2,458.72	49.17	37	-12.17	-0.50
2,600.01 to 2,800.00	311	2,689.14	53.78	37	-16.78	-0.62
2,800.01 to 3,000.00	238	2,898.76	57.98	37	-20.98	-0.72
3,000.01 to 3,200.00	167	3,085.03	61.70	37	-24.70	-0.80
3,200.01 to 3,400.00	28	3,246.35	64.93	37	-27.93	-0.86
3,400.01 to 3,600.00	86	3,496.32	69.93	37	-32.93	-0.94
3,600.01 to 3,800.00	75	3,709.10	74.18	37	-37.18	-1.00
3,801.00 to 4,000.00	433	3,963.86	79.28	37	-42.28	-1.07
Above 4,000	63	4,456.05	90.92	37	-53.92	-1.19
General average	249.51	4.99	37	32.01	12.83	

Source: FIEL. based on data from the Office of the Secretary of State for Social Security.
Note: [1] Based on INSSJyP($).   [2] The data on social insurance allowances is for December 1992 and includes all Retirees and Pensioners of the National Social Insurance System.

ers, this program generates a net benefit representing more than 12 percent of the average income provided by the system.

Reform Proposal

Until late 1991, although the authorities acknowledged the serious decline of the social services system, they failed to realize that the root cause was the design of the system itself. It was only in early 1992 that it was officially recognized that the organizational problems and resultant incentives constituted one of the main causes of the crisis in all of the social service organizations. This shift in the perception of the authorities led the executive branch to prepare a draft reform calling for significant changes in the system.

A year after the appearance of the official reform proposal, it had still not been sent to the National Congress, presumably as a result of strong opposition from powerful political sectors and union organizations. The government decided to hasten the reform of the existing system and issued an Executive Decree. For the first time, this enabled beneficiaries to choose the social service organization they wish to join from among the existing organizations, except those reserved for management personnel.[9]

Although this was a step forward, the reform of the health care sector could benefit from:

- freedom to choose from a wide range of institutions and periodic information for beneficiaries about different insurance plans and incomes coming from premiums freely determined by insurers;
- a minimum health plan defined by the state and mandatorily offered by all organizations with a maximum price: and,
- system financing based on basic wage contributions (1 to 2 percent of the wage) to a fund that is redistributed among the beneficiaries according to their risk of disease and income level, with shared voluntary contributions to the system and the obligation to defray the cost of the minimum health plan.

Family Allowances System

In Argentina the system of family allowances was initiated in 1957 with the creation of the Family Allowance Fund for Personnel in Private Commercial Companies and the Family Allowance Fund for Personnel in Industry. At the start, the only benefit the funds provided was an allowance for each child under

---

[9] Unlike the exhaustive original reform proposal, this second version leaves a number of important aspects to be defined in the subsequent regulations, which makes it compatible with a wide range of health insurance models.

15 years of age or disabled. In order to finance this system, a Family Allowances Compensating Fund was created within both funds, financed with a mandatory employer contribution. The system was designed to have a redistributive impact because individuals without family responsibilities would finance those who did. In 1965 a Family Allowances Fund was created for longshoremen. In 1969 the various family allowances systems were unified, with the same coverage and a uniform contribution rate established for all workers. The Family Allowances Fund for the Personnel of State Enterprises was created at the same time. The law was repealed by Decree 651/73 and replaced by a decree establishing that the payment of family allowances for the personnel of these enterprises would be made from the current income of the enterprises themselves. The last important change in the system was Decree 2284/91 (Deregulation of the Economy), which dissolved the three existing funds and transferred the management of the system to the National Social Security Administration.

At present, the Family Allowances Funds grant the following benefits: marriage, prenatal care, maternity care, childbirth, adoption, spouse, child, large family, primary and preschool education, secondary and higher education, primary and preschool student aid, annual vacation supplement and child under four years of age. The benefits vary according to the economic capacity of each province. The system is financed with an employer contribution of 7.5 percent of the total wages paid to workers. For the Patagonian provinces of Chubut, Santa Cruz and the National Territory of Tierra del Fuego, the contribution is 3 percent.

Diagnosis

In 1991, the population covered by the system rose to nearly 3 million individuals. In addition to this population, 2,100,370 public sector employees (public administration and state enterprises) also receive family allowances, making the total target population 5,082,243. Each month on average, a total of 7,644,342 family allowances are paid to private sector personnel. To this must be added primary and preschool student aid, of which there are approximately 1,424,800 cases each year. As far as the real growth of family allowances is concerned, the benefits have shrunk with the passage of time. For a typical family (i.e., a married worker with two children, one in primary school and the other in secondary school) the real level of monthly benefits in 1992 was 19.5 percent below the average of the 1980-92 period.

Traditionally, the family allowances system has had large surpluses, so that its net income is used for other purposes (expensive procurements, building management expenses). In the March-October 1992 period, under the new (ANSES, *Administración de la Secretaría de Seguridad Social*; Social Security Secretariat Administration), the family allowances system received contribution revenues totaling US$545 million, whereas reimbursement expenses and direct benefits payments totaled US$226 million. This means that the system had a surplus of US$319 million. Consequently, there is still a great deal of room for reducing the companies' contribution rate or raising the average level of the services provided.

Family Allowances and Income Distribution

Based on information from the Permanent Household Survey, the distribution of the benefits obtained by the population through family allowances was calculated, according to quintile of income.[10] The results indicate that the 20 percent of the population who earn the least receive only 4.4 percent of the monthly family allowances, while the 20 percent who earn the most receive 25.5 percent of such payments. The imbalance in the distribution of family allowances is chiefly a reflection of the fact that the population with the lowest income also has the lowest level of employment in the formal labor market and, therefore, is not entitled to family allowances.

Considering only the population covered by the system, the payment of benefits is distributed in similar percentages for the various quintiles of income so that the average payment received by households in the form of family allowances does not differ substantially. Although the 20 percent of the population who earn the least receive the smallest average benefit, the difference among the remaining quintiles is not remarkable, as can be seen in Table 2.18. This shows that although the payment of family allowances is, on the whole, proportionally distributed, it is nevertheless a progressive benefit, given the sharp contrast between the incomes of the population.

Reform Proposal

In the highest income levels, the benefits of this system represent only a small fraction of the total income. This suggests the possibility of restricting the beneficiary population to the lowest income sectors. The only benefit that should remain unchanged (i.e., available to all income levels) is the maternity benefit, since its elimination would discriminate against women entering the labor market. All of the other benefits should be completely overhauled and a single benefit established to subsidize the education of children. In other words, an educational allowance should be established, from preschool to age 21. The purpose of the proposed subsidy would be to encourage human resources training. To deter-

---

[10] This survey is conducted by the National Institute of Statistics and Censuses (INDEC) for the federal capital and greater Buenos Aires, where 33 percent of the country's total population is concentrated.

Table 2.18. Distribution of Family Allowances

Quintile[1]	Average monthly family allowance ($)	Income Distribution (average index=100)
I	47.1	27.2
II	60.9	49.0
III	53.0	73.1
IV	52.0	106.6
V	51.3	244.2

Source: FIEL, based on INDEC data, 1989.
Note: Quintile I represents the lowest income group; Quintile V, the highest.

mine the maximum income eligible for this benefit, the combined income of the parents should be taken in to account to prevent horizontal inequity (for example, households not eligible because the head of the family earns more than the maximum amount, but the family income is less than in other households in which both parents work but have salaries below the ceiling).

Unemployment Allowance

Universal unemployment insurance has never existed in Argentina but instead only partial systems covering only a certain segment of the population. The oldest system still functioning is the one in the construction sector. Temporary arrangements were the rule for other workers until the passage of the National Employment Act. The Unemployment Fund for Construction Workers (1980) consists of monthly employer contributions to individual bank accounts in the worker's name. The 12 percent for personnel with less than one year's seniority and 8 percent for all others. When a worker leaves, regardless of the reason, he or she is entitled to compensation from the Fund. This system replaced the advance notice system. The National Employment Act established a system of comprehensive unemployment benefits for workers covered by the Labor Agreement Act whose employment has been involuntarily terminated. This system entered into force in March 1992.

The length of time that contributions were made to the National Employment Fund determines the duration of benefits, with a minimum of four months for those who have contributed for 12 months and a maximum of 12 months for those who have contributed for 30 or more months. The amount of the benefit is set for the first four months at 80 percent of the net amount of the best monthly wage in the six months preceding termination of the labor agreement, and decreases from then on. The compensation is subject to a minimum of 120 pesos and a maximum of 400 pesos. The system is financed with an employer contribu-

Table 2.19. Distribution of the Unemployed According to Length of Previous Employment
(Percentages)

	Federal capital and greater Buenos Aires	Other areas of the country
Less than one month	34.6	28.1
1-3 months	27.4	20.2
3-12 months	34.8	39.5
More than 12 months	3.2	12.2

Source: Labor Ministry and Tenuous Employment Analysis, National Technical Assistance Program for the Social Services Administration in Argentina, 1989.

tion equal to 1.5 percent of the wages of salaried employees and a contribution of 3 percent of the total wages paid by public service companies, if any.

The large amounts collected in 1992, together with the level of the average allowance (estimated at US$300), suggests that the likelihood of the system not being financed with its own funds at the current contribution rate is extremely low. In fact, according to information obtained from the Permanent Household Survey conducted by the National Institute of Statistics and Censuses (INDEC, *Instituto Nacional de Estadísticas y Censos*) the average length of employment is four months.

Table 2.19 shows that the probability of losing one's job after 12 months is less than for the other categories. Since the federal capital region and greater Buenos Aires contain a third of the country's total population, it is estimated that for the country as a whole, 10.5 percent of those who are unemployed held their previous job longer than 12 months, which means that only 10.5 percent are eligible to collect the allowance. The rate of increase in the number of unemployed individuals in the eligible population necessary to ensure that the payment of unemployment allowances is fully covered by the system's income is calculated as follows:

$$\Delta d/e = (w/s \cdot t/p)/(1 + w/s \cdot t/p)$$

where Δd = increase in the number of unemployed individuals necessary to deplete the funds;

  e = level of employment;

  w = average wage of the covered population;

  s = average allowance;

  t = rate of contribution to the National Employment Fund; and,

  p = percentage of the unemployed population who previously held a job for more than 12 months (population eligible to collect the allowance).

Given that the average allowance paid in the first month was approximately US$360, and given the percentages of collection thereof, it is estimated that the average payment will climb to $US306. Assuming an average wage of US$580, and given that only 10.5 percent of the unemployed are eligible to receive the allowance:

$$\Delta d/e = 0.2131$$

This means that a 21.3 increase (in the number of unemployed individuals) is required. But in order for the income to continue dwindling (remember that the allowance is not permanent), the total number of unemployed individuals must alsoat least remain the same. That is, if the covered population re-enters the labor market at the end of the period, an equal percentage must leave it. Thus, 21.3 percent must be the highest unemployment rate in this population group.

Reform Proposal

Given the existence of employment arrangements that provide for severance pay, the population can be divided into three different groups according to whether they receive a payment covering the time they spend looking for work: (i) population with dual coverage (compensation plus allowance), or those governed by the labor contract law; (ii) population with single coverage (compensation, public administration, domestic service, and agricultural system); and (iii) population with no coverage, workers in the informal sector, the self-employed, and employers.

Although internalizing the costs of dismissal makes severance pay obligatory, penalizes companies with larger turnovers, makes adjustments in the labor market more difficult and creates inequities among workers since those who keep their jobs or voluntarily resign receive no payment from the company. This arrangement tends to discourage dismissal and creates a potential demand for "early retirement" payments as the end of the worker's active life approaches. Both the unequal coverage of the population and the heavy burden on the payroll of covering employment contingencies suggest the possibility of a simultaneous reform of severance pay and the unemployment allowance. Moreover, entitling the entire population to monetary compensation in the event of termination, regardless of the reason, would tend to increase equity among workers.

The proposal consists, first, of eliminating the current compensation and the unemployment allowance and replacing them with a new compensatory benefit. This "compensation" would consist of individual insurance obtained from an insurance company (perhaps a Pension Funds Administrator) with a monthly employee contribution of 4-4.5 percent, an amount similar to the current provision for severance pay. This system would eliminate the uncertainty concerning the costs of dismissal and, at the same time, would facilitate entering and leaving the labor market.

Work-related Accidents and Diseases

Argentina's legislation concerning work-related accidents, occupational diseases and accident-diseases aims to provide the worker and his family with adequate protection in case he becomes temporarily or permanently unable to work because of total or partial disability. Work-related accidents have been covered by legislation since 1915 in Argentina. Originally, the employer's liability was limited to accidents that occurred on the job (*i.e.,* in accordance with the "occupational risk" theory). The law provides the option of filing claim pursuant to specific legislation or the Civil Code. In 1940, the law was given greater interpretive scope by including accident-diseases under work-related accidents. In 1960, the employer's liability was extended to include accidents that take place while the worker is traveling to and from work. One of the most significant amendments provided that the right of action expired two years following acknowledgement of the disability, but since there is no deadline for such an acknowledgment, the right of action never really lapses.

Crisis of the System

The vagueness and imprecision of the provisions concerning accidents allowed the system to function as a substitute for unemployment insurance, with the number of such claims proliferating. This caused insurance companies to sustain enormous losses since, as a result of the very concept of an accident not being defined and the limits of liability not being specified (in the Civil Code), and in the absence of a period of prescription, insurance premiums were indeterminate. Despite this, the situation could be tolerated because in late 1989, all insurance company losses were covered by INDER, which held the state monopoly on reinsurance. Thus, there was a direct subsidy from the state to the beneficiaries of this regulation on work-related accidents. In March 1990, INDER decided not to grant reinsurance coverage in many areas of the country for various occupational diseases or accident-diseases. The initial reaction of the insurance companies was to renegotiate the contracts, establishing exemptions, lower coverage limits and higher premiums and thereby raising labor costs.

The Reforms of 1991 and 1992

In November 1991, Law No. 24028 was passed, repealing Law No. 9688 and replacing it with a new system. The new law limits the employer's liability to the term of employment. However, liability refers more generally to psychophysical injuries. It holds the employer liable for any accident that occurs and excludes occupational diseases. The introduction of the concept of psychophysical injury considerably expands the scope of covered incidents, giving rise to a subsequent increase in the number of lawsuits.[11] The maximum compensation is 55,000 pesos. The new method of calculating the compensation lowers it 35 percent from that available under the former system, which is in contrast to the raising of the maximum compensation (which was previously US$25,000. It is still possible to file suit under the Civil Code, without any limitations of any kind. There are limits on the right to institute legal proceedings, which, in addition to all the cases mentioned in the text, expires two years after termination of the labor relationship.

Proposal for an Alternative System

The system of compensation for work-related accidents could be appropriately based on economic incentives rather than the existing legislation. In such a case, the design of the system would provide for the internalization of costs (*i.e.,* the employer would be responsible for compensating damages). According to the principle of internalizing costs, the legislation must establish a system in which accidents are insurable. The current system, in which the amounts to be paid are extremely uncertain, complicates the determination of an actuarial premium. Therefore, the types of accidents eligible for compensation should be precisely determined, especially with respect to accident-diseases. Another alternative would be to include within the definition of accidents only those that are traumatic in nature and a specific list of occupational diseases, with all references to accident-diseases being eliminated. The latter would be covered by means of other mechanisms—some already established by law and some yet to be developed—aimed at retraining the victims of accident-diseases.

Those who suffer an accident-disease would have the initial option of having the company redefine their duties to adapt them to their new condition. If this is not possible, they would receive severance pay. Those who continue to work would not be entitled to file an accident claim (Law No. 24028) nor to file suit under the Civil Code, since they would be protected by the fact of having a job suited to their abilities. Those who were dismissed or who recently resigned (whereas the claim was not prescribed) would have the option of receiving their

---

[11] In late September 1992, Decree 1813 was issued to reduce the considerable incentives to file suit because of the high fees charged by legal advisers, experts and lawyers in legal proceedings concerning work-related accidents. This decree was an attempt to lower such costs by creating within the judicial system a group of experts and other advisers, which the disputing parties can consult. If either party decides to use this group, the other must necessarily use experts who are also members of it.

disability retirement, receiving severance pay and early retirement due to disability. Finally, anyone not covered by the legislation on disability ("low degree" of diminution of the ability to work) would have the option of joining a retraining program. These programs would be administered by private or public entities (companies, universities, unions, etc.) and would be financed with contributions from companies wishing to cover the accident-disease risk in this way.

Finally, in amending the existing legislation, more effective limitation of the principle of joint causality and eliminating the possibility of filing suit under the Civil Code should be considered. In cases of employer fraud (in which the industrial safety regulations are violated or a claim for damages is filed), the general coverage and compensation system be maintained but the limits doubled.

Bibliography

Barral, S. 1935. *30y 11575. Informe técnico y balance actuarial al 31-12-1933*. Buenos Aires: Caja Nacional de Jubilaciones Bancarias.

————. 1967. *Jubilaciones: bases para el estudio del equilibrio y la estabilidad de su régimen*. Buenos Aires: Academia Nacional de Ciencias Económicas.

Bovbjerg, R., P. Held, and M. Pauly. 1987. Privatization and Bidding in the Health Care Sector. *Journal of Policy Analysis and Management* 6(4):648-66.

Castañeda, T. 1989. *The Chilean Health System: Organization, Functioning and Financing*. Washington, D.C.: The World Bank.

Diéguez, H., J.J. Llach, and H. Petrecolla. 1991. Reflexiones sobre el gasto público social. *Desarrollo Económico*. 31(123):429-37.

Enthoven, A. 1978a. Consumer-Choice Health Plan (First of Two Parts). *The New England Journal of Medicine*. 298(12):650-658.

————. 1978b. Consumer-Choice Health Plan (Second of Two Parts). *The New England Journal of Medicine*. 298(13):709-720.

————. 1978c. Cutting Cost without Cutting the Quality of Care. *The New England Journal of Medicine*. 298(22):1229-1238.

Feldstein, M. 1985. The Social Security Explosion. *The Public Interest*. Fall (81):94-106.

Fernández, R. 1979. *Hacia una reforma de sistema argentino de previsión social*. Working Document No. 1. CEMA.

Fundación de Investigaciones Económicas Latinoamericanas (FIEL). 1987. *El fracaso del estatismo*. Buenos Aires: Editorial Sudamericana.

————. 1989. *Los costos del Estado regulador*. Buenos Aires: Editorial Manantial.

————. 1991a. *Argentina. La reforma económica 1989-91. Balance y perspectivas*. Buenos Aires: Editorial Manantial.

_____. 1991b. Reforma del sistema nacional de jubilaciones y pensiones. Buenos Aires, Argentina. Mimeo.

_____. 1992a. *Argentina: Hacia una economía de mercado.* Buenos Aires: Editorial Manantial.

_____. 1992b. Hacia una nueva organización del federalismo fiscal en la Argentina. Paper presented in the Eighth Convention of the Private Banks of Argentina, Buenos Aires, Argentina.

González García, G., *et al.* 1987. *El gasto en salud y en medicamentos, Argentina, 1985.* Buenos Aires: Estudios CEDES.

Instituto Nacional de Estadística y Censos (INDEC). 1989. *Módulo de utilización y gasto en servicios de salud.* Buenos Aires: INDEC.

Instituto Nacional de Obras Sociales (INOS). 1980-88. *Boletín Informativo.* Buenos Aires: INOS.

Instituto Nacional de Previsión Social, Gerencia Económico-Financiera. 1990. *El sistema previsional argentino. Desarrollo de un diagnóstico.* Buenos Aires: Instituto Nacional de Previsión Social, Gerencia Económico-Financiera.

Larroulet, C., ed. 1991. *Soluciones privadas a problemas públicos.* Santiago de Chile: Instituto Libertad y Desarrollo/The Center for International Private Enterprise (CIPE).

Ministerio de Salud y Acción Social. 1985. *Argentina: Descripción de su situación de salud.* Buenos Aires: Ministerio de Salud y Acción Social.

Ministerio de Trabajo y Seguridad Social, Secretaría de Seguridad Social. 1992a. *Las inequidades en el régimen nacional de previsión social vigente.* Programa Nacional de Asistencia Técnica Para la Administración de los Servicios Sociales en la República Argentina (PRONATASS), Gob. Arg/BIRF/PNUD/ARG88/005. Buenos Aires: Ministerio de Trabajo y Seguridad Social, Secretaría de Seguridad Social.

_____. 1992b. *Régimen de previsión de trabajadores independientes.* Buenos Aires: Ministerio de Trabajo y Seguridad Social, Secretaría de Seguridad Social.

———. 1992c. *Sistema nacional de previsión social: Su evaluación y situación a fines de la década del '80*. Buenos Aires: Ministerio de Trabajo y Seguridad Social, Secretaría de Seguridad Social.

Panadeiros, M. 1988. *Sistema de atención médica en la Argentina: propuesta para su reforma*. Working Document No. 17. Buenos Aires: Fundación de Investigaciones Económicas Latinoamericanas (FIEL).

———. 1991. *El sistema de obras sociales en la Argentina: Diagnóstico y propuesta de reforma*. Working Documento No. 29. Buenos Aires: Fundación de Investigaciones Económicas Latinoamericanas (FIEL).

———. 1992. *Gasto público social: El sistema de salud*. Working Document No. 34. Buenos Aires: Fundación de Investigaciones Económicas Latinoamericanas (FIEL).

Schultess, W., and R. Lo Vuolo. 1991. Transformación del sistema previsional de autónomos: Paso inicial para la reforma en la seguridad social. *Desarrollo Económico* 30(120):547-71.

CHAPTER THREE

Financing Social Security in Brazil

Francisco E. Barreto de Oliveira, Kaizô Iwakami Beltrão,
and André Cezar Medici

This chapter describes the growth of Brazil's social security system and diagnoses its social insurance, health care, and social welfare programs. Using a model developed by the Institute for Research in Applied Economics (IPEA, *Instituto de Pesquisa Econômica Aplicada*), the administration of the current system is projected to the year 2030 in accordance with three coherent macroeconomic hypotheses predicting different rates of growth. The projections reveal a pattern of expenditures increasing faster than income, indicating the necessity of financing ranging from 3 percent to 6 percent of gross domestic product (GDP) in the best and worst case scenarios.

Based on these projections, the need for a thorough and immediate reform of the social insurance system is discussed. This reform should achieve greater social justice and maintain the long-term economic and financial equilibrium of the system, while at the same time respecting the rights of those covered by the old system.

A proposal is presented for reforming the system within a theoretical framework that includes basic and supplementary social insurance, health care and social welfare. Economic and financial projections of the performance of the proposed system in the same period are also presented, using the same macroeconomic hypotheses. The results of these projections indicate a trend toward the stabilization of expenses in the three hypothetical cases, ranging from 7 percent to 8 percent of GDP.

Social Insurance

Since its inception, the Brazilian social insurance system has grown considerably as a result both of political successes in the democratic arena and of the paternalistic and authoritarian actions of the state. The recent crises in the social insurance and welfare system, although a source of public concern, have also had the very beneficial effect of encouraging open debate about certain aspects formerly restricted to the state bureaucracy.

Institutional Growth

Although Brazil's oldest social insurance regulation dates back to 1543 during the colonial period, the Eloy Chaves Act (Decree-Law No. 4862 of January 24, 1923) is considered the cornerstone of the Brazilian social insurance system. The Eloy Chaves Act provided for railroad retirement and pension funds. In the twenties and thirties the system was expanded to include other professional categories, so that by 1937 there were 183 different funds.

In 1930, urban wage-earners enjoyed the greatest political and economic clout in the country. The Ministry of Labor, Industry, and Trade was created, and social insurance began to receive greater attention from the state.

Then a new era dawned, during which enrollment in the system was determined by professional category. The Retirement and Pension Institutes were formed, and social insurance coverage was extended to virtually all urban workers and to a large segment of the self-employed.

The first positive step toward correcting the disparity among professional categories caused by the organization of the Brazilian social insurance system was the enactment of the social insurance "Organic Law" (LOPS, *Lei Orgânica da Previdência Social*) of August 26, 1960. Six years after the passage of the LOPS, the various institutions were combined to form the National Institute of Social Insurance (INPS, *Instituto Nacional da Previdência Social*) on November 21, 1966.

The process of extending coverage to professional categories not yet included in the system began in 1963 with the Rural Workers Assistance Fund and continued in 1969 with the Basic Plan (neither of which was very successful). The process ended in the seventies with the inclusion of domestic workers (1972), regulation of the mandatory enrollment of self-employed workers (1973), insurance coverage for those over 70 years of age and the disabled without insurance (1974), and the extension of social insurance and welfare benefits to rural workers and their dependents (1976). Social insurance was thus expanded to include every wage-earner in the country.

In 1974 the former Ministry of Labor and Social Insurance was split to form the Ministry of Social Insurance and Welfare (MPAS, *Ministerio da Previdência e Assistência Social*), which is responsible for formulating and implementing social insurance, medical care and social welfare policy. With the creation of the National Social Insurance and Welfare System (SINPAS, *Sistema Nacional da*

Previdência e Assistência Social) in 1977, each function of the system became the responsibility of a specific agency; in addition, several new entities were created and the functions of others already in existence were redefined.

In the process of creating different minimum wages, the government established two new parameters in August 1987: the National Wage Base and the Minimum Reference Wage. This affected social insurance in two ways: it eliminated the connection between benefits and the minimum wage to cut expenses, and it eliminated the correlation between the minimum wage and the wage percentages contributed by subscribers to increase income.

In 1987 the Unified and Decentralized State Health Systems Development Program (SUDS, *Programa de Desenvolvimento de Sistemas Unificados e Descentralizados de Saúde*) was also created. This system was intended to reinforce and develop quality comprehensive health care and to decentralize the activities of the National Institute for Medical Assistance and Social Security (INAMPS, *Instituto Nacional de Assistência Medical da Previdência Social*).

The federal constitution adopted in 1988 introduced substantial changes and established the basic principles of universal coverage, equivalent urban and rural benefits, selectivity in the granting of benefits, guaranteed benefit levels, equity in financing, diversification of the financing base, decentralization and worker participation in the administration of the system.

In March 1990, during the Collor administration, the Ministry of Social Insurance and Social Welfare was dissolved and its responsibilities were transferred to other ministries. Welfare became the responsibility of the Ministry of Social Action, and health care, of the Ministry of Health. Social insurance came under the control of a National Secretariat within the newly created Ministry of Labor and Social Insurance (MTPS, *Ministério do Trabalho e Previdência Social*). Other institutional changes included the formation of the National Institute for Social Insurance (INPS, *Instituto Nacional da Previdência Social*), an autonomous federal agency attached to the MTPS through the merger of the INPS and the IAPAS, and the transfer of the INAMPS to the Ministry of Health.

On July 24, 1991, the president of the republic promulgated Laws No. 8212 and 8213. The first, which established the organization of social insurance, instituted the financing plan. The second concerned social insurance benefit plans and introduced various changes, the most significant of which are:

- the risks covered by social insurance, as well as the minimum and maximum values of the benefits granted, were made the same for all contributors to the system, eliminating the inequities of the former plan that separated the urban population from the rural population;
- a man became eligible for a pension upon the death of his insured wife (already provided for in the Constitution);
- a proportional retirement for women was established;
- the age of eligibility for old-age retirement by rural workers (men) was

Table 3.1. Trend of Social Insurance Revenues by Category, 1971-91
(New cruzados)

Years	Total Revenue	Total contributions	% Total Revenue	Union revenue	% Total Revenue	Other Revenue	% Total Revenue
1971	12,184	10,166	83.44	1,338	10.98	680	5.58
1972	17,912	15,300	85.42	1,755	9.80	857	4.78
1973	25,577	22,266	87.05	2,169	8.48	1,142	4.46
1974	36,863	32,733	88.80	2,569	6.97	1,561	4.23
1975	55,717	49,148	88.21	3,479	6.24	3,090	5.55
1976	90,495	79,793	88.17	5,560	6.14	5,142	5.68
1977	138,937	124,594	89.68	9,856	7.09	4,487	3.23
1978	213,748	188,038	87.97	12,743	5.96	12,967	6.07
1979	330,861	304,315	91.98	16,600	5.02	9,946	3.01
1980	636,003	582,687	91.62	33,139	5.21	20,177	3.17
1981	1,368,675	1,199,131	87.61	130,428	9.53	39,116	2.86
1982	3,363,258	2,962,519	88.08	325,347	9.67	75,392	2.24
1983	6,636,897	5,944,064	89.56	545,733	8.22	147,100	2.22
1984	19,873,470	17,081,372	85.95	2,198,035	11.06	594,063	2.99
1985	70,365,069	63,077,826	89.64	3,092,098	4.39	4,195,145	5.96
1986	197,701,615	181,553,308	91.83	7,678,447	3.88	8,469,860	4.28
1987	646,270,876	526,025,201	81.39	5,266,980	0.81	114,978,695	17.79
1988	4,006,540,902	3,550,725,000	88.62	23,954,162	0.60	431,861,740	10.78
1989	71,747,097,000	54,159,107,000	75.49	14,267,572,000	19.89	3,320,418,000	4.63
1990	2,044,543,388,000	1,621,929,302,000	79.33	187,559,630,000	9.17	235,054,456,000	11.50
1991	8,904,715,040,000	7,241,992,374,000	81.33	912,149,746,000	10.24	750,572,920,000	8.43

Source: MPAS, 1971-79; DATAPREV, 1980-90.
Note: For the 1982 Union contribution, the balance sheet did not include as income the ORTN CR$180 billion payment to banks to retire social insurance debt. In this table, that amount is included.

lowered from 65 to 60 years (provided for in the Constitution);
- female rural workers became eligible for old-age retirement at 55 years of age (provided for in the Constitution); and,
- all contributors to the system receive all benefits, except the family allowance, to which domestic workers and insured self-employed workers are not entitled.

During the interim government of Itamar Franco, the ministerial structure was again changed in October 1992. The MTPS was split to create the Ministry of Labor and the Ministry of Social Insurance, with the INPS absorbed by the latter and the Ministry of Social Action renamed the Ministry of Social Welfare.

Income Growth of the Social Security System

For analytical purposes, the income of the social security system can be divided into three major categories:
- Income from contributions, which includes the compulsory payroll contributions of urban companies (employee and employer share, including the contributions made to finance worker's compensation insurance) and contributions from the basic earnings of self-employed, independent, domestic and temporary workers and urban and rural employees. Also included in this income category are the 2.5 percent tax on the first-stage marketing value of rural goods and the legally established percentages contributed by rural workers on the uncultivated land they own;
- State contributions from a variety of sources (rates on the prices of automotive fuels, percentages of lottery revenues, regular Treasury funds, etc.); and,
- Other miscellaneous income such as rents, investment returns, loans, fines, etc.

Table 3.1, which shows the growth of income in the 1971-91 period, reveals that contributions represented, on average, 88 percent of the annual income. Nearly 98 percent of the income from compulsory contributions came from the payroll taxes on urban salaries.

The union made extraordinary transfers to the system in 1981 (Cr$ 50 billion) and 1982 (Cr$ 180 billion) to reduce the deficit. Also noteworthy is the growth of union involvement in the 1977-84 period to cover the deficit, which then shrank almost to zero in 1988. In fact, the momentary recovery of economic growth and, more significantly, the growth of real wages brought about by the Cruzado Plan provided the social insurance system with cash surpluses, which were invested in the financial market. Union contributions began increasing again in 1989 as a result of the hike in Finsocial rates included in the transfers and the increase in regular Treasury funds, both of which were used to cover the then-projected deficit.

Table 3.2. Growth of Revenues from Contributions and GDP Growth, 1971-91

Years	Revenue from contributions (in 1990 new cruzados)	Growth of contributions (%)	GDP (%)
1971	2,118,171,822,612	—	—
1972	2,676,260,333,970	26.35	11.1
1973	3,395,547,277,474	26.88	14.0
1974	4,044,615,206,980	19.12	9.5
1975	4,642,392,726,242	14.78	5.6
1976	5,342,140,465,852	15.07	9.7
1977	5,905,113,778,180	10.54	5.4
1978	6,297,729,656,572	6.65	4.8
1979	6,871,388,470,970	9.11	6.7
1980	6,997,172,096,061	1.83	9.2
1981	7,205,997,337,730	2.98	-4.4
1982	9,044,572,311,554	25.51	0.6
1983	8,855,838,866,904	-2.09	-3.4
1984	7,632,438,593,990	-13.81	5.3
1985	8,856,464,952,313	16.04	7.9
1986	10,764,313,950,403	21.54	7.6
1987	9,695,113,552,290	-9.93	3.6
1988	8,856,239,268,943	-8.65	-0.1
1989	9,231,647,407,484	4.24	3.3
1990	9,327,715,415,802	1.04	-4.4
1991	7,241,992,374,000	-23.04	0.9

Source: MPAS, 1971-79: DATAPREV, 1984-90.

Table 3.2 shows the exceptional growth of income from contributions in the 1970s to rates in excess of GDP growth rates. The increase in income, in addition to factors of an institutional nature, was due to the process of accelerated economic development and urbanization observed in the country, which caused an enormous jump in the number of contributors to the social security system.

Growth of Social Security Expenses

Social insurance and social welfare expenses fall into four major categories:
- the social insurance program, including all of the retirements, payments, assistance, pensions and other financial benefits paid to urban and rural affiliates and their dependents, including expenses related to worker's compensation insurance;
- medical, covering the same groups as social insurance and the entire population in emergency cases;
- social welfare, related to child and indigent care; and,
- general administrative and financial, including the costs of personnel and supplies for regular operations and possible financial expenses.

Table 3.3 reconstructs the growth of the expenses of the entities in the system as though they had all existed since 1971, based on the Consolidated Financial Statements of INPS, Ipase and Funrural. The table shows that, on average, social insurance and social welfare financial benefits (monthly life annuity income and social insurance coverage) account for two-thirds of the total amount spent by the system. This percentage drops between 1983 and 1989 to 52.43 percent of the total in the latter year, which is explained by the sudden decrease in the value of newly granted and existing benefits as a result of the indexing criteria then in use and the high rates of inflation.

The opposite occurs with INAMPS medical and administrative expenses, the percentage share of which falls between 1976 and 1983. As indicated earlier, the financial surpluses generated by the Cruzado Plan were used in their entirety, primarily to expand the health care programs. This enormous growth includes the establishment of SUDS (1987), which was designed to achieve optimum resource use.

IAPAS expenses for fiscal, financial and assets administration exhibit a general downward trend until 1983, except for fiscal year 1981. In 1981, expenses rose suddenly because this decentralized agency paid interest to the banking system as a result of it substantial indebtedness.

LBA (*Legião Brasileira de Assistência*) and FUNABEM are responsible for the social welfare expenses *stricto sensu* since they provide services to the uninsured segments of the population.

Growth and Diagnosis of Social Insurance

Contributors and Beneficiaries

The gradual incorporation of new subscribers as part of the on-going process of the universalization of coverage characterized the institutional growth of Brazil's social insurance system.

Given the established five-year waiting period, the first beneficiaries—retirees and pensioners—did not enter the system until 1929, establishing a ratio of passive to active subscribers of approximately 1:13. As the regular income from new funds being created for the beneficiaries of the system replaced the income from contributors, the ratio increased until it reached 1:8.59 in 1933. The creation of the Retirement and Pension Institutes caused the constant decline of the passive/active ratio, which was 1:30.36 in 1938.

The enormous jump in the number of contributors followed a gradual increase in the number of beneficiaries. This meant that the ratio increased continually, with a few sporadic recoveries due, for example, to the establishment of the INPS in 1967, the inclusion of domestic workers and the official enrollment of self-employed contributors in 1973. Other measures, such as the creation of

Table 3.3. Trend of SINPAS Entities Expenditures, 1971-90

Years	INPS Cr$	%	INAMPS Cr$	%	IAPAS Cr$	%	LBA Cr$	%	FUNABEM Cr$	%	TOTAL
1971	7,684	65.68	3,265	27.91	631	5.39	78	0.67	42	0.36	11,700
1972	11,437	67.99	4,436	26.37	808	4.80	97	0.58	44	0.26	16,822
1973	15,735	67.78	6,230	26.84	1,077	4.64	118	0.51	55	0.24	23,215
1974	22,990	68.16	8,943	26.51	1,583	4.69	147	0.44	68	0.20	33,731
1975	34,290	65.13	15,377	29.21	2,659	5.05	225	0.43	98	0.19	52,649
1976	56,625	62.42	28,657	31.59	4,959	5.47	303	0.33	179	0.20	90,723
1977	89,459	64.92	42,115	30.56	5,045	3.66	866	0.63	324	0.24	137,809
1978	140,149	65.87	63,422	29.81	6,894	3.24	1,683	0.79	614	0.29	212,762
1979	229,088	68.83	91,791	27.58	7,305	2.19	3,639	1.09	991	0.30	332,814
1980	464,415	68.01	186,773	27.35	20,236	2.96	8,737	1.28	2,652	0.39	682,813
1981	1,015,381	68.26	362,112	24.34	84,344	5.67	19,280	1.30	6,467	0.43	1,487,584
1982	2,240,086	72.19	722,678	23.29	92,853	2.99	35,815	1.15	11,550	0.37	3,102,982
1983	5,003,083	74.08	1,479,425	21.91	177,671	2.63	70,019	1.04	23,057	0.34	6,753,255
1984	14061824	70.54	5,051,148	25.34	604,099	3.03	163,128	0.82	55,302	0.28	19,935,501
1985	46,839,749	69.08	18,130,820	26.74	2,122,749	3.13	542,581	0.80	174,052	0.26	67,809,951
1986	129,462,320	70.05	46,588,658	25.21	5,328,206	2.88	2,931,038	1.59	504,700	0.27	184,814,922
1987	316,391,227	53.19	225,090,990	37.84	21,556,793	3.62	25,419,133	4.27	6,413,070	1.08	594,871,213
1988	2,326,015,126	53.29	1,657,712,292	37.98	177,964,869	4.08	172,167,548	3.94	30,732,376	0.70	4,364,592,211
1989	38,261,565,000	52.43	24,825,530,000	34.02	6,270,537,000	8.59	3,132,294,000	4.29	491,459,178	0.67	72,981,385,178
1990	1,262,367,988,000	62.64	647,700,729,000	32.14	37,129,716,000	1.84	52,596,900,000	2.61	15,499,461,000	0.77	2,015,294,794,000

Source: MPAS Financing Group for data to 1977, FPAS General Balance Sheets and LBA and FUNABEM Balance Sheets to 1979 and DATAPREV for data from 1980 to 1990, and LBA and FUNABEM/CEBIA Balance Sheets for the 1987-90 period..
Note: The data for fiscal years before 1978 were estimated for the purpose of reconstructing SINPAS expenditures from 1971 on.

Pro-Rural in 1971 and the establishment of social insurance coverage for people over 70 years of age and the disabled in 1974, caused a substantial rise in the number of beneficiaries and also contributed to the 1:2.8 passive/active ratio in 1981.

Financial Benefits

Tables 3.4 and 3.5 show the number of urban and rural beneficiaries with continuing benefits arranged by major category at December 31 in the 1971-90 period.[1] This shows that even for urban benefits the number seems exceedingly high in the period under consideration.

Table 3.6 provides an overview of the composition by number and value of urban social insurance benefits. It is clear that retirements, while representing approximately 48 percent of the continuing urban social insurance benefits, account for roughly 67 percent of the total expenses. Monthly life annuity payments, on the other hand, account for less than 4.5 percent of the expenses.

An analysis of the increase in rural social insurance beneficiaries should be approached with some caution since these programs were created very recently, with little or no waiting period. And although the administrative control systems of urban social insurance can be considered somewhat flawed, in rural areas control is extremely erratic. But even taking these reservations into account, there is no denying the fact that the growth rates of the number of rural beneficiaries are high during the period in question, especially in the rural employment program.

Equity in Social Insurance

Equity in the social insurance system in Brazil is fairly complex. Tables 3.7 and 3.8 show the distribution, by wage bracket, of the number of contributors and payroll amount and the number of beneficiaries and value of the benefits. The reader might, at first glance, be led to conclude that the benefits are concentrated in the lowest income sectors, which would indicate the existence of a redistributive program.

Evaluation of the degree of equity of the Brazilian social security system begins with an analysis of the distribution of the benefits granted to the various categories of beneficiaries.

Table 3.9 shows the impact of the benefits included in the model, by sex and wage bracket.

---

[1] The benefits are of two types: continuous (retirements, allowances, pensions, etc.) and one-time (funeral grant, birth grant, and savings fund).

Table 3.4. Urban Social Insurance: Number of Beneficiaries Maintained as of December 31, 1972-90

Types	1972	1974	1976	1978	1980	1982	1984	1986	1988	1990
Retirements										
Disability	511,089	614,265	816,544	970,329	1,100,001	1,233,393	1,355,138	1,455,976	1,533,499	1,578,02
Years of service	313,892	368,529	449,409	567,641	641,873	780,102	9,422,604	1,052,917	1,106,035	1,141,223
Old-age	137,320	150,886	173,861	210,074	267,874	361,487	469,557	593,866	699,200	842,873
Special	34,169	45,485	58,841	77,812	92,865	115,008	158,969	211,012	247,607	279,494
Pensions	710,670	831,846	973,887	1,210,168	1,231,050	1,407,682	1,779,081	2,008,855	2,198,231	2,476,251
Payments										
25%	43,928	28,529	20,359	11,249	7,499	13,777	11,962	12,863	15,605	16,037
20%	48,945	86,349	120,696	120,515	12,015	111,973	88,394	94,156	108,529	148,038
Monthly life annuity										
Disability	—	—	331,666	427,091	451,933	489,887	498,196	495,300	490,812	485,118
Old-age	—	—	414,209	499,372	469,590	467,718	423,398	396,350	370,393	340,021
Illness/accident	578,504	649,101	732,861	883,787	697,172	753,534	986,900	911,990	810,327	824,651

Source: INPS.

Table 3.5. Rural Social Insurance: Number of Beneficiaries Maintained as of December 31, 1972-90

Types	1972	1974	1976	1978	1980	1982	1984	1986	1988	1990
Employee										
Disability retirement[2]	[1]	46,017	121,893	179,570	204,620	351,070	433,238	458,737	472,294	483,304
Old-age retirement	[1]	940,408	1,251,570	1,312,165	1,392,502	1,574,597	1,712,126	1,771,624	1,819,706	1,938,905
Pensions	[1]	77,884	227,098	322,735	447,987	59,595,750	735,494	853,448	957,451	1,093,351
Disability social insurance coverage	—	—	211,421	277,190[1]	114,218	1,673,845	207,964	242,832	262,138	291,401
Old-age coverage	—	—	[1]	[1]	209,991	229,742	264,346	304,915	315,905	334,974
Employer										
Disability retirement	—	—	—	—	985	8,911	12,328	12,806	12,935	12,589
Old-age retirement	—	—	—	—	19,269	96,959	109,809	112,670	114,039	113,434
Pensions	—	—	—	—	1,681	14,712	22,841	29,688	35,217	43,621

Source: INPS.
Notes: [1] The benefit exists, but no data are available.
[2] Up to 1978 the total disability coverage also includes the total coverage.

Table 3.6. Continued Social Insurance Benefit, Urban, 1980-90
(Averages)

	Percentage share of the total	
	In number	In value
Retirements	47.99	67.17
Pensions	26.46	18.75
Monthly Annuity	13.19	4.49
Auxiliary	10.45	8.16
Others	1.91	1.43

Source: DATAPREV, 1980-90.

Table 3.7. Contributors and Payroll Amount per Wage Bracket, 1989
(Percentage)

Wage bracket	Number of contributors			Value of payroll amount		
	Men	Women	Total	Wage bracket	Men	Women
1-2[1]	32.4	40.3	35.1	8.1	14.9	9.9
2-3	17.0	15.8	16.6	8.1	11.5	9.0
3-5	16.9	13.2	15.7	13.7	15.9	14.3
5-10	13.4	10.0	12.2	20.7	22.2	21.1
+10	20.3	20.7	20.4	49.4	35.5	45.7

Source: DATAPREV.
Notes: [1] Wage bracket 1-2 is the lowest; +10, the highest.

Table 3.8. Beneficiaries Maintained and Total Amount of Expenditures with Benefits, per Wage Bracket, 1989
(Percentage)

Wage bracket	Number of benefits			Expenditures with benefits		
	Men	Women	Total	Men	Women	Total
1-2[1]	67.7	86.0	72.2	30.8	59.3	35.6
2-3	9.1	5.5	8.2	9.6	9.1	9.6
3-5	10.3	4.3	8.8	17.3	11.2	16.2
5-10	11.8	3.8	9.9	36.1	17.8	33.0
+10	1.1	0.4	0.9	6.2	2.6	5.6

Source: DATAPREV, 1989.
Notes: [1] Wage bracket 1-2 is the lowest; +10, the highest.

Table 3.9. Benefits Granted in 1990 per 1,000 Urban Contributors, by Benefit Bracket

	Men			Women		
Benefit	Bracket 1	Bracket 2	Bracket 3	Bracket 1	Bracket 2	Bracket 3
Old-age retirement	3.12	0.83	0.53	6.4	1.62	0.9
Disability retirement	5.38	1.59	1.35	4.76	1.17	0.8
Years-of-service retirement	1.12	2.2	2.38	0.52	0.9	1.01
Auxiliary	33.62	6.08	3.65	29.3	4.5	2.58
Special	0.45	1.45	0.56	0.09	0.11	0.04

Source: SINTESIS/DATAPREV, PNAD-90/IBGE.
Notes: Bracket 1 - Benefits from 1-3 minimum wages.
          Bracket 2 - Benefits from 3-10 minimum wages.
          Bracket 3 - Benefits over 10 minimum wages.

Among women old-age retirements have the greatest impact, while among men either the number of disability or length-of-service retirements is greater, depending on the wage bracket. Therefore, it would appear that income and sex have a great deal to do with the type of retirement the contributor will probably have. Contributors with the lowest incomes receive a proportionately larger number of old-age or disability pensions, while the highest income brackets receive the largest proportion of special and length-of-service retirements. The basic explanation for this is that there is a sufficiently longer waiting period (in years of contribution) for the benefits of length of service and special retirements, male contributors with large incomes being the ones who contribute for the longest time.

Any detailed analysis of equity for rural populations will be skewed, chiefly because of the lack of disaggregated data at the desired levels. For example, the records of benefits granted do not mention the beneficiary's sex.

Preliminary results indicate a substantial financial transfer from younger to older generations. This transfer is not so closely related to the nominal values of the benefits granted as to the distortion of direct contributions to the system since the earlier generations began their period of contributions with much lower rates (3 percent) and these rates increased considerably in value in the period studied (1930-90) until reaching the current levels (8-10 percent).

Figure 3.1 shows the replacement level (projected value of the benefit over the projected value of the contribution) for cohorts identified by date of birth (1900-80), for contributors of both sexes, in the first wage bracket, which pays benefits of one to three minimum wages.

Equity in the Brazilian social insurance system is characterized by substantial intergenerational transfers, chiefly because there is no correlation between the value of the nominal benefit and the value of the direct contributions made

Figure 3.1. Level of Return by Sex Wage Bracket 1

Source: TDI/IPEA No. 73.

during the individual's entire contribution period but rather between the value of this benefit and the last 48 monthly contributions. Intragenerational transfers are less numerous and appear to be slightly biased in favor of female contributors and contributors with higher wages.

Growth and Diagnosis of Health Care

In the past, the health care system in Brazil was divided between the Ministry of Health, which was primarily responsible for preventive care, and social security, which bore the burden of nearly all curative interventions. Although this irregular situation has been corrected, health care in Brazil is still a fairly problematic issue, which is clearly reflected by indicators such as infant mortality (over 75 deaths per thousand children under one year of age).

Physical Infrastructure

In 1989 the health care system in Brazil consisted of 34,831 health care establishments, including hospitals, dispensaries, health centers and first-aid stations. Roughly 79.5 percent of these establishments provided only outpatient services, meaning that they had no admissions departments. The remaining 20.5 percent were hospital-type institutions (see Table 3.10).

Table 3.10. Trend in the Number of Health Units, 1976-89

| Year | Total | Health units | |
		In-patients	Out-patients
1976	13,133	5,310	7,823
1977	14,288	5,458	8,830
1978	15,345	5,708	9,637
1979	17,079	6,036	11,043
1980	18,489	6,103	12,386
1981	22,341	6,473	15,868
1982	24,018	6,650	17,368
1983	25,651	6,680	18,971
1984	27,552	6,861	20,691
1985	28,972	6,678	22,294
1986	30,872	6,920	23,952
1987	32,450	7,062	25,388
1989	34,831	7,127	27,704

Source: IBGE-AMS 1976-89.

Between 1976 and 1989 the number of health care centers operating in Brazil experienced annual geometric growth of 7.8 percent, with the fastest growth occurring in the public sector. In 1976 the public sector share was 51 percent, in 1986 it was 61 percent, and in 1989 it was 65 percent.

Between 1976 and 1989, the outpatient system expanded from 7,823 to 27,704 centers. Despite the reduction in private sector involvement, for-profit institutions also increased their share during the same period, thus reducing the percentage share of the philanthropic institutions.

Some of the accelerated growth of the federal health care system, especially in the early years of the 1980s, is explained by the investments of the Program for the Decentralization of Health and Sanitary Activities (PIASS, *Programa de Interiorização da Assistência e Saúde Saneamento*) and by the growth of the INAMPS outpatient system. After a while, PIASS centers still in operation were transferred to the states, spurring the growth of the state system.

With the proliferation of decentralization programs not only within INAMPS but also within the Ministry of Health itself, a surge in the municipal outpatient system occurred in 1984. In 1986, 25 percent of the outpatient clinics in the country were operated by municipalities.

The opposite occurred in the hospital system: (1) the inpatient system grew only slightly during this period; (2) the level of private sector participation was high; and (3) in the public sector, the hospital system grew more or less at the same rate as the federal and state systems and with less intensity at the municipal level. In the private sector, the contraction of the philanthropic and charitable system and the growth of the for-profit system are of particular note.

Table 3.11. Brazil: Hospital Beds, Consultations and Admissions per Person, 1981-86

Years	Hospital Beds per 1000	Consultations per person	Admissions per 1000
1981	4.17	1.95	141
1982	4.13	2.09	139
1983	4.05	2.27	113
1984	3.98	2.39	134
1985	3.77	2.40	128
1986	3.77	2.46	131

Source: IBGE-AMS, 1981-86.

Clearly, one of the adjustment strategies employed by INAMPS in the recent crisis consisted of increasing the volume of resources allocated to the public sector and reducing the rate of procurement of private sector services.

Between 1976 and 1986, the increase in the number of hospital beds was less than the projected population growth, as indicated in Table 3.11. In the private sector, the share of for-profit institutions grew, and nonprofit institutions dwindled.

Indicators of Service Output Efficiency

Certain changes in the installed capacity had a decisive effect on the output of medical services. Considering indicators such as the number of medical consultations per resident (2.46 in 1986) and the number of admissions per thousand residents (131 in 1986), it is clear in both cases that the output of services exceeds INAMPS projections (2 and 100, respectively; see Table 3.11). It is also clear that the regional distribution of these services is extremely uneven.

Using a ratio of 1.8 beds per thousand residents, there appears to be a surplus supply of inpatient beds in Brazil. A more detailed regional analysis, however, or one based on the social status of the patients cared for, will show that there are cases in which there are not enough beds, especially in the poorest regions and segments of the population. This is because 78 percent of the inpatient beds are in the private health care system.

Medical Personnel

It is estimated that there is a 75 percent surplus of medical personnel in Brazil (see Table 3.12). Yet, there is also a deficit of medical consultations, indicating low productivity and poor regional distribution.

There is also a 23 percent estimated surplus of dentists for Brazil as a whole.

Table 3.12. Health Care Workers Needed and Actual Number of Ambulatory System Workers, 1985

Regions	Health care workers needed (A)	Actual number of health care workers (B)	Shortage or surplus (C)	(C)/(A) %
Brazil	87,108	152,805	65,697	75.43
North	4,693	4,550	-143.0	-3.0
Northeast	25,485	29,665	4,180	16.4
Southeast	37,538	87,088	49,550	132.0
South	13,662	21,583	7,921	58.0
W. Central	5,730	9,919	2,611	73.1

Source: Actual number of health care workers-AMS-85 (total of specialist and resident health care workers, who work daily, one, two, three or four times a week).
Note: It is assumed that, on average, all jobs are 20-hours per week or 1,056 hours per year.

At the regional level, only in the north is there a deficit, which is estimated at 34 percent.

Everything suggests that Brazil, despite its adequate installed capacity, needs substantial investments in health care in some areas of the federation, especially in the northern, northeastern and west central regions.

Economic and Financial Aspects

In 1989, Brazil spent an estimated 4.77 percent of GDP on health care. Of this amount, 2.94 percent of GDP was federal spending, 0.51 percent was state and municipal spending, 0.4 percent was direct payments by families and 0.92 percent (nearly one percent of GDP) was private spending channeled through companies and the private health sector. In 1989, the latter two segments served approximately 32 million people, a population sector that, although it contributed to the general system, did not receive services.

Health care spending in Brazil is still inadequate. It should be increased by at least 25 percent in order for the Brazilian people to have a minimal resource base to pay the costs of minimum, universal medical care.

In the health care sector, payments to third parties are for services provided under contracts and agreements between INAMPS and the private sector. Third-party payments, which in 1980 represented 63 percent of all health care spending, represented only 36.1 percent in 1986 (see Table 3.13). The reduction in the amount paid to private suppliers was the main reason for the decrease in costs.

The volume of investments is ridiculously low, given the needs of the sector. Recent calculations suggest that maintaining the level of replacement of the

Table 3.13. Consolidated Federal Health Care Expenditures, by Type of Expenditure, 1980-86
(Percentages)

Type of expenditure	1980	1982	1984	1986
Financing total	86.1	78.9	77.4	65.2
Personnel	16.4	18.3	16.3	21.7
Third-party services	63.0	55.4	56.1	36.1
Others	6.7	5.2	5.0	7.4
Current transfers	9.5	15.7	17.9	28.4
Intragovernmental	5.5	5.4	6.2	11.3
Intergovernmental	1.2	6.0	6.9	10.7
Other transfers	2.8	4.3	4.8	6.4
Investments	2.8	2.9	2.3	2.9
Financial investments	0.2	0.1	0.0	0.0
Capital transfers	1.4	2.4	2.4	3.5

Source: AMS-85.

installed capacity without scaling back the existing system would require an investment rate of 11 percent, much higher than the figure indicated in Table 3.13 (about 3 percent).

State and municipal health care spending in 1986 was nearly 30 percent of the consolidated federal spending. This is not much, given that these are the areas in which most of the general health care is provided to the public. Increasing the funds available to these entities would require either a tax reform that would change the current system of placing all the funds in the hands of the federal government, or some means of transferring more resources to state and municipal health programs.

Equity in Health Care

Analyzing the equity of health care in Brazil is made difficult by the near total lack of raw data. Although there are some household surveys concerning the use of services, little is known about supply and demand.

The decline in the quality of care provided by the public sector caused consumers with greater purchasing power to choose other types of care, such as group medicine, medical cooperatives and health insurance. Some companies, especially those owned by states, developed their own plans, which were generally expensive and of a high caliber.

A transfer from the private to the public sector has also occurred: cases involving extremely expensive and complex procedures as well as chronic-degenerative ailments generally not covered by private plans shift to the public sector.

Conclusions

In summary, the health care problem in Brazil is characterized by insufficient aggregate spending, growing inefficiency and ineffectiveness in the allocation of resources, poor regional distribution of supply as well as lack of organization in the health care system, and unclear relationships *(service commission)* and no incentives for efficiency between the public procurement agency and the private system of suppliers of medical and hospital services.

Growth and Diagnosis of Social Welfare

Social welfare programs in Brazil fall into the following two categories:
- financial benefits, consisting of monthly life annuity incomes for the elderly (over 70 years of age) and the disabled, for individuals not covered by social insurance and with no other source of income, equal to half of the minimum wage (an increase to the minimum wage has been proposed); and,
- welfare benefits, ranging from day care nurseries to the direct or indirect distribution of food by federal, state, municipal, and private entities through a complex system of agreements and contracts.

Because the financial benefits paid by the social insurance agencies were analyzed previously, only the welfare services are discussed in this chapter.

Institutional Growth and Diagnosis

In the thirties and forties, Brazil passed social welfare legislation reflecting the new relationship between the state and the various segments of society. In 1941 the Juvenile Welfare Service (SAM, *Serviço de Assistência ao Menor*, later known as *FNBEM, Funbem* and *CBIA*) was created within the Ministry of Justice and Domestic Affairs to guarantee justice for young children. The LBA was established a year later to facilitate cooperation with the state and to provide welfare services for the families of soldiers in the Brazilian Expeditionary Force (FEB, *Força Expedicionária Brasileira*).

The Federal Constitution of 1988 established social welfare as a right of the people, independent of any type of contribution. It also restricted welfare assistance to only the needy and the helpless. The Consitution provides protection for families, maternity, infancy and old-age and services and benefits for homeless children and adolescents, the elderly, the handicapped and the needy. It also guarantees the entire population a minimum monthly income, formerly available only to the elderly and the handicapped who had contributed at least once to the social insurance system. The municipalities are responsible for providing welfare services, leaving regulatory matters and coordination to the federal government.

In May 1990, the Ministry of Youth project was initiated to consolidate health and welfare services for children under 17 years of age by coordinating the ministries responsible for basic social policies and optimizing use of public funds. The target population consisted of 37 million children and adolescents, and 18 projects were to be carried out during the Collor administration. Project objectives included the promotion and protection of the health of pregnant women, children, and adolescents; childhood development; promotion of the legal rights of children and adolescents; prevention of birth defects and care for the handicapped; and support of community development.

The Child and Adolescent Statute (ECA, *Estatuto da Criança e do Adolescente*) signed into law by the president of the republic on July 13, 1990, replaced the Juvenile Code and plotted a new course for health care policy in this sector.

In late January 1991 the Collor II Plan established the Social Development Fund (FDS, *Fundo de Desenvolvimento Social*) to fund socially responsible investment projects, which excluded the financing of federal, state and municipal entities.

The Equity of Social Welfare

Any attempt to qualitatively evaluate the equity of social welfare services is hampered by the lack of data on individual households. In fact, the 1983 National Household Sampling Survey (PNAD, *Pesquisa Nacional por Amostra de Domicílios*) tried to obtain data on use of social welfare benefits and assistance, with disappointing results.

Although few evaluations have been made, the ineffectiveness and inefficiency of financial benefits and the lack of control over them are universally recognized, as is the existence of misrepresentation and fraud.

Conclusion

Social welfare services in Brazil are characterized by a complex institutional structure with occasional overlapping of coverage, insufficient concentration, and gaps in coverage; a nearly total lack of mechanisms to evaluate performance for cost efficiency; and lack of transparency and social control of the systems, which encourages paternalism and dependency, in addition to providing countless opportunities for fraud.

Projected Economic and Financial Condition of Social Security, 1990-2030

The following projections should be viewed as plausible hypotheses and not predictions. Thus, given the demographic, economic and institutional assumptions, the IPEA model projects the disaggregated economic and financial results of the social security system. The unemployment insurance programs, the Social Integration Program (PIS, *Programa de Integração Social*), the Public Official Equity Building Program (PASEP, *Programa de Formação do Patrimônio do Servidor Público*), and the Length-of-service Guarantee Fund (FGTS, *Fundo de Garantia por Tempo de Serviço)* are not included in the projections.

Methodology

The projection model consists of a demographic module, a module for generating the contributors to the social insurance system, a module for generating beneficiaries, a macroeconomic consistency module, and a module for generating income and expenses.[2]

Taking these modules in series and using the three macroeconomic hypotheses explained below, the financing requirements are obtained by means of the difference between the income and expenses projections for the social security system as a whole.

Macroeconomic Hypotheses

The model is little affected by the demographic variables, characterized essentially by tremendous inertia. Thus, in formulating the hypotheses, only the economic variables are taken into account.

The consistency module, which is discussed in greater detail in Appendix II, projects three hypotheses: hypothesis 1 or *public adjustment,* in which an adjustment is made to balance the public sector accounts, the result of which is a rate of growth; hypothesis 2 or *private adjustment*, in which internal savings are increased only by increasing the profits kept by companies and, finally, hypothesis 3 or *crisis*, in which it is assumed that no adjustments are made in the public sector, which causes a low level of growth and a fiscal deficit.

Results

Figure 3.2 shows the trend of the number of contributors and beneficiaries.

Figures 3.3 to 3.5 are projections of the expenses of each component of social security as percentage points of GDP for each hypothesis. In the most positive scenario (hypothesis 1), expenses grow from 8 percent in 1990 to 13.5 percent in 2030 and to nearly 15 percent in the least positive scenario (hypothesis 2).

---

2 Appendix II provides more details about the basic modules.

Figure 3.2. Evolution of EPA, Beneficiaries and Contributors of the System, 1923-80
(In millions)

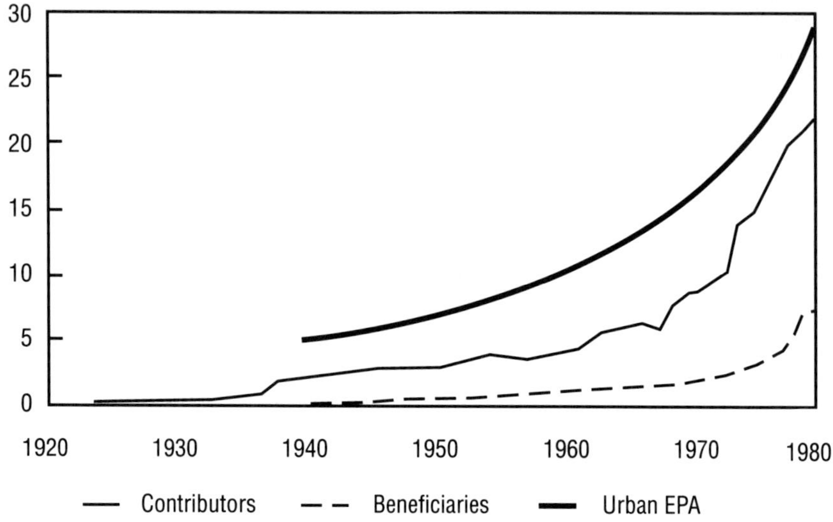

Source: TDI/IPEA No. 73.

Finally, Figures 3.6 to 3.8 show the growth of financing requirements, which vary in 2030 from roughly 4 percent of GDP in the most optimistic case to about 6 percent of GDP in the worst case. To understand the seriousness of the situation, remember that the federal budget of Brazil now equals six percentage points of the GDP.

The first important point to be made is that the projections are based on fairly optimistic hypotheses, even the most negative macroeconomic hypothesis.

Thus, the level of evasion probably will not change despite substantial increases in the contribution rates necessary to finance the system. The informalization of the economy is unlikely to slow, particularly in view of the tax increases needed to pay for social security.

A second and perhaps more important macroeconomic effect is that, in addition to the increases in the tax burden *stricto sensu*, the increases in the *contributive burden* projected for the near term will probably reduce savings, investments and, consequently, the growth of GDP itself. Even considering the beneficial effects of this redistribution, it will certainly adversely affect the growth of GDP.

The results indicate that although certain aspects of the current social insurance regulations are socially justifiable, they drive up costs considerably, raising serious doubts about the possibility of financing them without also fueling inflation. These rules also fail to correct certain distortions in the Brazilian social

Figure 3.3. Social Security Expenditures: Current System Scenario 1
(Percentage of GDP)

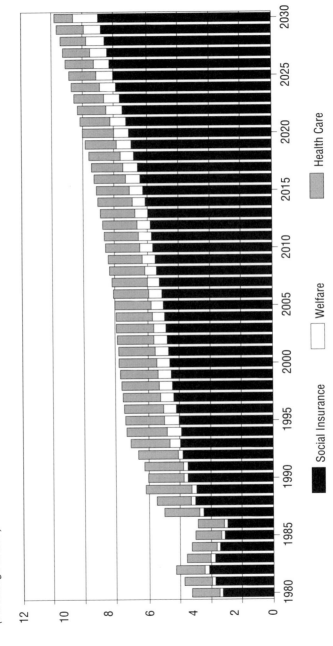

Social Insurance   Welfare   Health Care

Source: TDI/IPEA No. 73.

Figure 3.4. Social Security Expenditures: Current System Scenario 2
(Percentage of GDP)

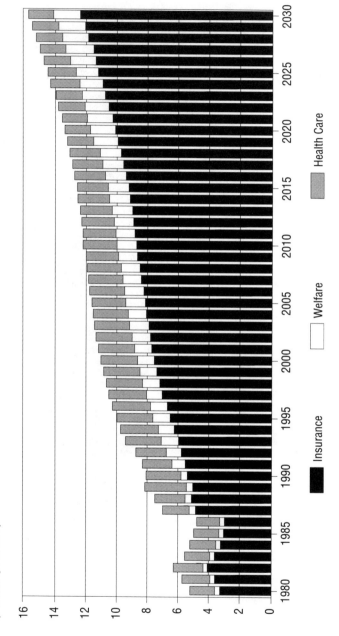

Insurance   Welfare   Health Care

Source: TDI/IPEA No. 73.

Figure 3.5. Social Security Expenditures: Current System Scenario 3
(Percentage of GDP)

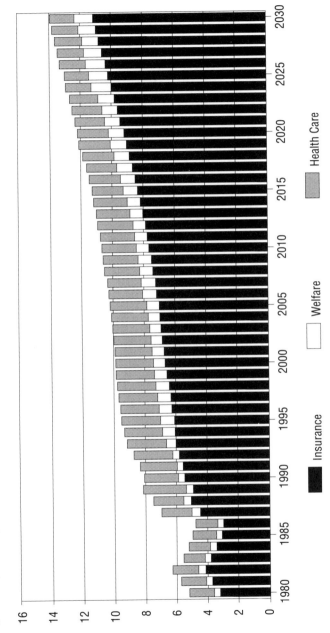

Source: TDI/IPEA No. 73.

Figure 3.6. Financing of the Social Security System: Scenario 1
(Percentage of GDP)

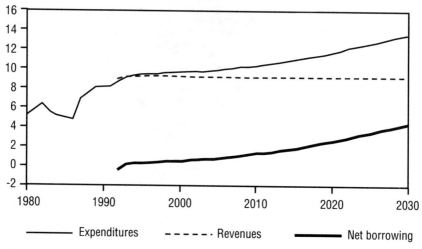

Source: TDI/IPEA No. 73.

Figure 3.7. Financing of the Social Security System: Scenario 2
(Percentage of GDP)

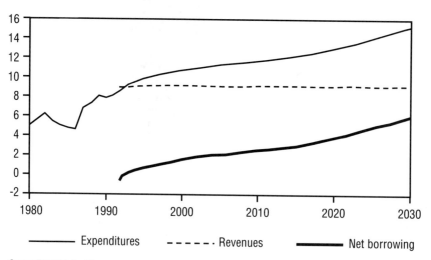

Source: TDI/IPEA No. 73.

Figure 3.8. Financing of the Social Security System: Scenario 3
(Percentage of GDP)

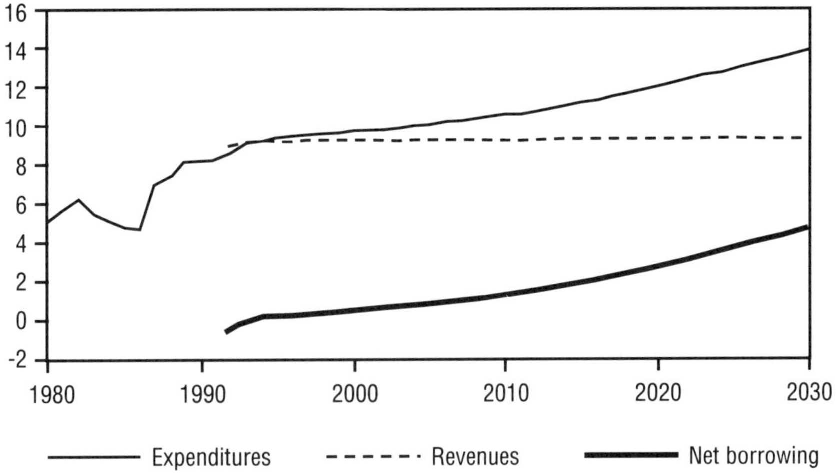

| | Expenditures | – – – – – · Revenues | Net borrowing |

Source: TDI/IPEA No. 73.

insurance system—the unrestricted length-of-service retirement, for example, an admittedly elitist and costly benefit.

Reform proposals should be based not on the principle of viability alone, but also, with equal or greater emphasis, on the principle of equity. It is essential that everyone understand who pays and how much, who receives and how much. For every right to receive there is a corresponding obligation to pay.

Social Security System Proposal

A summary of the principal features of one of the possible solutions for reforming the social security system is presented below. A more detailed discussion can be found in various documents prepared recently by the IPEA.

Basic Guidelines for Reform

The basic guidelines for social security reform proposals follow:
- total transparency of costs and the benefits of social security through clearly explaining the conflicts inherent in the distribution of income;
- maintenance of the social security concept but with effective separation of its components (social insurance, health care and social welfare) in design, financing and operation;

Figure 3.9. Social Security Expenditures: Proposed System Scenario 1
(Percentage of GDP)

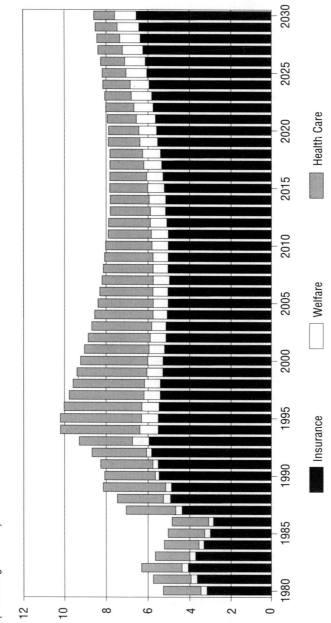

■ Insurance   □ Welfare   ▨ Health Care

Source: TDI/IPEA No. 73.

- absolute respect for the freedom and free choice of each individual, limiting insofar as possible state intervention in savings and investment decisions;
- respect for established rights and totally optional changes;
- preferential option for contributions paid directly by the individual;
- expansion of the tax base and reduction of nominal rates;
- protection of the resources that finance social security;
- social control, preferably exercised at the individual level, over all social security functions;
- decentralized administration and allocation of resources to avoid the concentration of political and economic power;
- explicit income policies instead of welfare benefits under state control; and,
- replacement of the state as provider of social services by the state as promoter of social services.

Basic Social Insurance

General social insurance includes:
- universal coverage (employees, employers, self-employed, rural and urban, including federal, state and municipal officials, civilian and military);
- compulsory affiliation;
- benefits: predefined benefits; minimum social insurance benefit, totally unrelated to the minimum wage; unforeseeable events (death, disability, sickness and involuntary unemployment), maximum benefit equal to three minimum wages on the date of the reform, adjusted on the basis of variations in the consumption pattern of social insurance beneficiaries; and foreseeable events (old-age and length of service), maximum benefit of one minimum wage on the date of the reform, adjusted on the basis of the criterion mentioned in the preceding paragraph; and,
- pegged contribution.

Financing

Basic financing includes:
- pay-as-you-go arrangement with contingency reserve;
- contributions paid solely by the employee, via payroll deductions, up to a limit of three minimum wages. All payroll-based employer contributions would be included directly in the salaries of workers who choose the new system; and,
- pegged income (Basic Social Insurance Fund).

Operations

State social insurance is centrally administered at the outset.

Worker's Compensation Insurance

General workers compensation includes:
- universal coverage;
- compulsory participation;
- predefined, more generous than usual benefits; and,
- pegged contribution.

Financing

Basic financing for worker's compensation includes:
- pay-as-you-go;
- contributions made solely by employers, with rates varying according to the risk of accidents and injuries at each company (based on the pattern for the sector to which the company belongs);
- tax base: payroll or others; and,
- pegged income (Sectoral Worker's Compensation Insurance Funds).

Operations

Worker's compensation operates as:
- essentially mutual insurance;
- decentralized operations (by sector of activity, geographic region, etc.); and,
- responsible organizations: employer mutual insurance companies, which set the rates, collect the premiums and administer the insurance.[3]

It may be possible to use and reorient existing structures and contributions to SESI, SENAC, SENAI, and SESC, employer organizations, currently financed by compulsory contributions based on the employer's payroll.

Social Welfare

Social welfare encompasses:
- residual clientele (Minimum Social Insurance System);

---

[3] The mutual insurance companies would be non profit organizations, formed by employers in each economic sector and geographic region. Employers who join the mutual companies would be jointly liable.

- universal coverage unrelated to contributions; and,
- minimum benefits (60 percent of the minimum wage on the date of the reform, adjusted according to variations in the basic consumer price index).

Financing

Basic financing for social welfare includes:
- pay-as-you-go;
- other tax bases; and,
- pegged income (Social Welfare Fund).

Operations

Social welfare includes both centralized and state operations.

Supplementary Social Insurance

Supplementary social insurance is essentially unrestricted in terms of obligation, financing, method of operation and financial system. A public system of supplementary social insurance is not advisable under any circumstances, as stated in the Constitution.

Health Care

General health care includes:
- universal coverage unrelated to contributions;
- health services financed by the State; and,
- decentralization of health services.

Financing

Basic financing includes:
- a pay-as-you-go system with financing from fiscal sources, with pegged incomes; and,
- a fixed, per-capita advance payment for health services by means of a bond issued to each citizen, equal to the average actuarial value of the cost of comprehensive health care.

The average value of the bond would be US$100 per person, varying according to the sex and age of the individual (or other easily measurable attributes).

Operations

Health care operations include:
- creation of HMOs contractually responsible for covering all of the affiliates' health risks in exchange for their bonds. The HMOs would have a financial interest in promoting preventive health care because it would reduce their costs;
- possibility of changing HMOs if the affiliate is not satisfied with their services; and,
- private and public system, to the extent that public hospitals could compete for users, with the bonds of the latter serving as a source of income.

Transition

Contributors who choose the new system will receive entitlement bonds equal to the current value of two-thirds of the contributions in excess of three minimum wages paid by the employee and the employer before the date on which the option was exercised. Affiliates use the bonds for their own private, supplementary social insurance plans. Bonds are based on union shareholding interest in state enterprises or long-term public debt.

Contributors who do not choose the new system, preferring to remain in the old system, keep all of the benefits of the old system, including the full retirement of public officials. The actuarial wage of each person not choosing the new system would be the expected value of the excess of financing over contributions converted into additional rates paid exclusively by the employee.

The salary increase resulting from the transfer of the employer's social contributions to the salary, less the cost of the new system, provides incentive to choose the new system.

Increases in the Tax Base

The tax base should increase because:
- strict correlation between the individualized record of contributions and the right to collect the benefit makes each insured individual his own accountant (those with no records are included in the Minimal System);
- cases of misappropriation are easily detected; and,
- calculation of the minimum expansion of the base is equal to the difference between the payroll subject to social insurance contributions and the Annual Social Information Ratio (RAIS, *Relación Anual de Informaciones Sociales*).

Maintaining Passive Subscribers as of the Date of the Reform

A payroll contribution will provide for passive subscribers, diminishing with time as the number of beneficiaries on the date of the reform decreases.

Evaluation of the Proposal

To see how the proposed system would work, social security expenses were projected by using the same macroeconomic hypotheses mentioned above. The results appear in Figures 3.9 to 3.11.

First, in all of the hypotheses, aggregate social security spending peaks at about 10 percent of GDP in the mid-nineties. This increase results from a rise in health care expenses. Note also that if the bond is assumed to replace state, municipal and private health care spending under the old system, the overall expenses of the new system would be virtually the same.

Second, in the mid-nineties annual expenses decline about 7 percent for hypothesis 1 and 8 percent for the other two. Expenses rise again in 2015, primarily as a result of increased social spending. These amounts are always lower than those obtained in the projections of the current system for the corresponding hypotheses, as shown in Figures 3.3, 3.4 and 3.5, where the total expenses tended to stabilize around 13.5 percent, 15.2 percent, and 13.9 percent, respectively.

Figures 3.12 to 3.14 compare social insurance spending for each hypothesis. Spending is the largest of the three components in both the current and the proposed system.

Figures 3.15 to 3.17 show the rates needed to finance the social insurance system. Expenses in 1994 would be financed with what is known as an integral rate, which would diminish over time and would be applicable to the entire salary. Under the proposed system, the incomes paid as the new benefit would be financed through the individual rate applied to the salary, with a ceiling of three 1994 minimum wages, adjusted by the index of social insurance services.

The Proposed Transition

Acknowledgment of Acquired Social Insurance Rights

Acknowledging rights acquired under the old system is a necessary condition for joining the new system through the insured individual's free and unconditional right to choose. The proposal described here considers the necessity of issuing to each insured individual who chooses the new system an acknowledgment bond equal to the current capitalized value of the contributions made to the old system before exercise of the option for amounts above a new ceiling established for the maximum contribution salary. To provide an incentive for saving and to avoid

Figure 3.10. Social Security Expenditures: Proposed System Scenario 2
(Percentage of GDP)

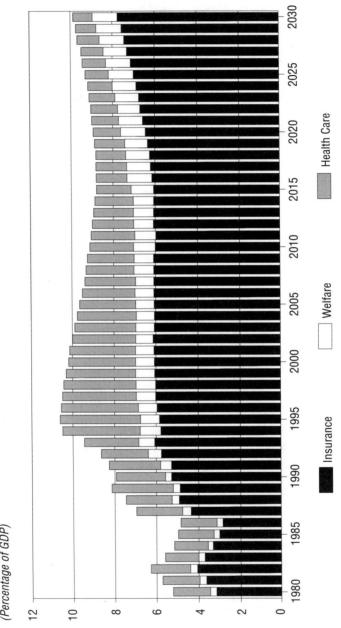

Source: TDI/IPEA No. 73.

Figure 3.11. Social Security Expenditures: Proposed System Scenario 3
(Percentage of GDP)

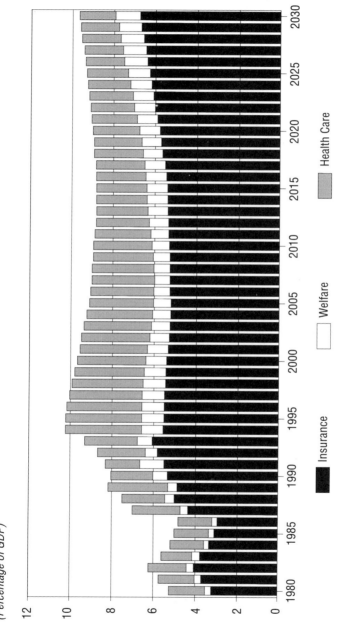

Source: TDI/IPEA No. 73.

Figure 3.12. Social Security Expenditures under the Proposed Systems Scenario 1
(Percentage of GDP)

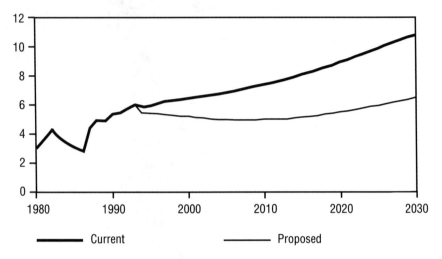

Source: TDI/IPEA No. 73.

Figure 3.13. Social Security Expenditures under the Proposed Systems Scenario 2
(Percentage of GDP)

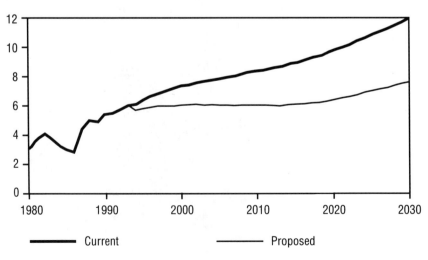

Source: TDI/IPEA No. 73.

Figure 3.14. Social Security Expenditures under the Proposed Systems Scenario 3
(Percentage of GDP)

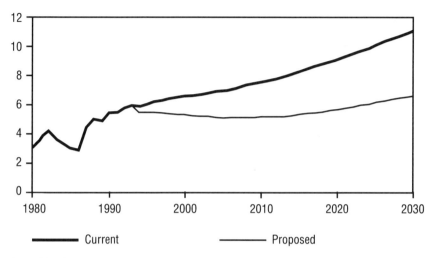

Source: TDI/IPEA No. 73.

Figure 3.15. Payment Quotas for the Proposed Financing Scenario 1

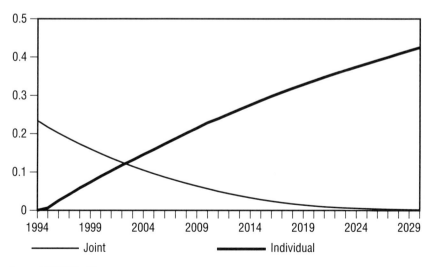

Source: TDI/IPEA No. 73.

Figure 3.16. Payment Quotas for the Proposed Financing Scenario 2

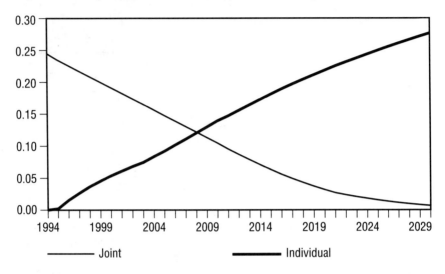

Source: TDI/IPEA No. 73.

Figure 3.17. Payment Quotas for the Proposed Financing Scenario 3

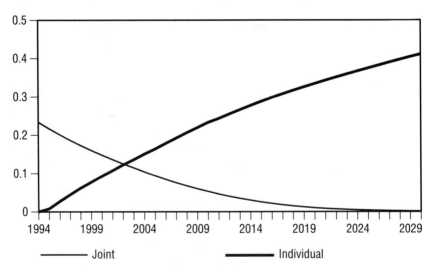

Source: TDI/IPEA No. 73.

immediate demands for funds, these bonds could be credited to institutions that provide supplementary social insurance, whether open or closed, as in accordance with the needs and preferences of each insured individual.

Base of the Bonds and Capital of State Enterprises

One of the critical problems of the transition is how to back the bonds with real assets. The union's substantial shareholding interest in state enterprises and in others in the private sector affords an excellent opportunity for achieving two objectives at once: backing the bonds and democratizing the capital of these enterprises. A subscription fund equal to the Union's total holdings in the productive sector of the economy should be created, with each bond receiving the number of shares equal to its value.

For distribution, the proposed arrangement would permit some degree of worker participation—through the social insurance organizations—in the capital of the state enterprises. Note also that the longer the period of contribution, *ceteris paribus*, the greater the value of the bond and, consequently, the greater the value of each individual's shares. Within this perspective, each contributor would have an interest in proportion to his own effort.

Operational Applications of the Bonds

One of the major difficulties in implementing the proposed reform is calculating the value of the bonds for each individual who chooses the new system. Under the current system, insured individuals must also prove their contributions for retirement purposes, especially in the case of length-of-service retirements. The solution would be to conduct a complete census of contributors to the social insurance system.

Finally, these difficulties with acknowledgment of the duration of the contributions are not inherent in the reform proposal but are, rather, deficiencies of the old system, due, as mentioned above, to the lack of adequate individual records.

Transfer of the Employer's Payroll Contributions

Not only to encourage affiliation with the new system but also to make it as transparent as possible, transferring the employer's payroll contributions directly to the salaries of those who choose the new system is fundamental to the transition.

Given that the change in the system would result in greater efficiency, it is very likely that those who choose the new system would receive a pay increase, which would be a powerful incentive for joining. By making the employee primarily responsible for verifying the collection of his contributions, the new financial system opens the possibility of a considerable expansion of the tax base.

Within the scope of a broader tax reform, a mechanism could be adopted similar to the one established for payroll contributions—exemption of the juridical person and payment by the natural person—for the existing contributions based on profits.

As part of a tax reform, contributions based on sales should be completely eliminated.

The Passive Subscriber Maintenance Fund

One of the most complex problems of any change in social insurance is maintenance of the *number* of old passive subscribers after the date of implementation of the new system. This number is usually large, especially in countries such as Brazil where the system is fairly old. One possible solution is to establish a *Passive Subscriber Maintenance Fund* for the passive subscribers of the old system, consisting of contributions paid exclusively by employees/natural persons, whether they choose the new system or not. Since this is a dwindling population group, the contributions would tend to diminish with the passage of time.

Procedure for Those Who Do Not Choose the New System

Obviously, for one reason or another, there will always be some workers who wish to remain in the old social insurance system. In keeping with the principle of guaranteeing acquired rights, the latter would be assured of all the rights conferred by the system they belonged to before the reform, including length-of-service retirement at the current replacement levels. It is therefore essential that an actuarial statement be prepared for each insured individual who chooses not to join the new system so that he completely finances any difference not covered by current employer and employee contributions.

The exact same procedure could be followed for individuals who belong to special social insurance systems, such as federal officials covered by the single legal system, legislators, officials of states and municipalities with their own systems and even military personnel.

The FGTS and PIS/PASEP Question

Any reform of social security must consider the so-called equity funds, the PIS/PASEP and the FGTS. This issue must be addressed because the current sources of financing these funds, which are payroll-based, would be used for other purposes under the proposed reform. The idea would be to create a *PIS/PASEP and FGTS Liquid Assets Fund* to provide budgetary and financial support for the exercise of rights acquired by the participants of both funds.

For equity accumulated by each worker in the FGTS, given that the proposal calls for a reasonable replacement of income in the event of involuntary unemployment, the length of time required for such deductions to accumulate would be fairly long. After a time, the same system of entitlement bonds for social insurance could be applied to the individual equity in both funds. In this case, upon retirement the bonds would be credited to the individual's account in a supplementary social insurance institution freely chosen by him for conversion to an equivalent monthly income. In this case, the right of overall deduction for retirement would be limited.

As for social insurance *bonds*, the backing could be obtained by increasing the union's shareholding interest and long-term public debt instruments, as determined by the exigencies of the fiscal and monetary policies.

Quasi-fiscal Contributions

Like other payroll contributions, the so-called quasi-fiscal contributions for SENAI, SESI, SESC and SENAC would be transferred, on an optional basis, directly to the worker's salary. In this case, every worker would choose to remain in the old system, thus receiving the services of the institutions financed by employer contributions, or to receive directly, in the form of wages, the product of applying the 2.5 percent rate to the yields that now pay for these services. A more radical reform of the system would include the possibility of making each company's deduction for these employer entities completely optional.

Final Considerations

The diagnosis of the Brazilian social insurance system indicates the necessity of an immediate and thorough reform, the objectives of which must be greater social justice and economic and financial equilibrium in the new system, together with acknowledgment of the rights acquired under the old system.

The current political climate in Brazil is extremely conducive to discussion, now that the process of amending the Constitution—which should be completed in October of 1994—has begun. Many of the provisions governing social security are set forth clearly and explicitly in the Constitution of 1988.

Also, from the macroeconomic viewpoint, the time is right for the introduction of social security reforms. Brazil is one of the few countries in the hemisphere that still has not implemented an adjustment plan to allow its inclusion in the new international order. Social security initiatives should therefore be incorporated within a larger series of macroeconomic measures, thus ensuring coherent policy in all sectors.

It is obvious, despite these positive factors, that the necessary social reforms will require considerable effort and expertise on the part of the government and the various sectors of society interested in the subject of social security.

Increased awareness and a change of attitude will be required of the Brazilian public as a necessary condition of social security reform. The limit of economic and financial mobility must be made clear, laying to rest the myth of a beneficent, paternalistic state capable of financing anything and everything. Above all, the public must understand who pays, who receives and how much is received in terms of benefits and services, and an explanation must be given of the cross subsidies and conflicting interests of the groups involved.

Finally, it is essential that the reforms include a restructuring of the system of incentives, regulations and state control. In fact, the discussion about privatizing social insurance makes no sense at all. Strange as it may seem, the success of a reform as liberal as the one proposed depends on the reinforcement of the state's basic, nondelegable functions. What is actually proposed is that the state, instead of remaining an inefficient supplier of all sorts of benefits and services, narrow its focus and concentrate on the tasks of promoting, regulating and controlling a new social security system.

Bibliography

Beltrão, K.I., and F.E.B. Oliveira. 1988. *Uma Análise Comparativa de Alguns Resultados do Suplemento Previdência PNAD* - 83 e Dados da DATAPREV. PNADs em Foco: Anos 1980, ABEP.

BEMFAM. 1987. *Pesquisa Nacional sobre Saúde Materno-Infantil e Planejamento Familiar, 1986.* Rio de Janeiro: BENFAM, IRD/Departamento de Educação e Comunicação Social da BEMFAM.

Berquó, E., and T. Merrick. 1983. *The Determinants of Brazil's Recent Rapid Decline in Fertility.* Washington, D.C.: National Academy Press, Committee on Population and Demography.

Camarano, A.A., I.I. Bertrão, and R. Neupert. 1988. *Século XXI: A Quantas Andará a População Brasileira?* Rio de Janeiro: IPLAN/IPEA.

Carvalho, J.A.M. de. 1980. Evolução Demográfica Recente no Brasil. *Pesquisa e Planejamento Econômico* 10(2):527-553.

Carvalho, J.A.M., and S. de M.G. Pinheiro. 1982. Fecundidade e Mortalidade no Brasil, 1970-1980, CEDEPLAR/UFMG. Belo Horizonte, Brazil. Mimeo.

CEDEPLAR. 1982. Fecundidade e Mortalidade no Brasil, 1960-1970. CEDEPLAR/UFMG. Belo Horizonte, Brazil. Mimeo.

CELADE/IBGE. 1984. *Estimaciones y proyecciones de población, 1950-2025.* Fascículo f/bra. 1. July.

DATAPREV. 1980-90. *Sistema Integrado de Tratamento de Séries Estratégicas (SINTESE).* Rio de Janeiro: DATAPREV.

FUNABEM/CBIA. 1987-90. *Balanço Contábil.* Rio de Janeiro: FUNABEM/CBIA.

Howard, R.A. 1960. *Dynamic Programming and Markov Process.* Cambridge, Massachusetts: Technology Presses.

IBGE/AMS. 1976-89. *AMS.* Brasília: Escola Nacional de Ciências Estatísticas/ Instituto Brasileiro de Geografia e Estatística.

IPLAN/IPEA. 1987. *A Evolução da Estrutura de Produção Agropecuária: Algumas Notas Preliminares.* Brasília: DIT, PNUD.

LBA. 1987-89. *Relatório Geral, 1989 - 1988 - 1987.* Rio de Janeiro: LBA.

_____. 1991. *Plano Diretor 1991-93.* Rio de Janeiro: LBA.

Leite, C.B. 1978. *A Proteção Social no Brasil.* 2nd ed. São Paulo: LTR.

Leite, C.B., and L.A.P. Velloso. 1962. *Previdência Social.* Rio de Janeiro: Editora Zahar.

Martine, G. 1986. Migrações de Ordem Rural numa Perspectiva Histórica: Algumas Notas. Brasília: IPLAN/IPEA. Mimeo.

Ministério da Previdência e Assistência Social. 1971-79. *Balanço do Fundo de Previdência e Assistência Social.* Brasília: MPAS/Grupo de Custeio.

Moreira, R.B. 1991. *Modelo Multissetorial de Consistência.* TD-217. Rio de Janeiro. Mimeo.

Muller, C. 1987. Censos Agropecuários. *Agroanalysis* 11 (6): 8-21.

National Academy of Sciences. 1979. Preliminary Report of the Panel on Brazil. Mimeo.

Oliveira, F.E.B., and M.E.E.M. Azevedo. 1984. *Previdência Social.* Working Document. IPEA/IPLAN.

Oliveira, F.E.B., H.M. Cabral, K.I. Beltrão, and S.J. Brito. 1990. *Metodologia de Projeção de Gastos Previdenciários e Assistenciais.* Working Document No. 4. IPEA/ESEP.

Oliveira, F.E.B., M.H.F. da T. Henriques, and K.I. Beltrão. 1986. Um modelo para Projeção de Tendências a Médio Prazo da Previdência Social Brasileira. *Previdência em Dados* 1 (2): 5-16.

Oliveira, F.E.B., *et al.* 1985. *Tendências a Médio Prazo da Previdência Social Brasileira: Um Modelo de Simulação.* TDI No. 73. IPEA/INPES.

_____. 1992. *Cenários da Previdência Social e Reflexos para os Fundos de Pensão.* Working Document. ABRAPP and EPGE/FGV.

Oliveira, L.A.P., and N. Silva. 1986. *Tendências da fecundidade nos primeiros anos da década de 80.* Anais do V Encontro Nacional de Estudos Populacionais. Águas de São Pedro, Brazil: ABEP.

Oliveira, L.A.P., and C.C. da S. Simões. 1988. *As Informações sobre Fecundidade, Mortalidade e Anticoncepção nas PNADs em Foco: Anos 1980.* ABEP/Nova Friburgo, RJ.

Vallin, J., and F.P. Meslé. 1988. *Les causes de décès en France. 1925-1978.* Working Document No. 115. INED-PUS.

Wong, L.R. 1986. *A Diminuição dos Nascimentos e a Queda da Fecundidade no Brasil dos Anos Pós-80.* Anais do V Encontro Nacional de Estudos Populacionais. Águas de São Pedro, Brazil: ABEP.

APPENDIX I

Summary of the Benefits of the National Social Insurance Institute

This Appendix explains the various types of financial benefits granted by the National Institute of Social Insurance (INPS, *Instituto Nacional de Previdência Social*) of Brazil. There are other programs administered by other government agencies that also provide financial benefits for workers, but they are not described here. They are: Unemployment Insurance, the Length-of-service Guarantee Fund (FGTS, *Fundo de Garantia por Tempo de Serviço*), the Social Integration Program (PIS, *Programa de Integração Social*), and the Public Official Equity Building Program (PASEP, *Programa de Formação do Patrimônio do Servidor Público*), which is part of the PIS.

A brief description of each benefit is provided below. The letters in parentheses mean: S - social insurance; A - social welfare; C - continuing benefit; U - one-time benefit. RMC means minimum contribution rule (*regla de mínimo de contribuciones*): for enrollments after July 24, 1991, a minimum of 180 monthly contributions; for enrollments before that date, between 60 and 180 monthly contributions, depending on the date of entry into force of the benefit requirement.

Annual Payment (S, C)

- *Recipient(s):* insured individual and dependents;
- *Amount:* December monthly income or proportional to the length of time benefit paid.

Length-of-service Payment (S, C)

- *Recipient:* insured individual entitled to length-of-service retirement who continues working;
- *Amount:* 25 percent of the retirement to which the worker would be entitled.

Special Retirement (S, C)
- *Recipient:* insured individual who has worked in occupations declared unhealthy, arduous or dangerous;
- *Amount:* 85 percent of the benefit salary, plus 1 percent of that salary for every 12 monthly contributions, up to a maximum of 100 percent.

Old-age Retirement (S, C)
- *Recipient:* insured individual;
- *Amount:* 70 percent of the benefit salary, plus 1 percent for every 12 monthly contributions, up to a maximum of 30 percent.

Disability Retirement (S, C)
- *Recipient:* insured individual;
- *Amount:* 80 percent of the benefit salary plus 1 percent for every 12 monthly contributions, up to a maximum of 20 percent.

Disability Retirement Due to Work-related Accident (S, C)
- *Recipient:* insured individual, except domestic workers;
- *Amount:* 100 percent of the contribution salary on the date of the accident or 100 percent of the benefit salary, whichever is larger; or 100 percent of the assistance for illness caused by accident if the latter, after adjustment, was greater than the contribution salary or the benefit salary.

Length-of-service Retirement (S, C)
- *Recipient:* insured individual;
- *Amount:* men, 70 percent of the benefit salary after 30 years of service, plus 6 percent for every full year over the 30 year minimum, up to a maximum of 100 percent; women, 70 percent of the benefit salary after 25 years of service plus 6 percent for every full year over the 25 year minimum, up to a maximum of 100 percent.

Length-of-service Retirement for Teachers (S, C)
- *Recipient:* insured teacher (certain categories) of courses recognized by the competent authorities;
- *Amount:* 100 percent of the benefit salary.

Worker's Compensation (S, C)
- *Recipient:* insured individual, except domestic workers;
- *Amount:* 30, 40 or 60 percent of the contribution salary or the benefit salary, whichever is larger; or 30, 40 or 60 percent of the amount of the assistance for illness caused by accident, if the latter, after adjustment, was larger than the contribution salary or to the benefit salary on the date of the accident.

Illness Benefit (S, C)
- *Recipient:* insured individual;
- *Amount:* 80 percent of the benefit salary plus 1 percent for every 12 monthly contributions, up to a maximum of 92 percent of the benefit salary.

Allowance for Illness Caused by Work-related Accident (S, C)
- *Recipient:* insured individual, except domestic workers;
- *Amount:* 92 percent of the insured individual's contribution salary in effect on the date of the accident, or the benefit salary if it is larger.

Funeral Grant (S, U)
- *Recipient:* insured individual. The insurance is paid to whoever has paid the costs of burying the insured individual;
- *Amount:* determined by the Ministry of Social Insurance.

Birth Grant (S, U)
- *Recipient:* insured individual;
- *Amount:* determined by the Ministry of Social Insurance.

Imprisonment Relief (S, C)
- *Recipient:* insured individual. The insurance is paid to the insured individual's dependents;
- *Amount:* 80 percent of the value of the retirement to which the insured individual would be entitled on the date of imprisonment, plus as many 10 percent increments of that retirement as there are dependents, up to a maximum of two. The amount of the benefit cannot be less than one minimum wage.

Personal Grant (S, U)
- *Recipient:* insured individual;
- *Amount:* one-time payment equal to the sum of the amounts related to the insured individual's contributions, adjusted in the same way as savings deposits, with day 1 as the anniversary date.

Death Allowance (S, C)
- *Recipient:* insured individual. The insurance is paid to the dependents;
- *Amount:* 80 percent of the retirement pay collected by the insured individual or to which he was entitled on the date of death, plus as many 10 percent increments of the amount of said retirement as there are dependents, up to a maximum of two. The benefit cannot be less than one minimum wage.

Pension for Death Due to Work-related Accident (S, C)
- *Recipient:* insured individual. The insurance is paid to the dependents;
- *Amount:* 100 percent of the contribution salary or the benefit salary, whichever is larger, on the date of death; or 100 percent of the amount of the sickness assistance or the disability retirement, regardless of the number of dependents.

Monthly Life Annuity (A, C)
- *Recipient:* insured individual;
- *Amount:* one minimum wage.

Family Salary (S, C)

- *Recipient:* insured individual, except domestic workers;
- *Amount:* equal to the number of children or other dependents under 14 years of age or disabled, in an amount determined by the Ministry of Social Insurance and based on the insured individual's monthly wage bracket.

Maternity Benefit (S, C)
- *Recipient:* insured individual;
- *Amount:* for insured individual domestic workers, equal to the last contribution salary; for self-employed workers, equal to the last remuneration equivalent to one month's work.

APPENDIX II

Modules of the Projection Model

This Appendix describes the five basic modules of the projection model: demographic module, module for generating contributors to the social insurance system, module for simulating the subpopulation of beneficiaries, macroeconomic consistency module and module for generating income and expenses.

Demographic Module

This module makes demographic projections by the components method, providing separate projections of rural and urban mortality rates by sex, age and calendar year, as well as fertility. It was assumed that in the future emigration would decline to levels similar to those observed in the sixties and seventies. Specific rates of activity by sex, age and place of residence were used to calculate the economically active population. The number of contributors was estimated using the rate of formalization, the proportion of formalized employees and the percentage of individual contributors (self-employed, employers, domestic workers, etc.) from the Ministry of Social Insurance. The base year of the projections is 1980, the last year for which census information is available, given that the 1991 census has not yet been published. This module is described in Oliveira *et al.,* 1985.

Module for Generating Contributors

Although information about the number of contributors is presented in various sections of this chapter, the fact is that the Ministry of Social Insurance has no precise data of this type. When the various funds of the social insurance institutes were consolidated, keeping individual contribution records were replaced by records kept according to company, which was then abandoned in favor of records showing only the total amounts collected by each unit of the federation.

Given this limitation, the population of contributors was estimated for the base year (1980) by combining data from various sources—RAIS, Demographic Census and several estimates obtained from the Secretariat of Planning of the IAPAS concerning the total number of self-employed workers, domestic workers, and so on (not identified by sex). A common problem in all of the lists was the existence of records with incomplete information, mostly no mention of sex or age. This module is described in Oliveira *et al.,* 1985.

Module for Simulating the Subpopulation of Beneficiaries

Three different groups of beneficiaries were considered: those admitted before 1988 (date of promulgation of the Constitution), between 1988 and 1992 (date of the decree regulating the supplementary laws) and those admitted after that date.

For the first group, whose benefits were restructured in accordance with the number of minimum wages at the time they were granted, the average value of the benefits was used, calculated year by year starting in 1980 on the basis of data provided by DATAPREV. This value was adjusted in 1991 and in February 1990 the lower limit was raised from 0.915 of the minimum to one minimum wage.

The members of the second group (*i.e.,* insured individuals whose benefits were granted between the date of promulgation of the Constitution and the date of the regulations of the supplementary laws) in principle obtained only an increase in the lower limit of the benefit to one minimum in 1990.

The third group—insured individuals who have collected the benefit since 1992—would be entitled to the advantages granted by the Constitution and presently regulated by the supplementary laws.

The method used consisted of simulating year by year the distributions by sex and individual ages of the populations of beneficiaries of the general social insurance system, the rural worker program and the rural employee program. In other words, for each calendar year between 1981 and 2030, an attempt was made to estimate each of the shares defined for the base year, in terms of number of individuals and their composition by sex and age.

Using several simplifying hypotheses, a possible representation of this process is a First Order Markov Process, wherein year by year the growth of the population is accompanied by stochastic transitions of individuals between the various possible statuses. The status of beneficiary is, in both cases, a subset of statuses encompassing the various types of benefits considered. The transitions from entry into the system and exit from it are particularly interesting because they permit determining the number of beneficiaries each year.

Associated with each possible transition is a probability, which in this version of the model is assumed to be constant over time, except in cases related to mortality, monthly life annuities and coverage.

Another methodology was used to calculate pensions. Based on the historical series, data for the future were projected. Using the component method to generate the pensioners contingent would have required a lateral model of family structure to allocate dependents to deceased beneficiaries. This model, which is in the process of development, was not used. This module is described in Oliveira *et al.,* 1985.

Macroeconomic Consistency Module

This is a multisectoral consistency module designed for long-term economic planning in Brazil; its projections are based on assumptions about the external situation and the behavior of national economic agents. Therefore, aspects related to the short term or to the dynamics of the growth process are not considered.

This model uses coefficients estimated on the basis of a social accounting matrix to examine the relationship between the productive sectors and the participation of the agents—families, private and public enterprises and the public sector—in the income generated; it assumes that the income is unequally distributed among families and that this inequity can be represented by a law of probabilities; it assumes that the consumption of goods and the investment in housing made by families are functions of the income estimated on the basis of a family budget survey; and it assumes that the investments—differently comprised between sectors for the various commodities—are determined in such a way that in the year of the projection, productive capacity is fully used in all sectors. The main results are gross domestic product and sectoral investments, national accounts, public sector accounts and balance of payments, exchange rate, cost of labor, employment generated and growth of the average income of the various social sectors. This module is described in Moreira, 1991.

Module for Generating Income and Expenses

The projections of the income and expenses of the social insurance system take into consideration the provisions of the Constitution and of Laws No. 8212/91 and No. 8213/91, which regulated the organization and financing of social security and the social insurance benefits plan respectively. Social insurance, health and social welfare expenses were included. Oliveira, Cabral, Bêltrão, *et al.*, 1990, provide more detailed explanations of the hypotheses used.

The calculation of social insurance expenses was based on two subgroups of accounts: (i) disbursements for benefits, comprising the basic costs, representative of the percentage of expenditures on benefits according to the rules in effect before the Constitution of 1988 and the additional costs resulting from the changes introduced by that constitution and the laws establishing regulations for the constitutional provisions; and (ii) personnel and administrative expenses, which include the personnel costs of auditing, collection and economic and financial administration of the system.

The provision of each type of medical service was calculated year by year as a proportion of the 30 percent of the total social security budget, except unemployment insurance, as determined by the temporary provisions of the Constitution.

For income, in accordance with the provisions of the Constitution and the

Financing Law, the following were used to project social security contributions: contribution salaries, billing, profits, and the results of the first-stage marketing of the output of rural producers, small-scale fishermen and miners. In the absence of better estimates, the growth of income was assumed to be equal to the growth of contribution salaries.

The financing system, which serves as the basis for the simulations, is of the simple pay-as-you-go type, with no maintenance of a contingency reserve. For this reason, neither income nor financial expenses were considered.

Since only one budget is provided for social security, costs were calculated and presented for the system as a whole. In addition to the system's own income, the funds in the Treasury were also considered. These were calculated to cover all personnel and administrative expenses related to the auditing and collection of contributions and the payment of social insurance and welfare benefits.

CHAPTER FOUR

The Chilean Experience

Patricio Mujica Riveros

Until the mid-seventies, one of the most salient features of the Chilean social security system was the state's growing involvement as provider and regulator of social services. This arrangement was ultimately subverted by poor management and the steady expansion of benefits without any specific means of financing.

The reform of the system began in the early 1980s with the changeover from the traditional pay-as-you-go system administered by the state to one that is mixed in terms of both administration (private and public) and the criterion for determining benefits (individual capitalization and pay-as-you-go). The state monopoly on the provision of social services was thus replaced by a system that promotes the involvement of private institutions and decentralized public agencies, independent of the central government.

This experience kindled a spirited debate and has since become an essential point of reference for the design and implementation of social security reforms throughout the region. In this chapter, the Chilean experience is examined and evaluated with a view to identifying the lessons to be learned from each of the programs in the Chilean social security system.

The second section describes the recent growth and the redistributive impact of the social welfare programs. The main conclusion is that evaluating the effectiveness of social welfare programs requires examining both the level of social spending associated with these programs and their distribution among the various income groups. In Chile, substantial progress in sharpening the focus of social welfare programs, which occurred after the reform, was accompanied by a significant reduction in the resources used to finance them. This suggests that the use of partial indicators can distort the evaluation of social policy.

The third section examines the health insurance system. The growth of the private health system has increased the options available to contributors and has stimulated competition in the provision of health insurance. Nevertheless, the benefits of privatizing the system have not been evenly distributed, and a number of transparency problems remain. Another problem, which has to do with the incentives built into the system, tends automatically to exclude certain population groups. The problems of the public health system are due primarily to poor organization and management.

The fourth section describes the pension system and its achievements. Despite progress, the evidence suggests that the operation of a capitalization system requires additional regulatory efforts to ensure transparency and to extend the benefits to self-employed workers. The final section summarizes the most important lessons to be learned from the reform of the Chilean social security system. The design of social security systems in Latin America has become a central issue in the current debate about the state's role in the promotion of economic and social development.

The financial crisis that erupted in the early eighties revealed a number of organizational and functional problems in most of the region's social security systems. In response, some countries initiated radical reforms of their systems, while others instituted emergency plans aimed primarily at solving the problems of underfinancing and inefficiency. Owing to the scope and permanence of the changes and the swiftness of their implementation, studying the reform of the Chilean social security system provides some valuable insights into the design and execution of social security reforms throughout the region.

The main objective of this chapter is to examine and evaluate the reform of the Chilean social security system for specific recommendations for the design of social security systems in the region. The specific objectives of this chapter encompass the following: assessing the level of coverage of the various programs of the Chilean social security system; measuring the redistributive impact of its social welfare programs; gauging the cross subsidies within the system; and simulating the pensions and social insurance funds in various situations.

Reviewing the Chilean experience should provide a frame of reference for answering some of the following questions.

- What are the determinants of the coverage of social security systems?
- What constraints limit including the informal sectors in the different programs of the social security system?
- What determines the redistributive impact of social welfare programs?
- What role should the state play in providing and regulating social services?
- What regulatory framework should be established to guarantee an equitable and efficient social security system?
- Is there any trade-off between efficiency and equity in the organization of social security systems?

This chapter is organized according to the three major programs that make up the Chilean social security system. In the following sections the operation of Chile's social welfare programs, health insurance system, and social insurance system is described and evaluated. The final section summarizes the major conclusions of the chapter.

Social Welfare Programs

Through the social welfare programs, the state generally effects financial transfers to individuals to augment the incomes of disadvantaged families or individuals whose income is temporarily insufficient or who are in a specific state of need.

Chile's principal social welfare programs are financial assistance and work-disability benefits. One conclusion suggested by our analysis of the recent growth of financial assistance expenditures is that the decrease observed in the latter half of the 1980s is the result not only of an automatic adjustment process set in motion by the economic recovery but also of a policy of reducing the real benefits of the social welfare programs.

Financial Assistance

Currently, the state makes financial transfers to individuals through four social programs: the one-time family grant (SUF, *subsidio único familiar*), welfare pensions (PASIS, *pensiones asistenciales*), family allowances, and unemployment benefits.

Table 4.1 summarizes the 1980-90 trend of monetary subsidies. The table shows that after a period of growth culminating in 1982, the social spending associated with financial transfers began a steady decline in 1985. The cumulative reduction in financial assistance in the 1980-90 period is approximately 40 percent in real terms.

The growth of financial assistance before 1982 is a result of the creation of various social programs designed to lessen the impact on income of the general decline in the level of economic activity in this period. The cutback in financial assistance spending coincides with the recovery of economic activity that began in 1985.

Nevertheless, to determine whether the reduced spending on financial assistance is merely the result of a natural adjustment process initiated by the recovery of economic activity or signals a decline in the real value of financial assistance, Table 4.2 shows the trend of the real unit value of financial assistance in the 1981-92 period. The table indicates that the real value of each of the state's financial assistance programs declined steadily between 1981 and 1989. It also shows a change in this trend in 1990.

Table 4.1. Monetary Subsidies, 1980-90
(Millions of 1990 pesos)

Year	Single family subsidy	Welfare pensions	Family allowance	Unemploy. subsidy	Total monetary subsidies
1980	--	13,775	94,520	15,859	124,154
1981	--	18,262	96,114	17,344	131,720
1982	--	22,977	93,880	29,333	146,190
1983	12,028	27,123	84,048	26,683	139,882
1984	18,232	34,872	73,175	15,050	141,330
1985	19,719	35,436	4,467	13,282	132,904
1986	15,505	35,188	53,809	8,373	112,876
1987	12,098	28,246	45,085	5,220	90,659
1988	11,165	31,600	40,231	4,045	87,041
1989	9,549	27,456	32,215	2,466	71,686
1990	9,952	29,265	31,174	1,697	72,088

(Percentage of GDP)

Year	Single family subsidy	Welfare pensions	Family allowance	Unemploy. subsidy	Total monetary subsidies
1980	—	0.21	1.47	0.25	1.94
1981	—	0.27	1.42	0.26	1.95
1982	—	0.40	1.61	0.50	2.51
1983	0.21	0.47	1.28	0.46	2.42
1984	0.30	0.57	1.19	0.25	2.30
1985	0.31	0.56	1.02	0.21	2.11
1986	0.23	0.53	0.81	0.13	1.70
1987	0.17	0.40	0.64	0.07	1.29
1988	0.15	0.42	0.53	0.05	1.15
1989	0.12	0.33	0.39	0.03	0.86
1990	0.12	0.35	0.37	0.02	0.85

Source: Superintendency of Social Security.

Redistributive Impact

Table 4.3 presents the distribution of monetary subsidies by decile of per capita autonomous income in 1990, based on the socioeconomic characterization survey (CASEN, *encuesta de caracterización socioeconómica nacional*) published by the Ministry of Planning (MIDEPLAN, 1992).

Despite the fact that the financial assistance tends to be concentrated in the low-income households, its distribution is not always consistent with a preferential allocation of assistance to the most disadvantaged groups. In fact, households in the first decile receive a lower percentage than households in the second decile. This could mean that the assistance is filtering through to low-priority

Table 4.2. Trend of Real Unit Value of Monetary Subsidies, 1981-90
(Base 1981)

Year	Single family subsidy	Welfare pension	Family allowance
1981	100.0	100.0	100.0
1982	98.0	104.2	103.6
1983	79.0	96.0	85.5
1984	77.5	110.5	82.0
1985	73.4	86.7	71.3
1986	61.3	82.9	59.7
1987	62.8	75.3	49.9
1988	54.7	75.6	43.5
1989	46.8	56.1	37.1
1990	54.2	81.0	—
Bracket I	—	—	58.7
Bracket II	—	—	42.7
Bracket III	—	—	29.5
1991	56.9	87.0	—
Bracket I	—	—	60.0
Bracket II	—	—	48.2
Bracket III	—	—	24.2
1992	61.7	112.8	—
Bracket I	—	—	67.2
Bracket II	—	—	59.1
Bracket III	—	—	23.8

Source: MIDEPLAN (1992), Superintendency of Social Security, INP.

Table 4.3. Distribution of Monetary Subsidies, 1990
(Percentages)

Decile	Single Family allowance	Unemployment subsidy	Welfare pensions	Family subsidy	Total subsidies
1	6.3	50.6	30.3	28.7	14.7
2	15.3	6.5	15.2	21.9	15.8
3	13.4	10.6	14.6	16.4	13.9
4	12.3	17.6	7.6	12.8	11.8
5	11.2	3.2	10.4	7.1	10.3
6	10.0	4.4	9.0	6.5	9.2
7	9.2	3.3	5.3	2.5	7.5
8	8.4	1.0	4.7	2.2	6.7
9	7.2	1.3	1.8	1.0	5.3
10	6.7	1.0	1.1	0.6	4.8

Source: MIDEPLAN, 1992.
Note: Decile 1 represents the lowest income group; decile 10, the highest.

Table 4.4. Share of Monetary Subsidies, 1990

Decile	Autonomous allowance	Family allowance	Unemp. subsidy	Welfare pensions	Single family subsidy	Total subsidies
1	100.0	5.8	2.4	7.0	4.9	20.1
2	100.0	5.0	0.1	1.3	1.4	7.8
3	100.0	3.3	0.1	0.9	0.8	5.1
4	100.0	2.4	0.2	0.4	0.5	3.5
5	100.0	1.8	0.0	0.4	0.2	2.4
6	100.0	1.3	0.0	0.3	0.2	1.8
7	100.0	1.0	0.0	0.2	0.1	1.3
8	100.0	0.7	0.0	0.1	0.0	0.8
9	100.0	0.4	0.0	0.0	0.0	0.4
10	100.0	0.2	0.0	0.0	0.0	0.2
Total	100.0	0.9	0.1	0.2	0.2	1.4

Source: Author's calculations based on MIDEPLAN, 1992.

Table 4.5. Trend of Worker Disability Subsidies Health System Total, 1986-90
(Percentage of GDP)

Year	Curative	Leave		Work-related accident	Total health subsidies
		Maternity	Illness		
1986	0.19	0.09	0.00	0.05	0.32
1987	0.22	0.11	0.00	0.06	0.39
1988	0.29	0.16	0.01	0.07	0.53
1989	0.32	0.10	0.01	0.08	0.50
1990	0.35	0.11	0.01	0.08	0.54

Source: Author's calculations based on MIDEPLAN, 1992.

sectors, which would require a change in the recipient groups or more effective control of the process of allocating the assistance.

Table 4.4 shows the impact of financial assistance on the level of autonomous household income for each decile, indicating that the increase in autonomous income associated with the assistance decreases as the level of household income rises. For households in the first decile, the financial assistance increases income by an amount equivalent to 20 percent of the autonomous income. In contrast to this figure, the increase for the top decile is a mere 0.2 percent.

In short, the evidence indicates that social welfare programs have a significant impact on the purchasing power of the poorest households and that the effect on high-income households is insignificant. Nevertheless, the evidence also shows that there are leaks in some programs, suggesting that there is room for improvement in the distributive impact of these programs.

Table 4.6. FONASA: Trend of Worker Disability Subsidies, 1986-90
(Billions of 1990 pesos)

Year	Curative	Leave Maternity	Illness	Total health subsidies
1986	7,557	4,075	—	11,632
1987	7,434	4,079	143	11,656
1988	9,176	7,521	206	16,903
1989	9,564	3,711	194	13,469
1990	9,426	2,868	188	12,482

Source: Author's calculations.

Worker Disability Benefits

The Chilean social security system provides various benefits for those unable to work, which are provided through three basic programs:
- Maternity and child-care benefit;
- Sickness and medical benefit; and,
- Work-related accident benefit.

Workers are entitled to these benefits by virtue of their employment, unlike the transfers described above, and their value therefore depends on the beneficiary's income level. Following is a discussion of the recent trend of these benefits and an evaluation of their distribution.

Trend

The significant growth of worker disability subsidies in the 1986-90 period can be clearly seen. In fact, the cumulative growth between 1986 and 1990 is greater than 130 percent in real terms, but is not evenly distributed among the various social insurance systems. As Tables 4.6 and 4.7 show, the growth of worker disability subsidies tends to be associated with the increase in the benefits provided through the private health system. While some of the benefits provided through the public system increase slightly (sickness benefits) or are considerably reduced (maternity benefits), most of the benefits provided through the health insurance companies (ISAPRE, *Institutos de Salud Previsional*) increase substantially. This phenomenon reflects the growing importance of private insurance systems in the Chilean social insurance system.

Redistributive Impact

Unlike most of the social welfare programs that form the state social system, the distribution of worker disability benefits among the various population groups

Table 4.7. ISAPRES: Trend of Worker Disability Subsidies, 1986-90
(Billions of 1990 pesos)

Year	Curative	Leave Maternity	Illness	Total health subsidies
1986	4,903	1,736	64	6,703
1987	8,300	3,405	156	11,861
1988	12,691	4,729	252	17,672
1989	16,851	4,776	375	22,002
1990	19,826	6,166	511	26,503

Source: Author's calculations.

Table 4.8. Net Annual Maternity Subsidy Benefits per Household and Quintile of Income, 1990
(Percentages)

Quintile	Percentage	Cumulative
1	1.80	1.80
2	4.94	6.74
3	11.06	17.80
4	19.69	37.49
5	62.51	100.00
Total	100.00	

Source: MIDEPLAN, 1992; MINSAL.
Note: Quintile 1 represents the lowest income group; quintile 5, the highest.

tends to reflect the existing income distribution. Table 4.8 shows the distribution of maternity benefits, by quintile of per capita household income. The distribution reveals that a large percentage of benefits is concentrated in the upper quintiles. In fact, over 60 percent of the total maternity benefits go to the top quintile, while the percentage going to the first quintile is only 1.8 percent. A similar situation occurs with the other worker disability benefits. As shown in Table 4.9, as household income increases, so does the share of the total benefits received.

The Health Insurance System

The various reforms carried between 1979 and 1985 drastically changed the old health system and led to the proliferation of private health insurance companies. At present, the Chilean health system is a mixture of public and private organizations.

The two major types of health insurance are the system financed by compulsory worker contributions of 7 percent of their earnings and the work-related

Table 4.9. Net Annual Social Insurance Benefits per Household and Quintile of Income, 1990

(Percentages)

Quintile	Percentage	Cumulative
1	5.12	5.12
2	12.8	17.92
3	17.27	35.19
4	23.66	58.85
5	41.15	100.00
Total	100.00	

Source: MIDEPLAN, 1992; MINSAL.
Note: Quintile 1 represents the lowest income group; quintile 5, the highest.

accident and occupational disease system, financed by employer contributions and an additional, variable contribution determined by the degree of risk involved in the profession. There are other sources of financing health services, including the payments made by users for the care they receive and the government contribution, especially in the public system.

Every employee, whether active or passive, has the legal obligation of contributing to some public or private health insurance system. Self-employed workers can join any of the systems as voluntary contributors.

The Public System

In principle, contributors to the public system and their dependents have two health care options:

- Institutional—direct care in establishments of the National Health Services System and in clinics run by the municipalities; and,
- Elective—users choose the professional and the establishment from among those that have registered in this system.

People who receive institutional care are classified in four groups according to their income level, which determines the percentage of the services to be paid for directly by the user.

The public health system is financed with user contributions and a contribution from the government. It therefore operates as a pay-as-you-go system, since there is no direct correlation between the contributions and the benefits that the system provides its members.

The Private System

The private system consists of private companies that provide health insurance to pay the medical expenses of affiliates and their dependents.

Table 4.10. Health Insurance System Coverage, 1987 and 1990

System	1987		1990	
	Beneficiaries	Percent	Beneficiaries	Percent
Public	9,159,022	74.6	8,809,374	68.8
ISAPRES	1,065,237	8.7	1,927,331	15.1
FFAA	350,575	2.9	318,917	2.5
Private	1,549,198	12.6	1,550,091	12.1
Others	154,745	1.3	197,355	1.5
Total	12,278,777	100.0	12,803,068	100.0

Source: MIDEPLAN, CASEN 1987 and CASEN 1990 Surveys.

The relationship between the ISAPRE and their affiliates is established in a health contract, the cost of which depends on the risk of the family group and the quality of services associated with the plan. According to law, in no case can the plans offered by the ISAPRE be of a lesser quality or provide less coverage than the public system. The cost of each plan is financed with compulsory contributions plus an additional payment if the legally established contribution does not cover the cost of the plan.

Access to the Health Insurance Systems

Coverage

Table 4.10 compares the coverage of the various health systems between 1987 and 1990. In 1987, nearly 75 percent of the population described themselves as beneficiaries of the public health system. In 1990, this percentage had fallen to 69 percent. The private system's share rose from 8.7 to 15.1 percent between 1987 and 1990. The table also shows that a large percentage of individuals did not belong to any health insurance system.

Socioeconomic Profile of the Beneficiaries

Despite the rapid growth of the private health system in recent years, such growth has been unevenly distributed among the various social sectors. Generally speaking, family income level is the main element that distinguishes affiliation with one system or another. The average income of an ISAPRE affiliate is approximately four times larger than that of a beneficiary of the public system. The age structure of the beneficiaries is another important difference between the two systems. Table 4.11 highlights beneficiaries' socioeconomic and demographic differences according to health system.

Table 4.11. Beneficiaries by Age and Quintile of Income
(Percentages)

Public System

Quintile	Age Bracket				
	0-5	6-14	15-59	60 and over	Total
1	40.5	42.0	26.4	13.7	29.5
2	29.8	27.7	26.1	17.8	25.9
3	16.6	16.1	22.4	24.4	20.8
4	9.0	9.7	16.1	24.8	15.1
5	4.1	4.6	8.9	19.4	8.7
Total	13.0	16.9	58.9	11.2	100.0

Private System

Quintile	Age Bracket				
	0-5	6-14	15-59	60 and over	Total
1	4.8	5.5	3.6	2.9	4.0
2	10.5	10.9	7.0	2.8	8.0
3	13.6	16.9	14.7	8.3	14.7
4	27.4	26.5	26.2	18.6	26.1
5	43.6	40.2	48.5	67.4	47.1
Total	13.0	16.3	67.3	3.4	100.0

Source: MIDEPLAN, 1992.
Note: Quintile 1 represents the lowest income group; quintile 5, the highest.

The Public System

The profound structural changes that occurred in the late 1970s and, in particular, the health insurance reform initiated in 1981 significantly affected the evolution of the state health system in Chile. The privatization of the social insurance system drastically changed not only the financing structure of the public health system but also the state's role in providing health services and the socioeconomic profile of its beneficiaries.

Financial Structure

The decrease in government health spending in the 1980s reflects both the reduction of social spending in that period and changes in its composition. The social policy of the period favored financing specific programs aimed at compensating for income losses due to unforeseen circumstances to ensure a minimum level of consumption within the family group. This bias in the social policy was accompanied by a drastic reduction in social spending in other sectors, including health care.

Table 4.12. Public Health Financing, 1980-91
(Billions of 1991 pesos)

Year	Government contribution	Affiliate contributions	Others	Total
1980	118,291	68,501	25,087	211,880
1981	118,678	84,879	33,279	236,836
1982	114,086	78,282	59,133	251,501
1983	93,930	89,928	25,032	208,890
1984	89,134	94,912	18,884	202,929
1985	81,240	88,985	24,659	194,885
1986	75,438	96,987	21,905	194,329
1987	75,536	93,344	23,988	192,868
1988	83,255	106,561	28,783	218,599
1989	79,243	122,593	28,034	229,879
1990	90,173	121,829	17,163	229,165
1991	105,687	126,326	53,983	285,996

Source: Superintendency of ISAPRES, Research Dept.

Table 4.13. Distribution of Public System Affiliates by Quintile, 1990
(In thousands)

Group	1	2	3	4	5
A	1,542,034	944,940	541,695	274,048	108,134
B	680,786	747,750	619,206	440,092	182,792
C	112,184	2,000,183	202,100	175,694	100,534
D	78,243	146,755	189,216	191,946	204,192
Don't know	163,559	226,814	265,992	238,509	169,295
Total	2,576,806	2,266,442	1,818,209	1,320,289	764,947

Source: MIDEPLAN, 1992.
Note: Quintile 1 represents the lowest income group; quintile 5, the highest.

The reduction of government health spending drastically altered the financing structure of the public health system and led to an increase in the contribution rate, as indicated in Table 4.12. While in 1980 the government's contribution was just under 60 percent, by late 1991 it had fallen to 37 percent. The percentage of health costs financed by affiliate contributions, on the other hand, rose from 25 percent in 1980 to 45 percent in 1991.

Distribution of the Beneficiaries

Table 4.13 presents the distribution by quintile of beneficiaries of the institutional segment of the public health system. As indicated, the largest percentage of beneficiaries belong to groups in which free care is provided at state health

Table 4.14. Distribution of Public System Affiliates and Contributions, 1990

Quintile	Affiliates		Contribution	
	Percentage	Cumulative	Percentage	Cumulative
1	28.1	281.0	5.0	5.0
2	26.1	542.0	13.5	18.5
3	21.3	755.0	20.3	38.8
4	15.6	911.0	25.6	64.4
5	8.8	100.0	35.6	100.0

Source: MIDEPLAN, 1992.
Note: Quintile 1 represents the lowest income group; quintile 5, the highest.

institutions. This largely explains the recurring financial problems of the public health system and is also a reason for the cross subsidies in the system.

The existence of noncontributing groups in the context of a shrinking government contribution has led to a pay-as-you-go system characterized by net transfers from the middle and high income groups to the low income groups. Table 4.14 shows the size of the transfers generated by the public system. While the affiliates in the first quintile represent approximately 28 percent of the total number, their contributions amount to only 5 percent of the total collected. This situation contrasts with the contributions made by affiliates in the top quintile—35 percent of the total—despite the fact that their numerical share is only 8.8 percent.

State Involvement in the Provision of Health Services

Despite the sharp decrease in the resources allocated to the public health system, the state still provides the lion's share of all health services. As shown in Table 4.15, the state's share of the various health services is consistently larger than that of the private system.

The share of the public sector in the provision of health services is especially important in the case of hospital care. As far as services by days of hospitalization are concerned, the public sector share is 81 percent, while the obstetric care provided in public hospitals represents 84 percent of the system total.

The Private System

The growth of the private health system radically changed the financing of health care, the process of internal resource allocation and the distribution of the benefits provided by the system. The following section examines the efficiency, equity, and financing of the health system.

Table 4.15. State-supplied Health Care Services, 1990
(In thousands)

Services	State	Others	State percentage
Health check-ups	1,961.4	703.7	73.6
General consultation	1,336.0	618.9	68.3
Special and emerg. consultation	1,134.5	994.1	53.3
Total consultations	4,431.8	2,316.7	65.7
Lab tests	6,580.0	414.1	61.4
X-ray	2,925.0	264.1	52.5
Surgery	545.0	37.9	59.0
Days hospitalized	1,376.0	324.8	80.9
Obstetric care:	379.0	7.2	84.1
Normal	285.0	4.2	87.2
Caesarian	94.0	3.0	76.1
Dental care	1,457.2	4,465.9	24.6

Source: MIDEPLAN, 1992.

Table 4.16. Financial Trend of the ISAPRES System, 1986-90
(Billions of 1990 pesos)

Year	Oper. income (1)	Oper. expenses	Administive and sales expenses (2)	(2)/(1)	Capital and reserve profitability (%)
1986	47,221.7	33,892.0	11,161.5	0.24	50.8
1987	59,437.4	48,217.6	14,389.3	0.24	22.6
1988	78,962.3	65,193.2	17,178.4	0.22	20.9
1989	110,035.0	84,436.9	20,316.4	0.19	39.2
1990	130,060.6	98,901.7	26,089.0	0.20	40.5

Source: Superintendency of ISAPRES.

Financial Structure

Table 4.16 illustrates the financial trend of the private health system. It also shows the steady growth of income due to the increase in the number of affiliates. The constant rise of operating costs, which in fact exceeds the growth of income, can also be seen. The surge in operating costs is explained in large measure by the higher unit cost of medical services resulting from the introduction of more sophisticated techniques and procedures.

From this perspective, one of the greatest challenges facing the private health system in Chile is absorbing the higher operating costs associated with the process of technological innovation without excessively raising the cost of the health plans. This will in future require greater efficiency and perhaps a reduction in the operating margins of the health insurance organizations. The recent trend of administrative expenses and sales as a percentage of operating income suggests that the system has become more efficient, but the current downward trend of this indicator suggests that there is still some room for improvement. Moreover, the system's average return on capital and reserves, which at present is approximately 40 percent, indicates that the ISAPRE could easily absorb some of the increase in the system's operating costs.

The distribution of excess contributions generated by the system affects ISAPRE's profit margin. These surpluses come from the obligation to contribute 7 percent of the taxable income to finance health services. The current legislation requires affiliates to sign a health contract that cannot be changed for one year. This means that increases in income during the term of the contract generate excess contributions, which, given the legislation in force, are appropriated by the ISAPRE.

To eliminate the inequity in the distribution of excess contributions, various ways of returning these amounts to the affiliates have been suggested. Unfortunately, they all involve a considerable expense, which might eventually be passed on to affiliates in the form of higher health plan costs or reductions in the quality of the services provided. The advisability of establishing a system to guarantee the return of excess contributions to the affiliates will depend on the cost of administering it and the amount of such excess contributions.

Cross Subsidies

The private health system in Chile is based on individual contracts between the affiliates and the ISAPRE. The amount of these contracts must, in principle, be consistent with the level of services provided. The evidence suggests, however, that the policies followed by the ISAPRE in setting the prices for each type of contributor do not always reflect the technical cost. The difficulty of obtaining information to determine the appropriate cost for various groups of contributors and the necessity of simplifying the calculation of health plan prices has led the ISAPRE to adopt pricing policies that generally—but not always—ensure for each type of contributor some degree of balance between the contributions and the cost of the health services.

To identify the source of the cross subsidies in the ISAPRE system and to determine the amounts involved, the technical cost of the medical services provided for various groups of contributors was estimated. To do this, the cost of providing the services was calculated using a sampling from the ISAPRE open system for 1990, with the beneficiaries differentiated by age and sex. Finally, the cross subsidies for each type of contributor were defined as the difference between the technical cost of the plan and its price.

Table 4.17. Cross Subsidies, 1990
(Thousands of 1990 pesos)

Age	Single man	Married man	Single woman	Total
21-25	64,386.8	24,187.7	18,299.9	106,874.4
26-30	77,981.4	(34,116.7)	13,279.3	57,144.0
31-35	36,848.8	(28,791.9)	(54,227.5)	(46,170.7)
36-40	23,801.2	1,034.0	(51,188.4)	(26,353.2)
41-45	11,198.2	12,632.3	(31,983.4)	(8,152.8)
46-50	4,246.2	3,382.2	(26,388.6)	(18,760.2)
51-55	(271.4)	(1,950.4)	(18,807.1)	(21,028.8)
56-60	(1,588.2)	850.0	(9,415.0)	(10,153.0)
61-65	(4,337.1)	3,299.8	(15,793.0)	(16,830.7)
66-70	(1,245.1)	502.8	(2,852.3)	(3,595.2)
71-75	(2,075.6)	(173.8)	(5,834.5)	(8,084.0)
76-80	(744.1)	(343.1)	(1,419.7)	(2,506.9)
91-85	(430.5)	(369.8)	(1,582.5)	(2,382.8)
Total	207,770.7	(19,857.4)	(187,913.3)	

Source: Author's calculations.
Note: Negative amounts appear in parentheses.

Table 4.17 shows the size of the transfers by age and sex for the various types of contributors, assuming that the ISAPRE set their prices in such a way that the amount of the contributions is generally the same as the technical cost. The table shows that young affiliates subsidize older individuals in every category of contributors. Moreover, a net transfer is observed from single male contributors to married male contributors and, to a lesser extent, to single women.

Financing Health-care Expenses for Life

Financing health care during retirement is a central issue for the current health system in Chile. In retirement, the rising cost of medical care caused by aging coincides with a decrease in the level of disposable income, causing the contribution rate to rise significantly. An impossible financial burden will be placed on the public system if ISAPRE affiliates decide to switch to the public system upon retirement. The transfer of these contributors would cause not only a financing problem within the public system but could also adversely affect the stability and viability of the private health system. To determine the extent of restrictions on health care financing during retirement, the establishment of an individual capitalization fund was studied. The fund would finance a health plan for seniors with coverage and quality similar to those offered active affiliates.

Based on information about health spending per beneficiary by age and sex and using sampling data on the number of beneficiaries per contributor, health spending per average contributor was estimated.

To quantify the constraints that affect various population groups in terms of paying for health plans, an income equation was developed, based on data from the CASEN 1990 survey. The technical cost of the plans was compared with the amount of the compulsory contributions, in order to determine financing requirements during retirement. Simulations were made for a married male contributor, with a distinction being made between those with a college education and those who completed only high school. For each type of contributor, disposable income during retirement was determined according to the current rules for calculating pensions, assuming a return of 4.5 percent, a salary increase of 2.5 percent per annum and a 90 percent density of contributors.

To calculate the additional contribution required to finance health expenses during retirement, it was assumed that the retirement health plan would provide coverage similar to the one that the contributor was paying for at the time of retirement. Concerning the characteristics of the plans for active affiliates, two alternatives were considered.

Alternative 1: The value of the plan is the same as the value of the compulsory contribution (7 percent of taxable income).

Alternative 2: The value of the plan is equal to the average technical cost of the system.

The results of the simulation for each type of contributor are the following:

	University Education	High School Graduate
Alternative 1	1.17 percent	0.89 percent
Alternative 2	0 percent	1.21 percent

For the first alternative, the results show that the additional contribution needed during retirement to finance a plan with coverage similar to that provided before retirement is larger for high-income individuals (university education). Although no additional contribution is needed from this group to finance the average plan, an additional savings effort is naturally required of low-income individuals (secondary education) to pay for such a plan.

The Pension System

Description of the System

The social insurance reform of 1981 drastically changed the pension system. The new system, like the old, is compulsory for all employees and includes old-age, disability and survivor's pensions. Unlike the former system, however, severance pay and compensation are eliminated. In addition, self-employed workers can join the new system as voluntary contributors, on terms similar to those governing employees.

Table 4.18. Trend of AFP System Coverage, 1981-92
(Thousands of individuals)

Year	Affiliates (1)	Contrib. (2)	Work force (3)	Percentage	
				(1)/(3)	(2)/(3)
1981	1,400	—	3,594	39.0	—
1982	1,440	1,060	3,661	39.3	29.0
1983	1,620	1,230	3,768	43.0	32.6
1984	1,930	1,360	3,891	49.6	35.0
1985	2,284	1,558	4,019	56.8	38.8
1986	2,591	1,774	4,270	60.7	41.5
1987	2,890	2,023	4,354	66.4	46.5
1988	3,181	2,168	4,552	69.9	47.6
1989	3,471	2,268	4,675	74.2	48.5
1990	3,740	2,643	4,729	79.1	55.9
1991	4,109	2,487	4,797	85.7	51.8
1992[1]	4,281	2,546	4,840	84.9	52.6

Source: Statistcal Bulletin, AFP Superintendency.
Note: [1] Figures for June of that year.

In the new system, old-age pensions are financed with a compulsory, legally established contribution equal to 10 percent of the taxable wage. These contributions go into an individual account, thus creating a pension fund. The growth of the fund, in turn, depends on the value of the contributions and the return on the investments made for the fund.

Disability and survivor's pensions are backed by compulsory insurance paid for by the affiliate, through which the administrators transfer to the individual account an amount equal to the difference between the cumulative balance on the date of injury or death and the capital needed to finance the respective pension.

Finally, the new system establishes a state-guaranteed minimum pension for men over 65 years of age and for women over 60 who have contributed for no less than 20 years.

The system is administered exclusively by private companies, known as Pension Fund Administrators (AFPs, *Administradoras de Fondos de Pensión*). The primary responsibility of the AFPs is to insure affiliates against the financial risks associated with disability and death and to invest the contributions of their affiliates. In principle, the new system gives affiliates complete freedom to select and to change AFPs at any time and, upon retirement, to choose among the various types of retirement available.

The state's role in this arrangement is essentially one of supervision and control, and unlike the health system, the government does not compete with private institutions in the provision of benefits, except through the minimum pension and social welfare programs.

Table 4.19. Social Insurance Deficit, 1981-2030
(Percentage of GDP)

Year	Recognition bonds (1)	Operating deficit (2)	Total (1)+(2)	Year	Projections		
1981	0.01	1.19	1.20	1992	0.54	4.04	4.58
1982	0.08	3.12	3.20	1995	0.71	3.84	4.55
1983	0.17	3.53	3.70	2000	0.95	3.18	4.13
1984	0.20	3.70	3.90	2005	1.11	2.28	3.39
1985	0.24	3.36	3.60	2010	0.94	1.47	2.41
1986	0.32	3.38	3.70	2015	0.54	0.99	1.53
1987	0.38	3.42	3.80	2020	0.17	0.00	0.17
1988	0.36	3.04	3.40	2025	0.02	0.00	0.02
1989	0.53	4.17	4.70	2030	0.00	0.00	0.00
1990	0.63	4.13	4.76				
1991	0.71	4.08	4.79				

Source: Ortúzar, 1988; Arenas, 1992; and Arrau, 1992.

Growth of Contributors and Coverage of the System

Table 4.18 shows the growth of affiliates and contributors to the new system in the 1981-92 period.

The number of affiliates has increased steadily since the inception of the new system. After the wholesale transfer that took place in the early months of the new system's existence, the number of affiliates kept growing until they represented nearly 86 percent of the work force in late 1991. However, if the coverage of the new system is measured in terms of affiliates who actually contribute, this figure drops to 52 percent of the work force.

The proportion of affiliates who contribute, which was approximately 75 percent in 1981, shrank to about 60 percent in late 1991, in part because of the way that changes in the employment status of workers are recorded. Unemployed workers and, in general, those who leave the work force voluntarily or who retire, continue as affiliates but not as contributors.

The Social Insurance Deficit

The social insurance reform had a considerable impact on the fiscal budget owing to the decision of the authorities to recognize the past contributions of active workers who transfer to the new system and to continue payments to current beneficiaries of the old system.

Table 4.19 summarizes the social insurance deficit and projects it through the year 2030. As shown in the table, in the 1981-90 period, the deficit grew approximately four times. The largest component of the social insurance deficit

Table 4.20. Trend of Pensions, 1981-91
(Thousands of December 1990 pesos)

Year	Public system	Private system
1981	15.8	n.a.
1982	15.6	30.9
1983	15.1	29.9
1984	15.4	25.9
1985	13.9	25.5
1986	13.8	26.9
1987	13.6	27.7
1988	14.3	30.5
1989	14.5	32.9
1990	14.1	33.2
1991	—	32.7

Source: Banco Central de Chile, 1991.

is the operating deficit, and its considerable impact reflects the amount of income lost by the old system as a result of the wholesale transfer of contributors to the new system. The table also reveals the growing importance of disbursements to pay for acknowledgment bonds. From a value of less than 1 percent of the overall deficit in 1981, acknowledgment bonds accounted for roughly 15 percent in late 1991. Projection of the fiscal deficit indicates that it will continue growing until the year 2000 and will then stabilize at about 1 percent of gross domestic product (GDP).

Pensions

Table 4.20 summarizes the growth of the average amount spent on pensions in the public and private systems. The amount paid by the AFPs increased 7 percent in the 1981-90 period. This growth contrasts with the decline in the value of pensions paid by the public system, which was roughly 8 percent.

Tables 4.21 and 4.22 show the results of projecting the pensions of the current system in alternative scenarios (with and without fixed commissions) and for various categories of contributors. The results lead to the following conclusions. First, regardless of the initial income level, upon retirement individuals experience a significant drop in the level of their income. The reduction in disposable income can in some cases amount to more than 50 percent. Second, the results indicate that the redistributive impact of the fixed commissions is appreciable. Pensions as a percentage of income correlate positively with the level of taxable income. Finally, the tables show that the drop in income during retirement is proportionately larger as the level of education decreases.

Table 4.21. Pension Projections (without Fixed Commission), 1981-91
(1990 Pesos)

Real return = 4.5 percent per annum

| | Educational level | | |
	Higher university	Higher nonuniversity	Secondary education
Taxable income:			
Starting	245,513	111,708	44,580
At retirement (1)	789,984	298,331	221,431
Disposable income:			
Starting	213,596	97,186	39,020
At retirement (2)	687,286	259,548	192,645
Old-age pension (3)	344,983	153,606	115.582
(3)/(1)	43.7%	51.5%	52.2%
(3)/(2)	50.2%	59.2%	60.0%

Real return = 5.5% per annum

| | Educational level | | |
	Higher university	Higher non-university	Secondary education
Taxable income:			
Starting	245,513	111,708	44,850
At retirement (1)	1,164,871	448,529	346,096
Disposable income:			
Starting	213,596	97,186	39.02
At retirement (2)	1,013,438	390.22	301,104
Old-age pension (3)	557,549	253,023	197,910
(3)/(1)	47.9%	56.4%	57.2%
(3)/(2)	55.0%	64.8%	65.7%

Pension Funds

Table 4.23 summarizes the trend of the pension funds. The unprecedented growth of the pension funds administered by the AFPs is reflected in the increase in the value of the funds as a percentage of GDP—from 0.9 percent in 1981 to 34.5 percent in 1991—and is the result of the interaction of a number of factors. First, in this period, the AFPs paid a small number of pensions, owing to the relatively low average age of their affiliates. Second, the growth of the funds reflects the high return on investments in the stock market. Finally, the growth of the funds starting in 1989 reflects a significant increase in taxable wages as a result of the greater dynamism of the economy.

Table 4.22. Pension Projections (with Fixed Commission of 550 Pesos), 1981-91
(1990 Pesos)

Real return = 4.5% per annum

	Educational level		
	Higher university	Higher nonuniversity	Secondary education
Taxable income:			
Starting	245,513	111,708	44,850
At retirement (1)	789,984	298,331	221,431
Disposable income:			
Starting	214,824	97,744	39,244
At retirement (2)	691,236	261,039	193,752
Old-age pension (3)	341,097	149,292	110,290
(3)/(1)	43.2%	50.0%	49.8%
(3)/(2)	49.3%	57.2%	56.9%

Real return = 5.5% per annum

	Educational level		
	Higher university	Higher non-university	Secondary education
Taxable income:			
Starting	245,513	111,708	44,850
At retirement (1)	1,164,871	448,529	346,096
Disposable income:			
Starting	214,824	97,744	39,244
At retirement (2)	1,019,262	392,463	302,834
Old-age pension (3)	552,050	246,824	190,066
(3)/(1)	47.4%	55.0%	54.9%
(3)/(2)	54.2%	62.9%	62.8%

Figure 4.1 shows the real annual yield of the pension funds. The high yield of the system, which for the 1981-91 period averaged 14.4 percent per annum, does not necessarily reflect a trend that can be easily projected and, of course, is not representative of equilibrium values in normal conditions. In particular, the high yield of shareholding investments reflected the adjustment process of an incipient market that may not be easily reproducible over time.

The amount accrued in the pension fund is significant and exerts considerable pressure on the price of currently available assets. Therefore, new types of investment are needed for the pension funds in order to alleviate the pressure on the assets in the AFPs' current portfolio, reduce the risk of retirement savings and improve the long-term yield of these resources.

Table 4.23. Pension Fund, 1981-91

Year	Billions of pesos	
1981	11,695	
1982	44,495	
1983	99,474	ν. .
1984	159,576	8.4
1985	281,807	10.9
1986	433,377	13.4
1987	644,728	15.5
1988	885,875	16.4
1989	1,329,268	19.6
1990	2,244,481	26.5
1991	3,769,243	34.5

Source: Statistical Bulletin SAFP.

Tables 4.24 and 4.25 (See Appendix I for further information) show the results of projecting the growth of the pension funds in the four scenarios, in terms of the rate of return of the funds and the speed of convergence of the growth rate of affiliates with its long-term value. The alternatives considered are summarized below:

Alternative	Rate of Return	Speed of Adjustment
1	4.5	40
2	4.5	50
3	5.5	40
4	5.5	50

The long-term projections of the pension fund suggest that regardless of the scenario considered, the fund will continue growing at relatively high rates but with a downward trend. On the other hand, the projection of the model indicates that the pension funds will by the year 2000 represent nearly 50 percent of GDP and that this percentage will continue growing until the year 2010.

Summary and Conclusions

The Social Welfare Programs

The growth of the social welfare programs and their distribution among households following the reform of the social security system are in large measure a reflection of the changes in the institutional framework mandated by social policy

~ure 4.1. Real Annual Return of Pension Fund, 1981-91
(Deflated by the consumer price index)

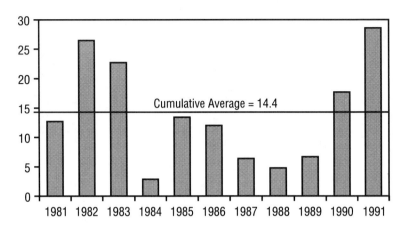

Cumulative Average = 14.4

Source: Statistical Bulletin SAFP.

in the latter half of the 1970s. These reforms included a redefinition of the state's role in social policy. The government's traditional monopoly in social services was replaced by a system that emphasizes the need to supplement the efforts of the state with more active participation on the part of private enterprises. In the current system, the state's action is focused on the poorest segments of the population.

Redefining the state's role in social security made possible a significant tightening of the focus of social welfare programs. However, the downside of this reorientation was a cutback in the resources allocated to social welfare programs. Chile's experience with social security reform suggests that the attempt to transfer a full range of social activities to the private sector can cause a significant decrease in aggregate social spending. Therefore, evaluating the distribution of social welfare programs requires examination of their level and degree of focus.

The Health Insurance System

Despite the gains in most of the indicators traditionally used to measure the health status of the population, there are still some serious deficiencies in health care that affect both the public and the private systems. The problems of the public health system derive from a long-standing financial constraint imposed by the reform of the social security system as well as poor organization and management. The problems of the private health care system, on the other hand, have to do essentially with its lack of transparency, the tendency to over-use health care

Table 4.24. Pension Fund Projections, 1991-2030
(Growth rate)

Year	Alternatives			
	1	2	3	4
1991	—	—	—	—
1992	12.33	12.33	12.33	12.33
1993	14.14	14.11	14.14	14.11
1994	12.60	12.56	12.60	12.56
1995	10.55	10.49	11.64	11.58
1996	10.14	10.07	11.23	11.16
1997	9.75	9.67	10.82	10.74
1998	9.36	9.27	10.43	10.35
1999	8.99	8.90	10.06	9.97
2000	8.64	8.55	9.70	9.61
2001	8.31	8.21	9.37	9.27
2002	7.99	7.89	9.05	8.95
2003	7.69	7.59	8.74	8.64
2004	7.33	7.23	8.38	8.28
2005	7.00	6.90	8.04	7.94
2006	6.69	6.59	7.73	7.62
2007	6.40	6.30	7.44	7.33
2008	6.13	6.03	7.17	7.06
2009	5.88	5.77	6.91	6.80
2010	5.65	5.54	6.68	6.57
2011	5.43	5.32	6.46	6.35
2012	5.80	5.69	6.85	6.74
2013	5.61	5.50	6.65	6.54
2014	5.36	5.26	6.39	6.28
2015	5.20	5.10	6.22	6.12
2016	5.05	4.95	6.07	5.97
2017	4.13	4.02	5.13	5.01
2018	4.84	4.75	5.87	5.77
2019	4.72	4.63	5.74	5.65
2020	4.61	4.52	5.63	5.54
2021	4.52	4.43	5.53	5.45
2022	4.43	4.35	5.45	5.37
2023	4.37	4.29	5.38	5.30
2024	4.23	4.16	5.23	5.17
2025	4.11	4.05	5.11	5.05
2026	4.00	3.95	5.00	4.94
2027	3.91	3.86	4.90	4.85
2028	3.82	3.78	4.82	4.78
2029	3.75	3.72	4.75	4.71
2030	3.69	3.66	4.69	4.66

Source: Author's calculations.

services, inefficiencies in budgeting resources and a structure of incentives that tends automatically to exclude specific population groups. Another problem affecting the health care system as a whole is equity in the distribution of benefits.

Table 4.25. Pension Fund Projections, 1991-2030
(Percentage of GDP)

Year	\multicolumn{4}{c}{Alternatives}
	1	2	3	4
1991	34.36	34.46	35.46	34.46
1992	35.28	35.28	35.28	35.28
1993	37.63	37.63	37.63	37.63
1994	39.79	39.77	39.79	39.77
1995	41.50	41.45	41.91	41.86
1996	43.12	43.05	43.98	43.90
1997	44.65	44.54	45.98	45.86
1998	46.06	45.91	47.90	47.74
1999	47.36	47.17	49.73	49.53
2000	48.54	48.30	51.47	51.22
2001	49.60	49.31	53.11	52.80
2002	50.53	50.19	54.63	54.27
2003	51.33	50.95	56.04	55.62
2004	51.98	51.54	57.30	56.81
2005	52.47	51.97	58.40	57.85
2006	52.81	52.26	59.35	58.74
2007	53.01	52.41	60.16	59.48
2008	53.08	52.42	60.82	60.07
2009	53.02	52.31	61.35	60.53
2010	52.84	52.08	61.74	60.85
2011	52.56	51.75	62.01	61.05
2012	52.46	51.60	62.50	61.48
2013	52.26	51.36	62.88	61.79
2014	51.95	51.00	63.12	61.96
2015	51.55	50.56	63.25	62.03
2016	51.09	50.06	63.29	62.01
2017	50.19	49.12	62.77	61.43
2018	49.64	48.54	62.69	61.30
2019	49.04	47.91	62.54	61.09
2020	48.40	47.25	62.32	60.83
2021	47.72	46.55	62.04	60.51
2022	47.02	45.82	61.72	60.15
2023	46.29	45.09	61.36	59.76
2024	45.52	44.31	60.91	59.28
2025	44.71	43.49	60.40	58.75
2026	43.86	42.65	59.83	58.17
2027	43.00	41.79	59.21	57.54
2028	41.11	40.91	58.55	56.87
2029	41.22	40.03	57.86	56.18
2030	40.32	39.15	57.14	55.47

Source: Author's calculations.

Public Health System

Substantial deterioration of the infrastructure, insufficient funds for operating expenses and an incentive structure that does little to promote efficient management are the main problems confronting the public health system. The biggest challenge facing the public health care system is developing a model for flexible, decentralized management that will enable it to adapt to the new needs that have arisen as a result of the change in the epidemiological profile of the population and the emergence of a highly competitive private system.

The current administration of FONASA (*Fondo Nacional de Salud*; National Health Fund) prevents it from offering flexible health plans, thus eliminating the possibility of providing benefits commensurate with the contributions of its affiliates. As a result, large numbers of individuals who can afford the plans offered by the ISAPRE have transferred to the private system. The lack of health plan flexibility has also resulted in cross subsidies from the middle- and low-middle-income groups to the low-income groups. Individuals who remain in the public health system and who have incomes higher than the average for this sector are forced to finance the poorest groups. The possibility of avoiding this "tax" is directly related to the individual's income level. The high income groups generally join the private system and thus escape this obligation.

Private Health System

The growth of the private health system has greatly increased the options available to contributors and has fostered competition in health insurance. However, the benefits and costs of privatizing the health system have not been equitably distributed. In addition, several problems related to the functioning of a private insurance system remain.

First, the privatization of a large segment of the health system helped to accentuate the regressiveness of the health system as a whole. The mass exodus of high-income contributors to the private system substantially reduced the funds available to the public system for redistributing benefits to the lowest-income groups. It is unclear, however, whether income redistribution is the most efficient alternative. Probably the message inherent in the experience of privatizing the Chilean health system is that this process requires additional government spending to compensate the low-income groups, which are the ones most affected by these reforms.

A second problem associated with private health systems is the discrimination practiced by the ISAPRE against older people and those with chronic illnesses. In both cases, the problem is largely a result of the transition from a public to a private system. When the contributors were in the public system they received an adequate level of health care at a reasonable cost. Later, with the growth of the private system, the situation of the beneficiaries of the public system deteriorated, prompting the change of system for those who could afford it. However, the ISAPRE rejected the elderly and the chronically ill because of the high cost of their health care. Once again, the problem is a result of the lack of specific mechanisms for financing the health care of these groups. The problem does not originate in the existence of private health systems, but rather in the difficulty of designing explicit transfer mechanisms for specific population groups.

Moreover, the experience of more than a decade of operating the new system suggests the existence of information and transparency problems within the private health system. The variety of health plans and the uneven distribution of information among users and health organizations can affect the choice of health plans as well as create induced demand and the over-use of health services.

The Pension System

After more than a decade, some interesting lessons can be drawn from the experience of the private pension systems and the problems caused by the transition from a pay-as-you-go system to an individual capitalization system.

The reform of the social insurance system helped streamline the pension system and standardize the requirements for obtaining and determining the amounts of benefits. The new system also freed the state from a series of responsibilities associated with providing services, thus enabling it to tighten the focus of social welfare programs. The AFPs have contributed to financial deepening of the new system. The growth of the pension funds has created a huge demand for investment instruments, which is one of the major explanations for the spectacular growth of the financial market in general and the stock market in particular.

From another perspective, examining the Chilean experience suggests that one of the basic determinants of the transition following the reform is the size of the acknowledgment bond and the methods used to finance it. The value of the acknowledgment bond determines the size of the social insurance deficit that the state must finance and, consequently, the constraint on fiscal policy. The impact of the reform on savings and investment depends essentially on the financing methods used. In most cases, a neutral financing policy will cause an increase in public debt. However, this public debt issue does not necessarily reduce private investment since it only reflects a shift from a contingent debt that is not recorded to one that is.

Despite the improvements in the organization and operation of the Chilean social insurance system, experience suggests that running a private system requires an additional regulatory effort on the part of the state to guarantee the transparency of the system, improve the yield of the pension funds and extend the benefits of the system to self-employed workers. Therefore, the three greatest challenges confronting the new pension system are expanding the coverage, increasing the transparency of the system and augmenting the investment opportunities of the pension funds.

System Coverage

One of the biggest challenges facing the current system is expanding its effective coverage. A distinction must be made, however, between the individual coverage associated with the variety of benefits provided by the system and the general coverage associated with the percentage of the work force included in the system.

In practice, neither of these two types of coverage is independent of the other, and it is likely that the expansion of one sometimes reduces the other. In Chile, the expanding coverage is greatly hampered by the structure of the social services provided by the system. Currently, the benefits are combined in packages that low-income workers can scarcely afford. One way of expanding the coverage would be to allow workers to determine the size of the package based on their preferences and their financial capabilities. Naturally, this can cause negative selection problems that must be considered and evaluated. Group affiliation is an efficient way of reconciling the expansion of coverage with the reduction of risks associated with the problem of negative selection.

System Transparency

Chile's experience indicates that the transparency of the system may be affected if there are no regulations guaranteeing the delivery of information to affiliates in a proper and timely manner. Failure to provide objective indicators of fund profitability and arbitrary delivery of information about past performance have helped erode the transparency and competitiveness of the system. This can create distorted incentives that will affect the long-term profitability of the pension funds.

Regulation of AFP Investments

The spectacular growth of pension funds in recent years requires a sufficiently flexible regulatory framework that recognizes the huge demand for existing investment instruments and promotes efficiency in the process of fund management.

The growth of resources available for investment has substantially exceeded the growth of authorized financial assets, causing an increase in the price of these assets and a corresponding reduction in the yield of the funds. Maintaining adequate long-term yields requires that financial innovation and diversification be encouraged. Consequently, the laws must be amended to avoid investment portfolio concentration, which is already beginning to surface.

Bibliography

Arellano, J.P. 1989. *La seguridad social en Chile en los años 90*. Working Document No. 27. Santiago: CIEPLAN.

_____. 1990. *El desafío de la seguridad social: el caso chileno*. Working Document No. 340. Santiago: PREALC.

Arrau, P. 1991. La reforma previsional chilena y su financiamiento durante la transición. *Colección de Estudios CIEPLAN (No. 32)*.

Banco Central de Chile. 1989. *Indicadores económicos y sociales 1960-88*. Santiago: Banco Central de Chile.

_____. 1991. *Indicadores económicos y sociales regionales 1980-89*. Santiago: Banco Central de Chile.

_____. 1989-91. *Boletín mensual del Banco Central de Chile*. Santiago: Banco Central de Chile.

Beyer, H., and J. Bordalí. 1989. *Fortalecimiento del sector privado: una alternativa para la salud*. Working Document No. 34. Santiago: Centro de Estudios Públicos.

Castañeda, T. 1990. *Para combatir la pobreza: política social y descentralización en Chile durante los ochenta*. Santiago: Centro de Estudios Públicos.

Comisión Económica para América Latina y el Caribe. 1990. Una estimación de la magnitud de la pobreza en Chile, 1987. Santiago, Chile. Mimeo.

Cheyre, H. 1988. *La previsión en Chile ayer y hoy: impacto de una reforma*. Santiago: Centro de Estudios Públicos.

Haindl, E., E. Budinigh, and I. Irarrázaval. 1989. *Gasto social efectivo: un instrumento que asegura la superación definitiva de la pobreza crítica*. Santiago: ODEPLAN-University of Chile.

Iglesias, A., and R. Acuña. 1991. *Chile: Experiencia con un régimen de capitalización 1981-91*. Santiago: Comisión Económica para América Latina y el Caribe.

Mesa-Lago, C. 1990. *La seguridad social y el sector informal.* Investigative Series about Employment. Santiago: PREALC.

Ministerio de Planificación (MIDEPLAN). 1992. *Población, educación, vivienda, salud, empleo y pobreza, CASEN 1990.* Santiago: MIDEPLAN.

ODEPLAN. 1989-91. *Informe social.* Santiago: ODEPLAN.

APPENDIX I

Calculating Old-Age Pensions

Old-age pensions are calculated in three stages:
- determining the longitudinal income profile;
- determining the individual's accumulated fund; and,
- determination of individual pensions, according to the regulations in force.

The Income Profile

The income profile is calculated using the results of the socioeconomic characterization survey (CASEN) conducted by MIDEPLAN in 1990.

The model developed is consistent with the human capital theory and assumes that incomes increase during the worker's life as a consequence of experience and the investment that individuals make in education. The following equation was developed:

$$W = \alpha_0 + \alpha_1 \cdot S + \alpha_2 \cdot S(2) + \alpha_3 \cdot E + \alpha_4 \cdot Z1 + \alpha_5 \cdot Z2 + \alpha_6 \cdot \alpha 1 + \alpha_7 \cdot \alpha 2 + \alpha_8 \cdot \alpha 3 + \alpha_9 \cdot \alpha 4 + \alpha_{10} \cdot (\alpha 1 \cdot S) + \alpha_{11} \cdot (\alpha 2 \cdot S) + \alpha_{12} \cdot (\alpha 3 \cdot S) + \alpha_{13} \cdot (\alpha 4 \cdot S) + \alpha_{14} \cdot (\alpha 1 \cdot S2) + \alpha_{15} \cdot (\alpha 2 \cdot S2) + \alpha_{16} \cdot (\alpha 3 \cdot S2) + \alpha_{17} \cdot (\alpha 4 \cdot S2)$$

where the variables are defined in the following terms:

W = natural logarithm of income
S = experience = age - education - 6.
$S(2)$ = experience squared.
E = years of formal education completed

In addition, the following fictitious variables were used:

$Z1$ = 1 if married,
0 if not married
$Z2$ = 1 if urban,
0 if rural
$D1$ = 1 if university graduate,
0 if not
$D2$ = 1 if subject has higher nonuniversity education,
0 if not
$D3$ = 1 if subject has vocational education or has completed vocational secondary education,
0 if not
$D4$ = 1 if subject has a high school diploma,
0 if not

Table 4.A1. Wage Equation Results

Variables	Men		Women	
	Parameters	T Test	Parameters	T Test
Interception	9.4242	305.12	9.3556	184.72
Experience	0.0266	13.32	0.0187	5.61
Experience	-0.0002	-8.28	-0.0002	-3.23
Education	0.0868	41.72	0.0872	29.24
Civil status	0.1781	13.73	0.0765	4.42
Zone	0.1338	10.42	0.0640	2.84
D1	1.1114	7.29	0.7452	2.67
D2	0.4977	4.03	0.1786	1.89
D3	-0.0153	-0.23	-0.0911	-1.32
D4	-0.0673	1.71	-0.1204	-1.30
D1*Experience	0.0030	-0.17	0.0330	0.83
D2*Experience	-0.0151	-1.05	-0.0079	-0.69
D3*Experience	0.0209	2.42	0.0231	2.17
D4*Experience	0.0166	3.57	0.0095	1.43
D1*Experience 2	0.0000	-0.39	-0.0007	0.57
D2*Experience 2	-0.0001	-0.04	0.0003	0.99
D3*Experience 2	-0.0004	-2.11	-0.0005	-1.88
D4*Experience 2	-0.0004	-3.71	-0.0001	-0.65

Source: Author's calculations based on data from INE and the Superintendency of AFPs.

Table 4A.1 shows the results of the income equation. The income equation enables us to estimate the wage profile of a representative individual with different levels of education. Since these initial results come from a cross sectional sampling from the 1990 CASEN survey (MIDEPLAN, 1992), an adjustment was made assuming a uniform annual increase in productivity over time and among various categories of individuals.

To define the various categories it was assumed that individuals with a university education begin to work at 24 years of age; individuals with a non-university higher education at 22 years of age and individuals with a high school education at 18 years of age.

Calculating the Individual Pension Fund

The formula for calculating the value of the fund accumulated by an individual at the time of retirement is:

$$D \cdot \frac{\frac{T}{\delta}}{t=1} \left[(T \cdot \underline{l}_t) - C \right]^{T-t}$$

where: T   =   Compulsory contribution rate
           D   =   Occupational density
           I_t =   Income in the period t
           r   =   Monthly rate of return
           c   =   Fixed commission
           T   =   Number of months of active working life

The fund accumulated depends on the rate of return, the compulsory contribution rate and the fixed commission, as well as the frequency of the contributions (occupational density).

The assumptions used to simplify determination of the amount are that the rate of return of the funds is constant with time, the compulsory percentage contribution and the fixed commission do not vary, and all individuals have the same occupational density.

Calculation of the Individual Pension

The rules governing calculation of old-age pensions in the new social insurance system are based on a life expectancy for beneficiaries, which, given a reference rate of return, permits the calculation of what is known as the required unit capital (CNU, *capital necesario unitario*), which is the amount needed to finance one peso of annual pension. Using the CNUs for each case, the amount of the fund accumulated at retirement determines the amount of the old-age pension.

The preferential rate of return for the CNUs will always be the same as the one used to determine the fund.

APPENDIX II

Disability and Survivor's Pensions

Despite the fact that the Chilean social insurance system is based on an individual capitalization arrangement in which pensions are determined essentially by the affiliate's own contributions, there are several exceptions. In particular, the disability and survivor's pensions granted by the system are a reflection not only of the affiliate's contributions, but also of the probability of various groups becoming subject to the conditions of need financed by such pensions.

Methodology

To illustrate the differences in the distribution of benefits, the distribution over time of the contributions and receipts associated with disability and survivor's pensions among various population groups were simulated.

The data required for the simulation were the mortality and invalidity rates for each age group, which were obtained from the National Institute of Statistics (INE, *Instituto Nacional de Estadística*)—1990 mortality—and the Superintendency of AFPs (June 1991-June 1992 invalidity).

The CNU for disability and survivor's pensions was calculated according to the existing rules, using reference rates of return consistent with the rest of the exercise.

The income profile was determined on the basis of data from the Superintendency of AFPs, using the following equation:

$$I = \alpha_0 + \alpha_1 \cdot Age + \alpha_2 \cdot Age \qquad (1)$$

Where:
I   = average taxable income
Age(2) = age squared.

The results are shown in Table 4A.2.

The results of the regression are for a cross-sectional sampling and, therefore, to the profile projected with them we apply a 2.5 percent annual growth rate for productivity.

An individual's income profile determines the contributions he or she will make to the system and the reference pensions for the potential beneficiaries of the insurance. To determine the amount accumulated in the account, it is assumed that the contributions begin at 18 years of age.

At each point, and assuming that none of the events has occurred previously,

Table 4.A2. Wage Equation Results

Variables	Men	Women	General
Interception	-172,544.96	-57,528.52	-104,173.41
Age	14,715,64	6,838.21	10,045.21
Age(2)	155.56	-72.46	-104.98

Source: Author's calculations based on data from INE and the Superintendency of AFPs.

Table 4.A3. Distribution of Disability and Survivor Insurance Benefits
(Benefits/contribution reason)

Real annual return = 4.5%

Age	Men		Women	
	(a)	(b)	(c)	(d)
15-20	0.00	0.00	0.00	0.00
21-25	0.03	0.03	0.02	0.03
26-30	0.08	0.47	0.05	0.06
31-35	0.14	0.72	0.12	0.12
36-40	0.25	0.92	0.20	0.21
41-45	0.41	1.20	0.34	0.34
46-50	0.57	1.17	0.43	0.43
52-55	0.54	1.14	0.39	0.39
56-60	0.00	0.78	0.00	0.00
61-65	0.00	0.00	—	—

Real annual return = 5.6%

Age				
15-20	0.00	0.00	0.00	0.00
21-25	0.03	0.03	0.01	0.02
26-30	0.07	0.38	0.05	0.05
31-35	0.12	0.57	0.10	0.10
36-40	0.21	0.70	0.16	0.17
41-45	0.31	0.78	0.25	0.25
46-50	0.35	0.60	0.25	0.25
52-55	0.09	0.52	0.08	0.08
56-60	0.00	0.00	0.00	0.00
61-65	0.00	0.00	—	—

Source: Author's calcualtions based on date from INE and the Superintendency of AFPs.
Notes: (a) man with no beneficiaries.
(b) man with wife and two children. Marries at 25 to a 20 year-old woman, has a boy at 27 and a girl at 31.
(c) woman with no beneficiaries.
(d) woman with two children, has a boy at 22 and a girl at 26.

the benefit associated with disability and survivor's insurance is equal to the difference between the total capital needed to finance the reference pensions and the amount accumulated in the account, weighted by the probability of falling into the various conditions of need.

Table 4.A4. Distribution of Disability and Survivor Benefits
(Percentage of taxable income)

Real annual return = 4.5%

	Men		Women	
Age	(a)	(b)	(c)	(d)
15-20	0.00	0.00	0.00	0.00
21-25	0.05	0.05	0.02	0.04
26-30	0.12	0.71	0.08	0.09
31-35	0.20	1.07	0.17	0.18
36-40	0.38	1.37	0.30	0.31
41-45	0.61	1.80	0.50	0.51
46-50	0.84	1.73	0.64	0.64
52-55	0.79	1.68	0.58	0.58
56-60	0.00	1.15	0.00	0.00
61-65	0.00	0.00	—	—

Real annual return = 5.6%

15-20	0.00	0.00	0.00	0.00
21-25	0.04	0.04	0.02	0.04
26-30	0.10	0.57	0.07	0.07
31-35	0.17	0.86	0.15	0.15
36-40	0.31	1.04	0.24	0.25
41-45	0.47	1.17	0.37	0.38
46-50	0.52	0.90	0.37	0.37
52-55	0.14	0.77	0.12	0.12
56-60	0.00	0.00	0.00	0.00
61-65	0.00	0.00	—	—

Source: Author's calcualtions based on date from INE and the Superintendency of AFPs.
Notes: (a) man with no beneficiaries.
(b) man with wife and two children. Marries at 25 to a 20 year-old woman, has a boy at 27 and a girl at 31.
(c) woman with no beneficiaries.
(d) woman with two children, has a boy at 22 and a girl at 26.

Results

The differences in the distribution of disability and survivor's pension benefits among various population groups are indicated in Tables 4A.3 and 4A.4. Except in a few cases, the expected benefit for each age group is less than the contributions. At the far ends of the distribution by age, the expected benefits are practically zero. As far as the young are concerned, this is explained by the scant risk of falling into any condition of need due to disability or death; in the case of the elderly, it is because the funds accumulated by these groups are sufficient to finance a disability or survivor's pension. In this case, the subsidy is redundant. Finally, as the simulations reveal, because the contributions are nondiscriminatory in terms of family size, single individuals who receive smaller benefits implicitly subsidize contributors with family obligations.

CHAPTER FIVE

The Social Insurance
Crisis in Venezuela

Gustavo Márquez and Clementina Acedo

In Venezuela, the social insurance system evolved in two clearly discernible stages. In 1940, the government and various political groups, among whom there was consensus about the need to establish a health care system to benefit workers and their families, took the initiative to develop a system.

In this initial stage, the sole focus of social insurance was medical care (*i.e.,* short-term insurance). The system contributed to the gradual development of an array of social welfare services in Venezuela. In the late forties and during the fifties, businesses and labor unions exerted no additional pressure to expand the insurance to include long-term risks (old age and disability) or to provide coverage outside the country's major industrial centers. This long phase coincided with the period of dictatorial government, during which no advances were made in the field of labor representation.

After the changeover to a democratic government in 1958 and the approval of the Constitution of 1961, the administration outlined the goal of a social security system with broader risk, population and geographic coverage. Pressure to provide coverage for long-term contingencies and for all workers began to mount, culminating in 1967 with the expansion of coverage to include old age and disability. In this new stage, which continued through the seventies and eighties, neither businesses nor unions exerted any significant pressure to improve the system or to modernize its organization and financing.

The acceleration of inflation in the early eighties did little to facilitate adjustment of the contribution limit or a shift to more profitable investments. Facing an explosive social situation and a serious economic slump, the government established unemployment insurance in 1989 under pressure from the unions.

As a result of the serious financial crisis afflicting the Venezuelan Social Insurance Institute (IVSS, *Instituto Venezolano de los Seguros Sociales*) in 1990, reorganization of the system was widely debated. Numerous subjects were discussed: raising the contribution limit, increasing the amount of pensions to the minimum wage, reestablishing the pension fund by paying off government debt, dismissing 35,000 idle workers, making some changes in the organization, separating the funds, selling the assets of the insurance system, abandoning the pay-as-you-go system, and switching to a capitalization arrangement.

The second half of this chapter examines some of these proposals, particularly those concerning changes in the contribution limit and adjusting the old-age pensions, using a model that simulates the trend of IVSS financial statements to the year 2030. The conclusions are not very encouraging because the severity of the social insurance crisis and the volume of resources needed make superficial changes in a few financing and benefits regulations irrelevant. Solving the problems of both the social insurance system and the IVSS will require profound changes that alter the system's underlying financial dynamics.

The first section of this chapter describes the history of the social insurance system. This backdrop provides the framework for analyzing the administrative and management problems currently facing the IVSS, the governing agency of the country's social security system. The IVSS has three parts, with representation for the parties involved and substantial state participation. This governing structure has determined the methods of administration, management and financial control of the IVSS in many cases, and it is a crucial element in explaining the current crisis in the system.

The second section develops a projection model to simulate the trend of IVSS financial statements between 1993 and the year 2030. The model uses a system of components with simplifying hypotheses and assumptions to focus attention on the impact of future demographic growth and on four policy solutions related to contributions and old-age pensions. The pension fund's loss of capital investment, the lack of control over costs, and the rationing systems used in providing medical services have brought on the crisis the social insurance system faces.

The third section presents a number of conclusions and policy recommendations. First, to ensure its financial stability, the pension system should be separated from the health care system and made one of the components of a competitive pension system. Second, to establish rational procedures to control both costs and access to the system, the role of insurer of medical contingencies should be separated from that of provider of medical care. Finally, system management should be decentralized.

Origin and Development of Social Insurance in Venezuela

The Compulsory Social Insurance Law was promulgated in Venezuela in 1940 and entered into force in 1944 during the Medina Angarita administration. However, its roots reach back to 1937, when the studies and the drafting of the bill began. Tito Gutiérrez Alfaro, then the director of the National Labor Office, presided over the committee in charge of formulating the proposal, aided by the International Labor Organization (ILO). Gutiérrez Alfaro maintained a steady correspondence with O. Stein, head of the social insurance section of the ILO in Geneva. Antonio Zelenka, another ILO consultant, conducted the necessary actuarial studies in Venezuela. This initial proposal greatly influenced the bill that was discussed in Congress and passed into law in 1940.

The first bill followed the general outline of the Labor Law of 1936, as revealed in the following articles:

- Article 127: "The federal executive, for the protection of employees and workers exposed to occupational risks, shall establish compulsory social insurance, to be paid for by employers through organizations or entities legally established in the country."
- Article 30: "The insurance shall also cover disability, maternity, old age and death not caused by work-related accidents and occupational diseases. In these cases, the insurance shall be financed with contributions from insured individuals, employers and state subsidies."

Clear from the start was the idea of full social insurance (covering short- and long-term contingencies), to be implemented in stages. The bill closely follows the guidelines set forth in the Labor Law of 1936 and those of the "Santiago Meeting" held by the American members of the ILO to establish a social insurance policy orientation.

Within this general orientation, a distinction must be made between "social security" and "social insurance" in terms of the type of contingencies provided for, the population coverage and the method of financing.

The purpose of social security is to establish a system to protect against adverse economic situations; its goal is universal coverage of the population against various risks. The system is financed through various sources such as taxes, direct contributions from the Treasury and payroll contributions. Social security encompasses the following:

- social insurance (old-age, disability and survivor's pensions), medical care and financial benefits for work-related accidents, medical care and benefits for illness and maternity, and unemployment benefits;
- family allowances;
- social welfare, consisting of direct transfers to the most vulnerable groups not eligible for social insurance benefits; and,
- public health care programs.

Social insurance, on the other hand, provides less risk and population coverage. Its purpose is to cover the contingencies that affect a worker's ability to remain in the labor market. Social insurance is financed through payroll-based contributions from insured individuals, employers and the state.

Most Latin American countries, although they aspire to social security, follow the social insurance model. Only pioneering countries such as Chile, Uruguay, Argentina, Cuba and Brazil have established social security systems or are close to achieving this goal. However, because of their excessive stratification, these systems have experienced financial and organizational problems (Mesa-Lago, 1989).

A second group of countries, including Colombia, Costa Rica, Mexico, Paraguay, Peru, and Venezuela, had a different experience. The social security systems in these countries appeared in the 1940s and 1950s. Seeking to avoid the problems created in the systems of the first group of countries, they were influenced by the new international trends in the ILO and the Beveridge Report. These countries chose social insurance, focusing on pension and maternity-illness programs.

This group of countries was generally characterized by scant industrial development and the predominance of the rural over the urban sector. A managing institution was created, restricted initially to the capital and the major cities and later extended to the entire country. These systems were based on minimal risk and population coverage. Venezuela is a clear example of this. Although more unified and limited, these systems also experienced serious financial and organizational difficulties (Mesa-Lago, 1989).

Decisions and Context

Since 1940, the main objective has been insurance covering both short- and long-term risks. Nevertheless, the risks, population, and geographic areas covered expanded gradually. The advisory group that proposed the law recommended this approach because it was consistent with the conditions in Venezuela at the time and with the necessity of developing the health care sector. This was a government initiative, taken in response to new ideas on social security, which prompted neither increased pressure from workers nor strong opposition in Congress (Acedo, 1982).

The Law of 1940

The 1940 law initially covered only short-term risks (*i.e.,* work-related accidents and maternity-illness), the idea being to protect the health and incomes of workers and their families, thereby improving the health of the population. The beneficiaries were workers with incomes below 800 bolívares per month who resided in the Federal District and in the Sucre District of the state of Miranda.

This decision was a response to pressing problems in Venezuela and was a way of combating social ills and the public health problems of that era. Administrative factors also played a role, such as limiting the geographic coverage of the system to urban areas with an established infrastructure and human resources with the necessary training.

Covering long-term risks (disability, old-age and survivor's benefits) was deferred since it would require a different administrative capability and longer contribution periods for benefits. The objectives were to instill the habit of contributing, to create the appropriate administrative conditions for expanding the territory and coverage of the system, and to collect the necessary statistical data.

At first, it was suggested that establishing insurance for long-term risks be deferred for four or five years. As it happened, however, the move to long-term insurance was proposed repeatedly until the promulgation of the new law in 1966, which entered into force in January 1967.

Theoretically, the insurance system has provided universal coverage since the beginning. In fact, the Law of 1940 extended coverage to "all who work for another, without regard to age, sex, nationality or income." However, given the criterion of gradual extension and the decision to cover short-term risks, it was proposed that geographic coverage be expanded in stages, starting in the country's more densely populated industrial centers. In 1944, the system covered workers residing in the Federal District and the Sucre District of the state of Miranda only. In 1945 the system was extended to the states of Aragua, Carabobo, and Zulia, which have the highest levels of income and relative development in the country and where a certain level of medical and welfare services was already being provided.

For funding, worker's compensation contributions were made only by the employer, in keeping with the universally recognized principle that such contributions are part of the company's overhead. These contributions were used not only for current expenses but also to establish a reserve fund for future obligations. Contributions to illness and maternity insurance were made by insured individuals and employers in equal amounts and consisted of 2.5 percent of the worker's wage. The government was responsible for the administrative expenses and for funding for the installation of sanitary facilities and equipment.

The Law of 1940 called for the creation of a central management organization to provide supervision and control of the various types of insurance, focusing on the administrative and financial aspects. Centralization was described as "vital" to the creation of a modern system, based on the law of large numbers and the attendant economic advantages.

Nevertheless, in this initial state there were limits to the creation of a totally centralized system, owing to the lack of transportation facilities to speed communication among the funds, insured individuals and employers. The proposed solution consisted of a less-centralized system through creation of a central agency with authority over the entire Republic, creation of a regional fund in each state that would be responsible for administering all of the insurance within its area, and limited financial autonomy for the illness-maternity section. Councils consisting of government, employer and worker representatives were to manage the first two organizations.

In all of these decisions the considerable influence of Stein's initial proposal and of the ILO recommendations is evident. Although social insurance was recognized as a universal social right, it was acknowledged that the country's unique situation, its lack of an organizational structure and enforcement capability, as well as its limited industrial development, prevented it from establishing a universal system at the beginning. Consequently, a more limited system was chosen, but one that could be expanded in stages.

New Decisions: 1946

A study conducted in 1946 during the government of the Revolutionary Junta revealed financial and administrative shortcomings in the social insurance system. Illness and maternity insurance operated with a monthly deficit of Bs 2 million (IVSS, 1946). Decree No. 89 of 1945 approved an additional credit of Bs 4 million to cover the deficit and to establish the state's contribution to illness and maternity insurance.

An amended law was recommended to centralize administration, the supposed remedy for the deficiencies observed. The response was Decree No. 239 of April 6, 1946, which placed all management responsibility (*i.e.,* "centralization, direct control and supervision") in the hands of a single organization, the IVSS (IVSS, 1946).

Expansion: The Law of 1966

Although from 1944 to 1945 the expansion of coverage to include all risks had already been provided for, it did not become a reality until 1966 with the promulgation of the new insurance law. It was through this law that social insurance acquired national significance for the first time.

In 1939 and in 1954 pension insurance bills were drafted that never reached Congress. In 1957, the Ministry of Labor entrusted its Office of Social Insurance with drafting a bill to expand coverage. In 1962, Dr. Rafael Alfonzo Guzmán, Director of Social Insurance at the Ministry of Labor, again drafted a bill and submitted it to the Ministry. For the purpose of updating it for presentation to Congress, Dr. Luis A. Mijares Ulloa and Dr. Víctor Masjuan Teruel were asked to prepare the studies and to draft the final version of the bill. The bill was discussed in Geneva with Dr. Antonio Zelenka, who was then the Chief of the Social Security Division of the ILO (IVSS, 1964). Finally, on June 22, 1966, the bill was approved by Congress as part of the new Social Insurance Law.

Expansion of coverage was delayed because it was not a high priority during the dictatorship of General Pérez Jiménez, nor could businesses and unions push for expansion. With the changeover to a democratic government, the subject of universal insurance coverage was again discussed in the context of worker's rights.

To evaluate the success of the policy of expanding social security, it is important to analyze how this system was established and through what type of organization.

Insurance as a social right was expanded in 1966 to cover all risks and to benefit the entire work force. The new law entered into force on January 1, 1967 and constituted a significant change in social insurance. The basic innovation was the expansion of coverage to include long-term risks through the granting of old-age, disability and survivor's pensions, establishing Bs 3,000 per month as the maximum wage for contributing to and receiving all of the benefits.

The insurance was expanded to include domestic workers and civil servants, who from this point on were subject to the partial system and collected only long-term pensions. Provisions were made but never carried out to include self-employed workers. As future benefits, their services could be extended for a period of not more than three years to regions of the country where this was necessary. Technical studies were prepared to expand insurance to include the risk of layoff or unemployment.

In 1966, the rights guaranteed by law were:
- comprehensive medical care;
- financial benefits for temporary disability; and,
- disability or partial disability, old-age, survivor's and wedding (one-time payment) benefits.

There are two systems: the partial and the general. The partial system consists of financial or long-term benefits, which are those included in the third category above, except wedding benefits. The general system grants all of the benefits (*i.e.,* medical care and financial benefits) covering short- and long-term risks.

Organization of the Social Insurance System

The user exercises his right to social insurance through a complex institution responsible for providing the services called for in the legislation. An analysis of organization that provides these services is therefore essential for identifying deficiencies in the system and the causes of user dissatisfaction.

The study of the organization of insurance shows that population coverage depends largely on the geographic distribution of the medical and administrative organizations that provide the services.[1] For each level of population coverage, the type of relationship between the user and the organization largely determines

---

[1] The years used were 1976, when the system of administrative units was consolidated, and 1988, the most recent year for which official data are available.

the existence and the possibility of solving conflicts between the insured and the organization.

The Organization

The IVSS is responsible for administering and controlling the various types of social insurance, as well as for providing the services. Attached to the Ministry of Labor, it is an autonomous organization with its own assets. Its headquarters are in Caracas and its jurisdiction covers the entire national territory (Art. 11 Reg).[2]

Financing

The IVSS is financed primarily with the contributions of employers and insured individuals. The current maximum contribution salary is Bs 15,000 per month, the amount to which it was raised in 1989. Contributions represent 70 percent of the system's income (Márquez, 1992), which is distributed among three legally independent funds:
- medical care;
- daily allowances; and,
- pensions and other financial benefits.

By law, these funds can be used only to pay the specific expenses of each individual fund. In the past, however, some of the pension fund was used to finance the deficit in medical care, as well as for investments in medical infrastructure projects and in public housing, the latter of which are vaguely provided for by the law (Art. 56 Law).

There is also an administrative fund financed with contributions from the executive branch, which is used to pay maintenance and administrative expenses. The law requires the state to contribute 1.5 percent of the contribution salaries. However, this item is approved late each year and in an amount lower (by almost 50 percent) than that specified by law. In 1980, the amount due was 584.8 million bolívares, but only 290 million bolívares were approved. In 1981, the law called for 670.5 million, the executive branch specified 525 million bolívares, and Congress approved 483 million.

IVSS investments are a third source of income for the system. To determine the total resources available for investment, the system's assets must be analyzed. In 1989, only 35 percent of the total assets was invested in financial instruments. The rest were invested in infrastructure (hospitals or administrative build-

---

[2] Law refers to the *Social Insurance Law* published in Official Gazette No. 1096 of April 6, 1964. Reg. refers to the *General Regulations of the Social Insurance Law* published in Official Gazette No. 4117 of August 16, 1989. In subsequent references these same notations will be used without further explanation.

ings) and other assets. A sizable percentage of the assets are in receivables resulting from contributor arrears, especially the government, and late payment of the contribution for administrative expenses (Márquez, 1992). As far as financial investments are concerned, the proper instruments have not been chosen, money having been invested for periods of many years at interest considerably below the market rate.

Administrative Structure

The IVSS is divided into medical units responsible for medical care and pharmacy services and into administrative units for all matters involving monetary benefits. For medical care, the system operates outpatient clinics, hospitals, treatment centers and labor medicine units. The administrative units comprise the regional funds, branch offices, auxiliary offices, agencies and subagencies.

Partial System: Administrative Units

Since the partial system is applicable throughout the national territory, there is an administrative unit in every state and two or three in the most industrialized states (Carabobo, Aragua, Miranda, the Federal District, Falcón, and Bolívar). As configured in 1976, this distribution reveals the slight growth of financial benefits throughout the country (see Table 5.1). In 1988 the situation had not changed much, the number of units having increased in only eight states.

This observation becomes more serious if we look closely at each type of unit and the work it does. All administrative and decision-making responsibilities are centralized in the presidency and the regional funds, the only units responsible for all of the system's functions (reception, classification, analysis, decision making and payment processing). The other units (agencies, subagencies, branch offices and auxiliary offices) merely receive and distribute the applications and documents sent to Caracas, except the branch offices, which can make payments (see Figure 5.1).

Located in Caracas, the presidency is the central administrative unit. The four regional funds are located in Caracas, Maracaibo, Puerto Ordaz and Valencia—all highly industrialized cities. In 1988, the number of administrative units in eight states doubled or tripled, although few of them actually performed all of the functions. In other words, the law was observed in the sense that there was at least one administrative unit in each state for the partial system or for long-term insurance (which is applicable throughout the country). However, these units did nothing more than receive applications and documents. The system is excessively centralized, and the main office is overburdened.

Even if the system were moderately efficient, it would still be difficult to process all of the data and respond to the requests of each state from the main

Table 5.1. Distribution by State of Medical Centers and IVSS Administrative Units, 1976 and 1988

States	1976				1988			
	Outpatient	Hospitals	Medical total	Administrative unit	Outpatient	Hospitals	Medical total	Administrative unit
Apure	—	—	—	1	1	—	1	1
Anzoátegui	1	3	4	1	2	2	4	3
Aragua	2	1	3	2	3	2	5	3
Barinas	—	—	—	1	—	—	—	1
Bolívar	4	2	6	3	2	2	4	3
Carabobo	4	2	6	2	11	2	13	2
Cojedes	—	—	—	1	2	—	2	1
Delta Amacuro	—	—	—	1	—	—	—	—
Distrito Federal	23	9	32	2	32	7	39	2
Falcón	1	3	4	2	3	2	5	3
Guárico	—	—	—	1	2	—	2	3
Lara	1	1	2	1	1	2	3	2
Mérida	—	—	—	1	—	—	—	1
Miranda	5	1	6	3	2	2	4	3
Monagas	—	—	—	1	—	—	—	1
Nueva Esparta	—	—	—	1	1	1	2	1
Portuguesa	—	—	—	1	—	1	1	2
Sucre	—	—	—	1	—	—	—	2
Táchira	2	1	3	1	3	1	4	1
Territorio Federal	—	—	—	1	—	—	—	—
Trujillo	2	1	3	1	2	2	4	2
Yaracuy	—	—	—	1	—	—	—	1
Zulia	7	1	8	1	7	1	8	2

Source: Méndez, 1976; IVSS, *Memoria y cuenta*, 1988; and IVSS, *Guía del asegurado*, n.d.
Note: For 1976, medical centers, outpatient clinics, and employee health centers were grouped under the Outpatient heading. The functions of these units are similar. For 1988, they are all considered outpatient units and only hospitals are shown separately.

Figure 5.1. Distribution of IVSS Administrative Units, 1976
(Number of units)

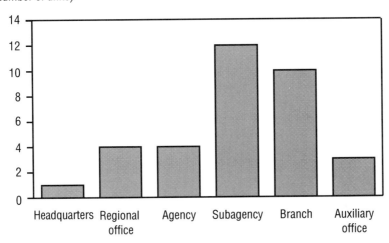

Source: Méndez, 1976; author's calculations.

office. Since the system operates slowly and is not sufficiently automated, the situation only gets worse, and the level of response is very low compared with the number of applications submitted. Users in the interior of the country must constantly travel to another city or to Caracas to process their claims. Even for users in Caracas, the situation is not ideal, given the congestion at headquarters.

General System: Administrative and Medical Units

The general system encompasses all the various types of short- and long-term insurance. There are many more medical units than administrative. In 1976, there were 77 medical units and 30 administrative units; in 1988, there were 120 medical units (including outpatient clinics and hospitals) and 40 administrative units. This is partly because medical care is more urgent and in greater demand among the disadvantaged segments of the population. It is also partly due to the fact that the medical units were established before the administrative units, which were created only in 1967. However, the medical units are not evenly divided among the states as are the administrative units since the general system covers only those areas where there is a medical infrastructure.

In 1976, there were 25 social insurance hospitals (32 percent of the medical units) and 52 outpatient clinics in Venezuela. In 1988, the number of hospitals had risen to 31, and the number of outpatient clinics, to 76.

Only hospitals provide full—or at least the most complete—medical services, including treatment for emergency cases and serious accidents. Hospitals provide outpatient consultations in general medicine and other specialties, hospitalization, surgery, emergencies and special services. In 1976, 36 percent of these hospitals were located in the Federal District, 12 percent were in Anzoátegui and an additional 12 percent were in Falcón (both of the latter are oil-producing states). In 1988, this concentration had decreased somewhat in the Federal District, increased in Falcón and Bolivar, and decreased in Anzoátegui. Hospitals are concentrated in the center of the country, but in regions such as Los Llanos there were no hospitals at all in 1976 and only one had been built by 1988.

Outpatient clinics provide consultations and care for serious cases and represent 58 percent of the medical units. Their functions include some types of outpatient consultations and certain auxiliary services such as pharmacy, infirmary and laboratory services. In 1976 there was a total of 45 outpatient clinics in 11 states; 38 percent of these were located in the Federal District. In 1988, there were 76 outpatient clinics in 15 states. The concentration increased in the Federal District (where the number of clinics rose from 23 to 32) while the number of hospitals decreased to two. New outpatient clinics were opened in Guárico, Apure (plains region), and Anzoátegui.

Structural and Operational Problems

Venezuela's medical and administrative services are excessively concentrated in the major urban-industrial centers (particularly in Caracas). This is understandable, given the demographic density and the growth of the labor market in these areas, but it forces people from the interior to travel to the capital in search of a broader range of medical services or to solve their administrative problems, which only makes things worse for the already overburdened central units.

The excessive centralization of services is more serious for collecting financial benefits than for obtaining medical care. In cities in the interior there are hospitals and outpatient clinics that provide medical services. But financial benefits are administered in the Caracas office and the office of the regional fund, which are much larger due to the centralization of administrative functions and decision-making powers. As a result, the system operates at low productivity, and users are inconvenienced when processing or applying for their pensions.

There is a shortage of medical units in certain areas of the interior, but in others more time is devoted to a smaller number of patients, which results in better-quality service. Problem areas suffer from shortages or delays in the supply of medicines, primitive sanitary conditions, equipment shortages, inadequate facilities for hospitalization and emergency and problems with paramedics.

Since its inception in 1944, the illness and maternity fund has operated with a deficit, financed with resources from the work-related accident fund. In 1966, the medical care fund also began operating with a deficit, which forced the various administrations of the IVSS to make illegal use of pension fund resources.

Although this made it possible to finance medical care and even to create a short-term infrastructure base, the possibility of carrying out an aggressive investment plan such as the one proposed for the pension fund was seriously diminished.[3]

IVSS data since 1980 indicate that the number of hospitals, the number of beds in relation to theoretical demand and the supply of medicines are all low. But most alarming is that spending is increasing without any correlation to the level of services provided, due to the large percentage going to hospital administration.[4] Unions are making exorbitant economic demands, especially of physicians, who have the highest concentration of human resources and consume 65 percent of the total income of the medical care fund. Yet, the services provided are neither sufficient nor adequate: the number of consultations (2.25 per beneficiary per year) was below the four recommended by the World Health Organization (Acedo, 1986).

These statistics are from the 1980s, when medical expenses were shielded from inflation by a number of exchange controls that froze the price of imported inputs. Conditions changed in 1989 and the hospital system is beginning to show signs of an alarming decline.

Because of service structure and use of human resources and equipment, the quantity and the quality of services provided suffers. This causes user dissatisfaction, but the possibility of demanding better service is undermined by an institution little concerned about customer service.

Representation: Management, Users and the Organization

The social insurance system is managed by representatives of employers, workers, and the government. These three parties are present on the Board of Directors, in the regional funds and in the administration of medical centers. Business owners are represented by *Fedecámaras*, workers by the League of Venezuelan Workers (CTV, *Confederación de Trabajadores de Venezuela*) and the state by representatives of the executive branch.

Once the system was established in 1967, there was little pressure from business and union representatives to improve the system. There seemed to be more interest in preserving influence with the executive branch than in updating and adapting the system to changing financial and organizational needs. For example, no changes were made in the organization to establish a decentralized service more attuned to the needs of users and the insured. For funding, there was no pressure to raise the contribution limit, to increase pension amounts or to pursue

---

[3] See Ministry of Labor, 1980-89, and J. Ramírez, 1970.
[4] See IVSS, 1980-88.

a more appropriate, effective and aggressive investment policy. The threat of bankruptcy would bring these questions to the fore. Certain aspects of routine management were also ignored, such as the supervision of memberships and the collection of contributions. The executive branch apparently was not subjected to much pressure from unions, from the insured or from business owners to pay the contributions it owed.

Union representatives, especially in medicine, staunchly defend their interests and demand better wages, despite the fact that supervision, evaluation, and medical and paramedical training are deficient.

Instead of helping users, the three-way management system is often an obstacle to resolving disputes between the insured and the organization. The Board of Directors of the IVSS, on which representation by a union representative is essential, is the only forum within the organization for solving users' problems. There is no such forum at the regional level, where there is no representation at all save one's own efforts with the director of the administrative unit. At the regional level, complaints are lodged with those directly responsible for administration of the system or service, so that deficiencies in the process can be corrected. The disadvantage is that the insured has limited ability to file complaints or claims with authorities whose essential functions do not include conflict resolution. To ensure greater impartiality in the final decision, disputes between the insured and the organization should be handled by an independent authority.

More flexibility is needed, as well as better management of the flow of information to provide more efficient service. Moreover, customer service must be recognized as central to handling disputes and settling claims locally.

Prospects for the Social Insurance System

In this section the financial position of the social insurance system in Venezuela is projected into the future. The projection explores the impact of expected demographic growth on the various income and expense components of the social insurance system to simulate the trend of a simplified financing structure.[5]

The lack of information about the demographic and financial variables of the system limits the projection.[6] But a great many of the limitations also result from the need to focus attention on the impact of the three elements we consider essential to the future of the social insurance system: the demographic transfor-

---

[5] Carmen Portela worked extensively on the calculations and the calibration of the projection model presented in this section.

[6] The IVSS has had no accounting records officially approved by the government since 1990. In 1989, the institute hired an outside auditor, who concluded that its accounting records were "unauditable."

Table 5.2. Venezuelan Social Insurance Institute Contribution Rates
(Percentages of wages up to the maximum taxable wage)

	System	
	Partial	General
Employee	2	4
Employer	4	9-11
State	1.5	1.5
Total	7.5	14.5-16.5

Source: IVSS, 1989. 108/109 Reg.
Note: The state contributions are to the administrative expenses of the IVSS and not as an employer. The employer's contribution in the general system varies according to the degree of risk associated with the line of business (Art. 109 Reg).

Table 5.3. Distribution by Fund of IVSS Revenues from Contributions

	General system	Partial system
Medical assistance fund	6.25	0.0
Daily compensation fund	1.00	0.0
Pension fund and other cash benefits	6.75	6.00
Total	14.00	6.00

Source: Author's calculations.

mation of Venezuela, the rules governing the financing of the system, and the calculation of old-age pensions.

To simplify, for example, we project medical expenses as a constant amount of resources per beneficiary. Obviously, demographic trends and advances in medical science could bring about enormous changes in the spending per beneficiary. This and many other simplifications should be studied by specialists in the various fields of interest in the social insurance system.

Financial Structure of the Social Insurance System

The Venezuelan social insurance system is financed primarily by employer and employee contributions, calculated as a percentage of wages, up to the maximum contribution. In addition, the state as such (not in its role of employer) helps finance the system with contributions to defray administrative costs. As indicated in Table 5.2, the contribution rates vary according to the risks insured.

The income from contributions is distributed among three funds: Medical Care, Daily Allowances and Pensions and other Financial Benefits (Art. 74 Law, Art. 112 Reg), depending from which system the contributions come, as shown

Table 5.4. Structure of Social Insurance System Revenues, 1970-88
(Percentages of total revenues)

Years	Contributions	Government contribution	Interest	Others
1970	82.9	11.3	5.8	0.1
1971	82.3	11.5	6.2	0.1
1972	81.8	11.4	6.7	0.1
1973	83.4	10.4	6.2	0.1
1974	67.2	16.5	16.2	0.1
1975	71.1	16.6	12.2	0.0
1976	74.7	13.1	12.2	0.1
1977	72.5	15.5	12.0	0.0
1978	75.4	13.3	11.3	0.0
1979	71.7	13.7	14.5	0.0
1980	76.0	11.9	12.0	0.1
1981	71.1	12.3	16.5	0.0
1982	70.2	12.7	17.1	0.0
1983	67.9	13.7	18.3	0.1
1984	67.3	13.4	19.2	0.1
1985	64.3	13.4	22.2	0.1
1986	60.6	13.1	26.0	0.4
1987	69.3	11.9	18.2	0.5
1988	71.8	13.7	14.4	0.2

Source: IVSS, 1980-88.

in Table 5.3. This distribution does not include the government contribution of 1.5 percent of the contribution salaries, which is the source of financing for the IVSS Administration Fund.

The system also receives income by investing the accrued reserve funds, which are the product of surplus income over expenditures, by fund. As far as the accounting is concerned, the investment funds consist of the surpluses less the deficits of all the funds. This means that if one fund has a deficit, it can get resources from another fund that has a surplus. Although this is clearly illegal (Art. 112 Reg), it has been the standard practice of all IVSS managers. It should be noted that although this arrangement reduces the capacity of the system as a whole to build reserves, it alleviates the pressure to recapitalize funds that have deficits.

Analysis of the structure of social insurance system investments (Márquez, 1992) suggests that the cumulative deficits of the medical care fund and the low return of IVSS financial investments are responsible for the decrease in the real value of the pension fund and other financial benefits. This decrease has raised doubts about the financial stability of the pension system and has revealed the financial and organizational problems of the medical care system.

One of the results of this process, as indicated in Table 5.4, is the small share of interest income in the total income of the social insurance system in 1987.

Table 5.5. Macroeconomic Projection Scenarios and Framework, 1991-2030

	The average old-age pension is set at one/third of the minimum wage	The average old-age pension is set at a figure actual to the minimum wage
The maximum taxable wage is adjusted every 10 years on the basis of the last five years' inflation.	Scenario 1-A	Scenario 1-B
The maximum taxable wage is set so high that it is effectively eliminated.	Scenario 2-A	Scenario 2-B

Source: Author's calculations.

Table 5.6. Macroeconomic Projection Variables, 1991-2030
(Interannual growth rates)

	Inflation	Real wage	GDP
1991-95	30.0	1.5	2.9
1996-2000	35.0	1.5	2.5
2001-05	20.0	1.5	3.0
2006-10	15.0	1.5	3.0
2011-15	10.0	1.5	3.0
2016-20	5.0	1.5	3.0
2021-25	5.0	1.5	3.0
2026-30	5.0	1.5	3.0

Source: Author's calculations.

Although no official accounting data have been available since then, the IVSS has often expressed concern about the decrease in the real value of the Pension Fund, associating that decrease with the return on financial investments.

A Projection Methodology

Three groups of basic elements affect the long-term financial position of a social insurance system: (i) the macroeconomic and demographic trend, (ii) the financing rules, and (iii) the rules governing the benefits of the system. The managers of the system obviously have no control over demographic growth; the other two elements must conform to it, given the projected macroeconomic trend. Therefore, the financing rules and the benefits of the system are the focus of the policy decisions of the system's managers.

This section is based on a demographic projection. Table 5.5 describes the financing and benefit rules used as simulation variables to develop four scenarios, within the framework of macroeconomic growth described in Table 5.6.

This exercise was constrained by the limits of the existing data. Part of the current crisis in the Venezuelan social insurance system is due to this very lack of data concerning the contributions and benefits of the system, or even of auditable accounting data since 1990.

The methodology used is based on a demographic projection:

- data from the OCEI (*Oficina Central de Estadística e Informática*, Central Office of Information and Statistics) Household Survey on the age and occupational structure of the work force is used to determine (i) the structure of the rates of participation by age and sex of the population over 15 years of age and (ii) the structure by age and sex of employees and workers in the modern segment employed in the public and private sectors in the second quarter of 1991;

- the number of employees and workers per employer obtained in the previous (ii) section is compared with the total number of contributors in the various categories of the social insurance system. Assuming that all contributors to the partial system are public employees and that all contributors to the general system are private employees, the total percentages of system coverage for each of the categories are obtained;

- this percentage of coverage is applied to all employee age groups in the public and private sectors to obtain the total number of contributors to the system;

- the contribution rule and several financing policy variants are applied to the average wage taken from the OCEI Household Survey to determine the total income per contributor to the system. The government contribution and the estimates of other income are added to this total. This total income is divided among each of the funds in the system;

- the percentage of the cohort eligible for retirement—men who turn 60 and women who turn 55 that year—and who actually obtain their retirement from the system, is calculated for the last five years (from 1985 to 1990);

- each of the expense components (pensions, medical care and daily allowances) is projected on the basis of its past performance and various benefit policy alternatives, thus obtaining a projection of the expenses per fund and the total expenses of the system; and,

- a fund-by-fund comparison of income and expenses provides an estimate of the system's total financial resources. Assuming a policy of investing surpluses (or financing deficits), a projection of the financial position of the system can be obtained.

This methodology obviously has serious limitations from the assumption of constancy in the structure of the labor market and from the lack of information about the structure by age and sex of the contributors to the system. Given these limitations, the methodology makes the best possible use of the available information and permits focusing the analysis on the impact of the projected demographic growth and the financing and benefit policies on the financial position of the system.

The Demographic Projection

The demographic structure fundamentally affects the composition of social investment demand, the use of human resources, and the demand for institutional mechanisms to transfer resources from one age group to another (the social insurance system, for example).

A country with a very young population needs schools and medical institutions that provide essentially preventive care and specialize in obstetrics and childhood diseases. Given this demographic structure, adult family members must spend some time caring for children that might otherwise be spent on income-producing activities. The need for institutional mechanisms to transfer resources to groups outside the labor market (from productive age groups to the young) is small, however, since most of these transfers occur within the family unit.[7]

On the other hand, a population with a large percentage of individuals who are no longer economically active will require proportionally fewer schools, more complex curative medical institutions and some mechanism enabling this group to receive some of the resources produced by society. In more rural and more traditional societies, this transfer mechanism is also internalized by the family unit through the concept of the "extended family." More urban, modern societies, however, generally have a highly institutionalized structure to ensure that this flow of resources exists in the form of pension systems.

The age structure of the population depends on the past trend of birth and mortality rates. Simultaneous reductions in the mortality and birth rates tend to cause an increase in the average age of the population and in the percentage of older groups in the total population. The long-term growth in Venezuela follows this demographic trend, especially after 1980, as shown in Table 5.7.

The demographic projection used in this chapter is the one proposed by the World Bank in its *World Population Projections,* which assumes net unit reproduction rates for the year 2010 that appear to be consistent with the long-term

---

[7] When the traditional nuclear family structure breaks down, this system of transfers is interrupted, creating conditions of extreme poverty in households headed by women. The need for institutional mechanisms enabling mothers to request and obtain child support payments is generally ignored, despite general acknowledgment of their importance.

Table 5.7. Demographic Indicators, 1936-90
(Percentages)

	1936	1941	1950	1961	1971	1981	1990
Birth rate	31.9	35.3	42.6	45.3	38.3	33.7	29.9
Mortality	17.2	16.4	10.9	7.3	6.7	5.0	4.7
Total growth	1.47	1.89	3.17	3.81	3.16	2.87	2.52

Source: Chen and Picouet, 1979, and OCEI, 1936-91.

trend of birth and mortality rates in Venezuela.[8] Table 5A.1 in the Appendix provides more detailed information about the age structure, total population and growth rates in various periods.

Venezuela's demographic growth in the coming decades, as can be seen in Table 5.8, suggests great changes in the composition of social investment demand, in the use of human resources and in the need for institutional mechanisms to effect intergenerational transfers of resources. Essentially, this process of demographic transition implies drastic changes in the shape of the population pyramid: from the typical steep-sided pyramid of countries in the early stages of demographic evolution to a pyramid that is broader at the more productive ages (between 25 and 45 years of age) and also at the more advanced ages, as shown in Figures 5.2 and 5.3.

Significantly, the absolute number of children under 15 years of age increases 5.6 percent between 1990 and 2030, the number of children under 5 years of age decreases 3.1 percent and the number of individuals over 60 increases 362 percent. Consequently, the population eligible for a pension (the group over 60) will almost triple its percentage of the total. This means that some of the resources going to children and young people in Venezuela today will have to be transferred to the elderly. This change is of vital importance to the social insurance system, in terms not only of the growth of the number of pensions but also the changes in the type (and costs) of the medical care that this population will demand.

The percentage of the young population (under 15 years of age) will decrease substantially, leveling the demand for schools and altering the structure of the demand for medical facilities. The percentage of children under 5 years of age in the total population will also shrink substantially, freeing up even more productive resources. At the same time, the percentage of 25-to-45 year-olds in the total population will increase, adding to the pool of fully productive human resources. A more conventional measure is provided on the last line of Table 5.9, which shows the quotient of the potentially active population (PET, *población*

---

[8] Bulatao *et al.*, 1990.

Figure 5.2. Population Pyramid, 1990 and 2030
(Thousands of men)

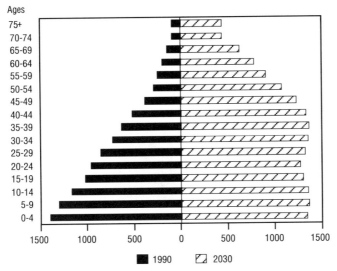

Source: Bulatao *et al.*, 1990.

Figure 5.3. Population Pyramid, 1990 and 2030
(Thousands of women)

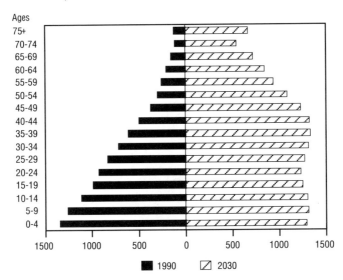

Source: Bulatao *et al.*, 1990.

Table 5.8. Demographic Indicators, 1985-2030
(Percentages)

	1985-90	1990-95	1995-2000	2000-05	2005-10	2010-15	2015-20	2020-25	2025-30
Birth rate	30.7	27.3	23.9	21.1	18.8	17.9	17.4	16.6	15.6
Mortality	5.2	4.9	4.7	4.8	5.0	5.4	5.8	6.3	6.9
Natural growth	2.6	2.2	1.9	1.6	1.4	1.3	1.2	1.0	0.9
Migration	0.8	0.5	0.3	0.2	0.0	0.0	0.0	0.0	0.0
Total growth	2.6	2.3	2.0	1.7	1.4	1.3	1.2	1.0	0.9
Total fertility	3.8	3.4	2.9	2.5	2.2	2.1	2.1	2.1	2.1
NRR	2	1.6	1.4	1.2	1.1	1.0	1.0	1.0	1.0
e(0) - both sexes[1]	70.1	71.0	71.8	72.6	73.1	73.6	74.1	74.6	75.1
e(10) - both sexes[2]	63.3	63.7	64.1	64.5	64.9	65.2	65.6	66.0	66.4
Infant mortality	36.0	31.1	26.1	21.6	20.3	18.9	17.5	16.2	14.8
q(5) - both sexes[3]	0.04	0.04	0.03	0.02	0.02	0.02	0.02	0.02	0.02

Source: Bulatao *et al.*, 1990.
Notes: [1] e(0) = life expectancy at age 0.
     [2] e(10) = life expectancy at age 10.
     [3] q(5) = probability of death within 0-5 age group.

Table 5.9. Population Structure by Age, 1990-2030
(Percentages)

	1990	2010	2030
Less than 5 years	13.85	7.87	7.52
Less than 15 years	38.29	27.62	22.66
Between 25 and 45 years	27.21	30.30	30.20
Over 60 years	5.57	8.23	14.43
	(PET/POP less than 15 and more than 60 years)[1]		
Maintenance rates	1.28	1.79	1.70

Source: Author's calculations based on information from Bulatao *et al.* (1990).
Note: [1] PET=potentially active population *(población en edad de trabajar)* between 15 and 60 years of age.
        POP= Population

en edad de trabajar, between 15 and 60 years of age) and its complement. A notable increase is observed in the potential capacity of Venezuela to support both the young and the old.

The Work Force

The structure of rates of participation in the work force by age and sex was obtained using data from the OCEI Household Survey for the second quarter of 1991. The rates of participation, as shown in Figure 5.4, exhibit a differential pattern with respect to age and sex, with greater participation by males. However, both sexes exhibit a similar pattern with respect to variation in the rates of participation by age.

To estimate the size of the work force (presented in Table 5A.2 of the Appendix) we assume that the level and structure of the rates of participation in the work force remain constant throughout the projection period. Changes in the composition of the work force are the result of changes in the age structure of the population and not of changes in the rates of participation. This is obviously an unrealistic assumption, but it does allow us the exercise to focus on the impact of changes in the demographic structure.

Structure of the Labor Market

According to law, affiliation with the social insurance system is compulsory for all employees (Art. 3 Law). This means that the coverage of the social insurance system is legally restricted to employees and wage-earners and, by way of exception, to specific categories of self-employed workers (Art. 3-6 Law, Art. 1-9 Reg.). On the other hand, given the limited amount of coercion that the system

Figure 5.4. Distribution of the Work Force by Age and Sex, 2nd Quarter 1991
(Percentage of the work force)

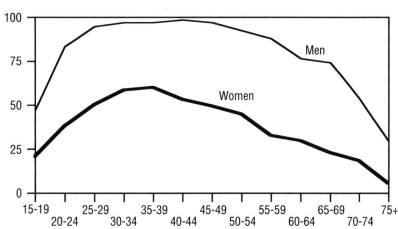

Source: OCEI, 1991.

can exert on employers and employees, it is generally assumed that employees and workers in the informal sector are not covered by the system.[9] Therefore, the theoretical coverage of the social insurance system is limited to employees and workers in the public sector and in the modern private sector.

Analysis of the data from OCEI reveals that the composition of employment in the labor market by occupational category and segment varies considerably according to sex and age, as shown in Table 5.10.

For the purposes of the projection, we assume that the percentage of each age group and sex in the categories of modern private and public employees and workers remains constant throughout the projection period. Using these percentages, we obtain the total number of employees and workers in each category, shown in Tables 5A.3 and 5A.4 of the Appendix.

Social Insurance System Coverage

For all potential insured individuals, the law provides two different systems of affiliation and coverage. The first, known as the partial system, provides coverage for permanent disability, old-age, death and marriage (the so-called "financial benefits" Art. 2 Law). The second, known as the general system, includes all

---

[9] The informal sector refers to all employees and workers in companies employing less than five people.

Table 5.10. Potential Coverage of the Social Insurance System: Second Half of 1991

(Percentages of modern sector employees and workers in the category over the total employed in the age and sex group)

Age	Women			Men		
	Private	Public	Total	Private	Public	Total
15-19	31.8	4.5	36.3	43.7	4.7	48.4
20-24	48.4	23.4	71.8	50.9	11.7	62.6
25-29	28.5	33.1	61.6	48.1	17.2	65.2
30-34	33.6	33.0	66.6	42.8	18.0	60.8
35-39	25.9	43.0	69.0	32.7	20.5	53.2
40-44	17.4	44.7	62.1	30.8	27.6	58.4
45-49	21.3	38.4	59.6	35.6	18.0	53.6
50-54	10.6	29.1	39.8	29.9	18.2	48.1
55-59	7.5	11.2	18.8	26.2	9.8	36.0
60-64	22.4	12.5	34.9	30.5	14.5	45.0
65-69	25.8	0.7	26.5	22.8	6.9	29.7
70-74	0.0	0.0	0.0	11.7	4.2	15.9
75 and +	0.0	0.0	0.0	25.7	0.0	25.7
Total	27.4	31.1	58.5	39.2	16.0	55.2

Source: Author's calculations based on OCEI, 1991.

of the "financial benefits" as well as coverage for medical care and temporary disability.

The *partial system* is for public employees subject to special labor provisions other than the Labor Law[10] and for private employees in areas where the IVSS has no medical facilities. Expansion of the system of medical facilities available to IVSS affiliates to the entire country caused a reduction in this latter category. The *general system* is for all modern private sector employees and workers and public sector employees with contracts subject to the provisions of the Labor Law.

Since the database makes no distinction between administrative employees and workers on the public sector payroll, a simplifying assumption was used, whereby all modern private sector employees are in the general system and all public employees are in the partial system. According to this assumption, the trend of the percentages of actual coverage of the social insurance system is that shown in Table 5.11.

---

[10] Public sector administrative employees are in a special class according to the Administrative Career Law, which provides for the irremovability of the employee after a period of probation. In contrast, public sector workers have contracts subject to the Labor Law, which also governs the contracts of private sector employees.

Figure 5.5. Projected Number of Subscribers by Insurance Plan
(Thousands of individuals)

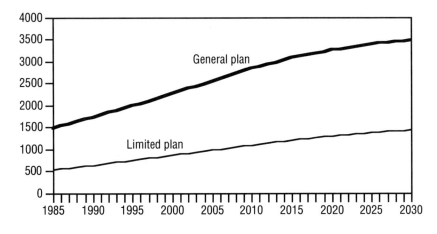

Source: Author's estimates.

Table 5.11. Affiliation with the Social Insurance System, 1977-91
(Percentages of the potentially covered population)

Years	General system	Partial system
1977	69.9	35.0
1978	72.6	35.1
1979	71.8	34.4
1980	70.9	43.3
1981	73.5	49.2
1982	69.9	50.0
1983	73.2	50.2
1984	77.0	51.0
1985	81.5	49.2
1986	74.0	51.1
1987	70.5	53.0
1988	71.0	53.0
1989	74.1	48.0
1990	77.5	49.1
1991	77.0	49.6

Source: Author's calculations based on OCEI, 1936-91, and IVSS, 1980-88.

These historical percentages of social insurance system coverage are measured in the projection model on the basis of data for the 1985-90 period. The results are shown in Figure 5.5 and in Table 5A.5 of the Appendix.

Contributions to the Social Insurance System

The social insurance system is financed primarily through the collection of premiums, calculated as a percentage of the contribution salary. The contribution salary has a nominal limit, above which the marginal contribution rate is zero. This means that average contribution rates decrease as total wages increase. In other words, the social insurance contribution is equal to

$$W \cdot t \qquad\qquad if\ W \le W_{max}$$
$$W_{max} \cdot t \qquad\qquad if\ W > W_{max}$$

where W =   monthly salary
        wmax =   maximum contribution salary
        t =   contribution rate.

Given the method of calculating the social insurance contribution, the average contribution rate depends on the relationship between average salary and maximum contribution salary and the shape of the wage distribution. Formally expressed, the total payroll contributions to the IVSS are equal to:

$$\sum_{W_i < W_{max}} W_i \cdot t + \sum_{W_i \ge W_{max}} W_{max} \cdot t = (W_{W_i} < W_{max} \cdot L_{W_i}, W_{max} \cdot L_{W_i} <_{W_{max}}) \cdot t$$

where L = employment in the corresponding group.

Multiplying and dividing by total L we obtain

$$\left(\overline{W}_{W_i < max} \cdot \frac{L_{Wi < W_{max}}}{L} \cdot W_{max} \cdot \frac{L_{W_i < W_{max}}}{L} \right) \cdot L \cdot t = (\overline{W}_{W_i < max} \cdot \overline{F} + W_{max} F) L \cdot t$$

where F+ = percentage of workers with salaries above the contribution limit.
      $F^- = 1 - F^+$

Since

$$\overline{W}_{W_i < max} < \overline{W}$$

this means that the contribution salary is always below the national average wage, and the larger F+ is, the greater the distance between the two.

Two stages are discernible in the historical relationship between the maximum contribution salary and the average wage in Venezuela. Up to the late sixties, the policy was to maintain a high maximum wage, making F+ close to zero, and the contribution salary practically the same as the average wage. Later, the elimination of periodic adjustments of the maximum wage caused a decrease in real terms. The acceleration of inflation in the seventies caused the maximum wage to decrease in real terms to levels below the average wage, making F+ almost equal to one.

In our projection we will use two different scenarios. In the first, F+ = 1 indicates a policy of not adjusting the contribution limit. As a result of this policy, contributions grow nominally at the same rate as the contributing population. In the second scenario, F+ = 0 indicates a policy of eliminating the contribution limit. In this case, and as a result of this policy, contributions grow nominally at a rate equal to the sum of the growth of the contributing population and the nominal growth of wages. The results of both projections are presented in Tables 5.A.5 and 5.A.6 of the Appendix.

The Benefits of the Social Insurance System

Retirements

When an insured individual who has made at least 750 cumulative weekly contributions reaches 55 years of age in the case of a woman or 60 in the case of a man, he or she is eligible for an old-age pension. The IVSS can lower the minimum retirement age for individuals who perform hazardous work, but in no case can such a reduction be more than five years.

Old-age pensions are calculated according to the following formula:

$$PV = \max \left\{ \begin{array}{l} Bs\ 2{,}000; \\ 0.4{\cdot}W_{ref}; \\ \{[(1+0.05{\cdot}(R-R_{min})){\cdot}0.3] + [0.01{\cdot}\max(0;\ trc(\tfrac{c-750}{50}))]\}{\cdot}W_{ref} \end{array} \right\}$$

where
PV	=	monthly amount of the old-age pension
C	=	total number of contributions
R	=	age at the time of retirement
R_{min}	=	minimum retirement age (55 for women, 60 for men)

$$W_{ref} = \frac{\sum_{t=R-5}^{R} \min (W_t; W_{max})}{5}$$

$$\max(a;b) = a \text{ if and only if } a>b$$

$$trc \left(\frac{C\text{-}750}{50} \right) = a \Rightarrow \frac{C\text{-}750}{50} = a, remainder$$

The formula for calculating old-age pensions creates two incentives for re-tiring late. The first term on the last line implies a 5 percent increase in the pension for every year that retirement is delayed beyond the minimum age. The second term on that same line means that for every 50 contributions beyond the required minimum of 750 contributions, the pension increases 1 percent.

The pension is established in nominal terms and is based on the average reference wages of the last five years. This method of calculation, often de-scribed as the pay-as-you-go system, is actually the same as a capitalization system with internal rates of return (TIR, *tasa interna de retorno*) determined by the length of the contributions and inflation during the individual's life (Márquez, 1992).

A worker with exactly 750 contributions who retires at the minimum age receives a TIR (implied by the formula for calculating the pension) that is nega-tive in real terms if the rate of inflation is 30 percent and slightly positive if the rate of inflation is 10 percent. Far from extremely generous, this formula is ex-tremely conservative for financing a retirement system, particularly with high rates of inflation (Márquez, 1992).

From a purely demographic point of view, it is interesting to note how the number of contributors per pensioner decreases (first column of Table 5.12), a phenomenon described earlier as the process of demographic maturation in Ven-ezuela.

Calculating the pensions in nominal terms has allowed their reduction in real terms to serve as a method of financial adjustment of the pension system. As indicated in the second column of Table 5.12, old-age pensions have decreased constantly in real terms since the early seventies. Measured as a multiple of the minimum wage (third column of Table 5.12), which compensates for the drop in real wages in the eighties, the downturn of pensions accelerated considerably in 1983. This decrease has reduced the share of pensions in the total spending of the social insurance system, as shown in the last column of Table 5.12.

For the purposes of our projection, we estimate the flow of new pensioners each year by applying a constant percentage (estimated for the 1985-90 period) to the cohort of contributors who reached 60 (men) or 55 years of age (women) the year before. Each of these groups is assigned a life expectancy at retirement, which allows us to construct synthetically dated cohorts of the retired popula-

Table 5.12. Selected IVSS Pension System Indicators, 1971-92

Years	Contributors per pensioned (individuals)	Monthly amount (1992 Bs.)	Minimum wage pension	Pensions as a percentage of total expenses
1971	2757.5	21,754	2.35	0.3
1972	94.3	16,327	1.81	7.0
1973	67.7	16,250	1.87	9.3
1974	49.0	14,720	1.23	11.8
1975	44.3	13,255	1.22	12.1
1976	39.2	15,752	1.56	15.8
1977	36.1	14,955	1.59	16.6
1978	34.9	14,399	1.64	18.5
1979	30.2	9,742	1.25	14.7
1980	31.1	12,832	1.00	16.8
1981	29.6	11,127	1.01	16.9
1982	30.1	11,757	1.16	18.7
1983	26.1	9,144	0.96	16.0
1984	24.3	8,473	1.00	18.1
1985	22.9	7,698	0.61	17.6
1986	21.1	7,014	0.46	15.9
1987	20.6	5,690	0.48	15.3
1988	20.6	5,112	0.43	15.8
1989	19.4	2,644	0.27	10.5
1990	18.4	3,172	0.45	10.6
1991	17.4	3,012	0.38	12.6
1992	17.4	2,874	0.32	10.2

Source: IVSS, 1980-88.

Figure 5.6. Contributors per Retired Worker in the Pension System, 1990-2030

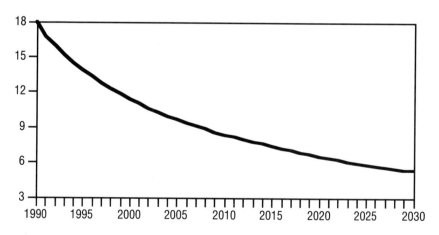

Source: Author's estimates based on Tables 5A.7 and 5A.8.

tion.[11] Assuming that the retired population at the beginning of the projection period has the same distribution by age as the general male (female) population over 60 (55) years of age, we obtain the total retired population on each date.

The initial number of retirees in each age group increases every year due to the influx of new retirees and is reduced by the death of retirees. Thus, on each date, the total number of retirees is equal to

$$\sum_{age/sex} stock^t_{age/sex} = \sum_{age/sex} stock^{t-1}_{age/sex} + \%ret_{sex} \cdot \sum_{sex} retir.cohort.^t_{sex} - \sum_{sex} cohort[(age-R) \geq e(R)]^t_{sex}$$

where e(R) = life expectancy at the age of retirement

The results of this calculation are shown in the first column of Tables 5A.7 and 5A.8 of the Appendix. Given the projected demographic trend, the number of pensioners per contributor in the system increases enormously in the projection period, as shown in Figure 5.6.

It was mentioned above that the decrease in the real value of pensions operated as a mechanism of financial adjustment in the pension system. Obviously, such a procedure has limitations, given that the amount of political pressure placed on the system to increase the pensions is directly proportional to the number of pensioners (increasing) and inversely proportional to the level of the pensions (at their lowest level). To some extent, such pressure is typical of an economy with mounting inflation, which was the case in Venezuela in the last decade.

The current debate in Venezuela clearly reflects this process: on the one hand, there is strong political pressure to increase the amount of the pensions to the level of the minimum wage; on the other, all of the groups involved reject the larger contributions that would be needed to finance such an increase.

Our projection exercise is based on two alternative scenarios. In the first, the results of which are presented in Table 5A.7 of the Appendix, pensions are kept more or less at their current real level (a third of the minimum wage), which implies periodic nominal increases of a percentage similar to that of the increase in real wages plus inflation. In the second scenario, pensions are adjusted in 1993 to the level of the minimum wage and are held at this real level throughout the projection period. Neither of the two scenarios involves fundamental changes in the institutional or financial structure of the pension system since both retain the liability structure of the current system, which is appropriate for a system with fixed contributions and undefined benefits.

---

[11] The life expectancy at the respective age (24.22 years for 55-year old women and 17.3 years for 60-year old men) was taken from Table 22, page 488, United Nations, 1992.

Table 5.13. Selected Indicators of the Medical Care System, 1970-92

	Beneficiaries		Expenditures		Exps. per beneficiary	
	Contributors	Families	Hospital admin.	Medical care	Hospital admin.	Medical care
Years	(Thousands of individuals)		(millions of Bs.)		(1992 Bs.)	
1970	611.8	1,254.6	9.2	461.1	1,538.13	7,867.07
1971	657.4	1,345.0	94.8	505.8	1,461.23	7,793.88
1972	707.2	1,445.7	98.5	533.5	1,373.07	7,438.13
1973	772.4	1,575.1	106.2	559.1	1,307.29	6,884.71
1974	839.1	1,717.4	129.3	625.7	1,346.22	6,516.88
1975	942.9	1,928.0	159.3	726.1	1,343.95	6,124.66
1976	989.2	2,023.6	200.6	833.1	1,498.30	6,222.82
1977	1075.7	2,207.5	223.9	880.9	1,423.81	5,601.31
1978	1190.8	2,443.4	266.3	930.6	1,428.00	4,990.46
1979	1184.3	2,960.7	266.7	1,038.3	1,116.25	4,344.95
1980	1220.6	3,051.6	119.8	1,632.7	400.21	5,454.37
1981	1285.4	3,213.4	326.7	1,839.5	892.26	5,023.49
1982	1269.9	3,242.3	309.6	1,823.1	770.10	4,534.80
1983	1216.8	3,042.0	434.7	1,908.4	1,076.44	4,725.68
1984	1265.8	3,164.6	295.7	1,881.3	627.48	3,992.60
1985	1334.2	3,335.6	244.5	2,303.7	441.99	4,164.00
1986	1454.1	3,635.2	277.9	3,339.4	413.22	4,965.41
1987	1557.4	3,893.6	387.5	3,885.2	419.80	4,209.32
1988	1727.4	4,318.4	555.9	5,130.1	419.42	3,870.62
1989	1712.3	4,280.9	—	8,565.2	—	3,534.17
1990	1803.0	4,507.4	—	14,885.3	—	4,147.13
1991	1866.1	4,665.2	—	14,721.7	—	2,952.77
1992	2034.5	5,086.2	—	22,366.0	—	3,140.97

Source: IVSS, 1980-88.

Medical Expenses

Individuals insured by the general system, pensioners and their immediate families are covered by a comprehensive medical policy that includes dental care
(Art. 7-8 Law, Art. 118-140 Reg). These services are provided in social insurance hospitals but can be subcontracted to third parties. Medical care is provided
for a period of 52 consecutive weeks for insured individuals, pensioners and
their families. For the families of old-age or disability pensioners, the period is
limited to 26 weeks.

If a beneficiary who has received medical care and has completed his treatment returns to seek medical care for another, different illness within the next
four weeks, the period of medical care shall be counted as if there had been no
interruption. Insured individuals who have exhausted their right to medical services regain it after contributing for 16 weeks. If the illness is a new one, however, only eight weeks are required. In any case, the beneficiary and the physi-

cian are not subject to any financial limits other than the reasonableness of the care and treatment provided in modern medical practice.

IVSS hospitals also conduct important and very expensive research and medical teaching tasks. This tends to raise the costs to users, even though it would be more appropriate if such costs were financed with different budget resources.

IVSS medical system expenses are determined in part by the system's institutional structure. Since the IVSS prefers to provide medical services in its own establishments, the facilities' administrative expenses (third column of Table 5.11) should be considered an integral part of this expense. Are these expenses excessive, given the nature of the medical facilities' principal activities? Could they be reduced through better use of subcontracting medical services? These are questions that demand a careful comparison with other medical facilities and with the cost of alternative methods of providing services.

Despite medical insurance coverage, the scope of activities carried out by the IVSS medical institution activities, and the inefficiency to be expected in a system with a captive market, medical expenses per insured individual have been shrinking steadily since the early eighties (as shown in Table 5.13). Earlier analyses of the IVSS show that this decrease in spending per beneficiary results from increased inefficiency, which lowers the effectiveness of distribution.[12]

The projection exercise assumes a constant real level of spending on medical care per beneficiary of 4,500 bolívares (at constant 1992 prices) and hospital administrative expenses equal to 10 percent of the spending on medical care. Both parameters are obviously arbitrary, but they roughly describe the situation of both expense items in the mid-eighties. Table 5A.9 of the Appendix presents projection results.

Both projection assumptions are conservative since they do not anticipate any great changes in the efficiency of the system nor any extraordinary increases in costs per beneficiary. In 1988, IVSS medical expenditures per beneficiary were less than 4,500 1992 bolívares. Even worse, the 1991-92 projections presented by the current IVSS administration place these expenses at levels below 3,000 1992 bolívares per beneficiary. This decrease in spending coincided with the worst crisis ever in the IVSS medical system, when medical facilities closed for lack of supplies and medicines.

In any case, the hypotheses of the projection model can be easily modified to incorporate more sophisticated—and possibly more realistic—assumptions.

Spending on Temporary Disability Benefits

Together with medical insurance, the IVSS provides income replacement in the

---

[12] For a detailed analysis of the distribution of the IVSS medical system, see Márquez, 1992.

Table 5.14. Daily Temporary Disability Compensation Expenditures, 1970-92

Year	Daily comp. exps. (millions of Bs.)	Exps. per contributor general system (Current Bs.)	(1992 Bs.)	Comp. as % of general system contributions (Percentage)
1970	80.3	611.80	19,482	12.30
1971	80.1	657.40	20,285	11.11
1972	86.1	707.20	21,227	10.70
1973	94.8	772.40	22,270	10.66
1974	114.6	839.10	22,343	11.57
1975	149.7	942.90	22,834	11.00
1976	164.7	989.20	22,260	10.41
1977	175.7	1,075.70	22,458	9.81
1978	184.4	1,190.80	23,206	8.58
1979	212.7	1,184.30	20,543	9.72
1980	255.5	1,220.60	17,421	8.02
1981	243.2	1,285.35	15,791	7.11
1982	238.7	1,269.92	14,253	6.74
1983	249.0	1,216.78	12,832	7.54
1984	218.8	1,265.84	11,902	6.30
1985	213.3	1,334.24	11,262	5.95
1986	224.8	1,454.09	11,004	5.33
1987	249.4	1,557.43	9,198	4.60
1988	279.5	1,727.37	7,879	4.10
1989	229.0	1,712.34	4,234	3.21
1990	447.0	1,802.95	3,170	2.40
1991	131.6	1,866.09	2,445	5.24
1992	181.0	2,034.49	2,034	5.33

Source: IVSS, Memoria y cuenta, 1980-88.

event of temporary disability caused by a work-related illness or accident. In-sured individuals in the general system who fall ill or who have an accident requiring a convalescence are entitled to a daily allowance while they are tempo-rarily unable to work (Art. 9-12 Law, Art. 141-47 Reg).

This allowance is granted for a maximum of 52 weeks for illness or acci-dent. If the insured individual is expected to recover, he will continue collecting the daily allowance beyond the 52 weeks. If the illness or accident requires hos-pitalization, the insured will collect a daily allowance equal to half of what he would receive if not hospitalized. Pregnant women are entitled to a daily allow-ance for six weeks before the due date and for six weeks afterward. The daily allowance will be equal to the daily equivalent of two-thirds of the most recent monthly wage.

Table 5.14 presents several disability compensation indicators. The allowance is related to the contribution salary, which enables us to project the total spending on allowances as a percentage (4.5 percent) of the total contribution income in the general system. Projection results can be seen in Appendix Table 5A.10.

Table 5.14 roughly describes the disability compensation system in the late eighties. The projection is conservative since it assumes that the current operating parameters of the system will remain constant. Changes in system organization, greater efficiency in the provision of medical care and better control over the use of this benefit could lower the costs. It is interesting that the current IVSS management has budgeted an even higher level of spending for the 1991-92 period than is projected here.

Spending on Other Financial Benefits

Everyone insured by the social insurance system (both the partial and the general system) enjoys the services described in this section. These services are not associated with medical care, and access to them has nothing to do with whether or not they were received through the insurance system. For the purposes of the projection, total spending on these services is considered in the aggregate and equivalent to 50 percent of the spending on old-age pensions, based on the budget projections prepared by the management of the IVSS for the 1991-92 period.

Partial Disability and Disability

If an insured individual becomes to some degree unable to work because of an occupational disease, work-related accident or ordinary accident, he is entitled to a pension (Art. 13-26 Law, Art. 148-161 Reg). If the work disability exceeds 5 percent but is less than two-thirds, it is considered partial disability; if the work disability exceeds two-thirds, it is considered disability. The degree of work disability is determined according to IVSS Regulation No. 3 of September 14, 1944.

If an accident or an occupational disease causes the disability, considerations of age or number of contributions do not affect the right to a disability pension. If the disability is due to an ordinary illness, a minimum of 100 weekly contributions in the last three years is required (or proof of having contributed 64 percent of the time) and if the insured is 35 years of age or older, he must also have a minimum of 250 weekly contributions. The total number of contributions is reduced 20 contributions per year for workers under 35 years of age and to a minimum of 100 weeks for a 27-year old worker.

In the case of more than 66 percent disability, the pension is calculated according to the following formula:

$$PI = \max \left\{ \begin{array}{l} \alpha \cdot W_{ref}; \\ Bs\, 2{,}000 + 0.3 \cdot W_{ref} + 0.1 \cdot \max\left(0;\, trc\left(\dfrac{C\text{-}750}{50}\right)\right) \end{array} \right\}$$

Table 5.15. IVSS General Administrative Expenses, 1970-92

Years	General Administration expenses (millions of Bs.)	Exps. per contributor (current Bs.)	(1992 Bs.)
1970	62.5	77.3	2,461.3
1971	63.6	73.7	2,273.7
1972	67.1	73.0	2,190.1
1973	85.3	85.5	2,472.6
1974	98.6	91.8	2,444.5
1975	123.4	102.8	2,488.8
1976	137.8	108.9	2,450.4
1977	148.2	107.0	2,234.4
1978	152.2	100.6	1,960.4
1979	152.9	100.4	1,742.2
1980	416.6	250.8	3,578.9
1981	261.6	145.5	1,787.4
1982	355.8	196.6	2,206.4
1983	348.5	196.9	2,076.1
1984	331.2	182.3	1,714.2
1985	391.9	206.7	1,744.4
1986	504.3	252.4	1,909.7
1987	574.5	267.3	1,578.7
1988	790.9	338.9	1,545.8
1989	1,922.2	835.0	2,064.8
1990	3,158.0	1,298.7	2,283.2
1991	2,565.0	1,016.1	1,331.0
1992	8,794.8	3,203.2	3,203.2

Source: IVSS ,1980-88.
Note: Starting in 1989, general administrative expenses were estimated at 60 percent of the total administrative expenses.

where	PI	=	disability pension
	C	=	total number of cumulative weekly contributions
	α	=	0.4 if the disability is due to ordinary illness or accident or 0.66 if the disability is due to occupational disease or work-related accident

The disability pension is increased 50 percent for workers who are paralyzed or who require constant care. If the partial disability is greater than 25 percent, the insured is entitled to a partial disability pension. The amount of the disability pension is calculated by multiplying the percentage of disability by PI. For 5-to-25 percent disability, the insured is entitled to collect a one-time payment calculated by applying the percentage of disability to three annual installments of the disability pension.

The insured is entitled to collect the disability pension six months after the start of the disabled condition and for as long as the condition continues. The partial disability pension will be paid whenever the individual stops collecting the daily allowances for treatment of the disability.

Survivor's Pensions

In the event of the death of an insured individual with no fewer than 750 weekly contributions, or of an insured whose death is caused by a work-related accident, or of a beneficiary of a disability or old-age pension, the immediate family (spouse, common-law spouse, minor or disabled children) is entitled to receive a survivor's pension (Art. 32-40 Law, 164-167 Reg). This pension is equal to an aliquot of the corresponding percentage of the benefit to which the insured or pensioner was entitled. If there is only one survivor, the percentage is 40 percent. The percentage increases 20 points for every additional survivor, up to a maximum of 100 percent.

Marriage

An insured individual who has made more than 100 weekly contributions in the last three years and who marries is entitled to a one-time payment of 7,000 bolívares (Art. 41-2 Law).

General Administrative Expenses

The administrative expenses of the social insurance system are financed with a special budget allocation from the state, equal to at least 1.5 percent of the total contribution salaries (Art. 69-70 Law, Art. 93-7 Reg). Although in the past the state's contributions have varied from this percentage, both up and down, in our projection we assume that this contribution is exactly equal to the legal minimum (see Tables 5A.5 and 5A.6 of the Appendix).

Table 5.15 shows that the spending per contributor to the system has tended to decrease in real terms. In our projection, the administrative expenses are considered part of the system's overhead and are estimated at 1,700 bolívares (at constant 1992 prices) per contributor. The results of this projection can be seen in Table 5A.11 of the Appendix.

Cost Evaluation of Alternatives

Evaluation of the financial soundness of the proposed policy alternatives is based on a reconstruction of the accounting of the various social insurance system funds to determine the total resources available for investment. The yield of these resources, calculated at market interest rates, accrues in the pension fund, which enables us to determine the current surplus or deficit of the system for each year in the projection period.

Table 5.16. IVSS Policy Costs
(current net value of nonaccrued deficits as a multiple of 1992 GDP)

	The average old-age pension is set at one-third of the minimum wage.	The average old-age pension is set at a figure equal to the minimum wage.
The maximum taxable wage is adjusted every 10 years based on the last five years' inflation.	Scenario 1-A 11.6 times	Scenario 1-B 26.6 times
The maximum taxable wage is set so high that it is effectively eliminated.	Scenario 2-A 4.1 times	Scenario 2-B 19.7 times

Source: Author's calculations.

To reproduce a simplified version of the system's financial structure, we used the 1988 IVSS accounting data on pension, medical care, daily allowances, and administrative fund totals. It is assumed that the algebraic sum of the amount available in each of these funds is invested at a real interest rate of 1 percent. The financial yields thus obtained accrue in the following period in the pension fund.

The value of the funds other than the pension fund in period t is equal to:

$$valueF_i^t = valueF_i^{t-1} + incomeF_i^t - expenseF_i^t$$

while the value of the Pension Fund is equal to:

$$valueF_{Pension}^t = valueF_{Pension}^{t-1} + incomeF_{Pension}^t - expenseF_{Pension}^t + max\left(0; i_t \cdot \sum_{i,Pension} valueF_i^{t}-1\right)$$

This calculation does not conform to "good actuarial practices" since the future debt contracted with current contributors is not included in IVSS liabilities. The pension fund will probably not be recapitalized in an amount actuarially consistent with those future liabilities.

Although this could be said to be a characteristic of pay-as-you-go systems in which today's contributors finance the pensions of yesterday's contributors, the IVSS was not structured this way until very recently, when inflation and the low financial yield of reserve fund investments forced the institute into this position.

The results of the calculations for the four scenarios are presented in Tables 5A.12 through 5A.15 in the Appendix. The current net value (VPN, *valor presente neto*) of the accrued deficits in each alternative (*i.e.*, the total that would have to be deposited today at a real interest rate of 1 percent to cover these deficits each year) is equal to a value ranging from 4 to 27 times the GDP of Venezuela in 1992 (see Table 5.16).

In each of the scenarios the system must operate with substantial current deficits, and it is not easy to imagine where the necessary financing will come from, given the current and foreseeable fiscal constraints. Even in the best of cases, in which the contributions increase and the current level of old-age pensions remains constant, IVSS finances are eroded by these deficits, and the volume of resources needed to make up such a loss is four times this year's total GDP. In the worst case, in which the contributions remain at their current level and old-age pensions increase, the foreseeable deficit of the system exceeds 3 percentage points of GDP each year, and the resources needed to make up the loss are 27 times this year's GDP, making this solution clearly unworkable.

Analysis of the projections reveals the sources of these deficits. In each of the scenarios, the cost of medical care is greater than the income received for it. The medical care deficits are covered by the surpluses of other funds, the pension fund in particular. This tends to decapitalize the pension fund and, as a result, to reduce the investment income of the entire system.

Even if pensions remain at the current level of one-third the minimum wage, the Pension Fund's required reserves tend to disappear. Nevertheless, it is clear that pensions cannot be kept at this level, if not because of pressure from current retirees, then because of what this tells current contributors about the future of the system.

Thus, the most realistic scenario of the four we propose is the one in which the contribution limit is eliminated and pensions are increased. But even in this scenario, the system sustains current losses and is undercapitalized, leaving its managers without many options other than requesting special government contributions, which at present seem hardly possible.

The equity of these special government contributions is questionable since they would represent contributions from society as a whole to a system that benefits only one group, and that not the poorest one, given that the social insurance system excludes workers in the informal sector. Furthermore, it is hardly believable that the coverage of the system can be expanded, given the financial outlook indicated by this projection.

The conclusions drawn from this analysis are not very encouraging for the future of the social insurance system. On the one hand, maintaining the current structure of contributions and benefits leads the system into bankruptcy in 10 years or less. On the other hand, none of the conceivable changes in the current structure does anything more than delay the crisis, leaving the underlying financial dynamic unchanged.

Solving this crisis will depend essentially on understanding its determinants. Two elements play a critical role: the depletion of pension fund reserves and the lack of control over medical expenses.

Obviously, a system that has sustained a loss equivalent to 40 percent of its reserve funds before reaching demographic maturity is bound to have serious financing problems. Since investment in low-yield public securities caused this loss, it is reasonable for the public to insist that it be made up with government funds and not additional contributions. Yet making up this loss would require resources equivalent to 6 percent of the total fiscal budget for 1993, making the IVSS one of the largest recipients of government resources, together with ministries such as Education and Health.

Politically, it is hard to see how IVSS contributors could be asked to help make up a loss arising not from normal operation of the social insurance system but rather from the state's appropriating IVSS funds to defray its own operating expenses. IVSS management's current difficulty in attempting to increase the contributions provide a clear example.

It is unclear whether a government contribution is consistent with maintaining a balanced fiscal budget that does not dilute the new resources of the social insurance system though inflation.

To reconcile these two contradictory requirements, it will first be necessary to reconstruct the medium-term reserve capacity of the IVSS Pension Fund through public securities paying market interest rates and with maturities spread over dates determined by an actuarial evaluation of the IVSS. Steps should be taken to solve the system's short-term liquidity squeeze.

The second crucial element in the social insurance crisis is the cost of medical care and the pressure that the deficits these costs generate exert on the system. Inferior medical services and a system incapable of rationally controlling costs characterize the current system. Long lines and low quality care are ways of controlling costs, but they have a negative distributive impact and contribute to capital shortages in the rest of the system.

Separating the role of insurer functionally and institutionally from that of provider of medical services provider is no doubt a complex solution, but it would permit reasonable planning and rationing based on a cost-medical benefit comparison for each of the covered procedures. Without this separation, the insurance system will be virtually eliminated financially.

Conclusions and Policy Recommendations

Organizing Venezuela's social insurance system around IVSS has become one of the system's principal weaknesses. The heavy involvement of the executive branch in managing and financing the system has eroded its financial reserves. Neither business nor union representatives have pressed for organizational and financial modernization of the system. Control and supervision of memberships, collection of contributions, and seeking of investment advice are handled in a complex, inflexible and generally inefficient manner.

This does not mean that the parties who make up this representative body do not exert pressure. Labor representatives, especially those from the medical field, exert a great deal of pressure, but only in defense of their own special interests and to improve their salaries. Yet, supervision and evaluation of medical care, as well as the management and training of human resources in the medical and paramedical fields, are still deficient.

There are no routine administrative procedures for solving the problems of users, except at the level of the board of the directors of the IVSS, where the insured must be represented by union representatives. If the user goes to a regional fund at which he has no formal representation, he must make his own case to the director of the administrative unit.

A more expeditious and flexible organization is needed, capable of handling information flows to ensure a more efficient service. Customer service must be central to settling disputes and claims.

Regional administrative decentralization by establishing local units with substantive functions beyond merely receiving documents is necessary. This would improve corporate affiliation and contribution collection, which are currently handled very inefficiently at the main office. Computerization of the system and access to complete information about the affiliate and his benefits would make paying benefits more flexible and less complicated. Local units should be capable of providing this information to the user, so that problems can be solved without a trip to the main office in Caracas and without having to resort to irregular methods.

There is a contradiction between sound financial management and the system's principles of solidarity that affects the handling of the reserve funds. Short-term insurance is financed with contributions made for long-term insurance, thus jeopardizing the financial stability of the latter. Together with a deficient investment policy, this process has prevented accumulation of the reserve funds needed to pay future benefits.

Widespread knowledge of the potential insolvency of the insurance system and the imprudent financing policy pursued in the last decade eroded system finances. The current fiscal austerity has precluded special budget allocations to help solve the problem, plunging the system into a liquidity crisis and raising doubts about its day-to-day operations. This crisis has already manifested itself in late pension payments, extension of the term of accounts payable and even closing of medical facilities for lack of supplies.

The current discussion is dominated by the public's perception that the injection of new resources without changing the way the system operates is simply a waste of money. This makes the work of the current management extremely difficult because it weakens their claim to needed funds. But this perception could change radically if a reasonable and workable plan were developed that would permit the medium-term recovery of pension fund reserves. Operating procedures to prevent further erosion of resources must also be established.

In the medium term, the plan should separate the pension fund from the medical system to prevent the siphoning off of resources that has weakened the system until now. Ideally, this plan should also create a competitive pension system that provides the IVSS Pension Fund with an incentive structure aimed at maximizing the yield of its financial reserves and that allows contributors to choose other providers if the IVSS fails to fulfill its financial responsibilities satisfactorily.

The medical system should also be reorganized. In the current structure in which the same system contracts and provides medical care, there are no provisions for establishing reasonable cost controls or for rationing services according to the cost and expected medical benefit of each procedure. On the contrary, the current system rations through long lines and low-quality service, which usually results in an even greater waste of resources.

The functions of medical service provider must be separated from those of the insurer to permit cost controls and to ration medical services on the basis of the expected medical benefit. This means that the IVSS should divest itself of the hospitals it now manages and that medical services should be contracted competitively, as is now the practice among insurance companies that sell health policies.

Local government authorities should be involved in administering hospitals. Decentralization would permit planning methods more in tune with the needs of the community, as well as greater control on the part of users. Private sector participation could also promote a more competitive system capable of providing better and less-congested service.

In these circumstances, increasing the contributions (by eliminating the contribution limit) could be presented to the public as necessary to continued operation of the social insurance system. The contribution limit in 1967 was the equivalent of 100,000 1992 bolívares, compared with the current limit of 15,000 bolívares. This reduction was not the result of a rational or responsible decision but rather a consequence of incompetent management of the IVSS in the 1967-89 period. Larger contributions and temporary short-term financing would enable the current management to overcome the crisis in the near future. But without such structural reforms, the crisis will continue.

Bibliography

Acedo, C. 1982. La implementación de los derechos sociales en un estado populista benefactor: el caso del seguro social en Venezuela. Caracas, Venezuela. Mimeo.

_____. 1986. *Necesidades jurídicas y acceso a la justícia de un nuevo sector: beneficiarios del seguro social.* Estudios Laborales. Volume I. Caracas: Universidad Central de Venezuela.

Bulatao, R., *et al.* 1990. *World Population Projections 1989-1990 Edition: Short- and Long-Term Estimates.* Baltimore: The Johns Hopkins University Press.

Chen, Chi-Yi and M. Picouet. 1979. *Dinámica de la población: el caso de Venezuela.* Caracas: UCAB-ORSTROM.

Gazeta Oficial. 1964. *Social Insurance Law.* No. 1096. Caracas, Venezuela: Instituto Venezolano de los Seguros Sociales (IVSS).

_____. 1989. *General Regulations of the Social Insurance Law.* No. 4117. Caracas, Venezuela: IVSS.

Instituto Venezolano de los Seguros Sociales (IVSS). 1946. *Seguridad social: síntesis de la labor cumplida.* Caracas: Editorial Elite.

_____. 1980-88. *Memoria y cuenta.* Caracas: IVSS.

_____. 1989. *Reglamento de la ley del seguro social: Art. 108-09 Reg.* Caracas: IVSS.

_____. N.D. *Guía del asegurado.* Caracas: IVSS.

Márquez, G. 1992. *El seguro social en Venezuela.* Occasional Papers Series No. 8. Inter-American Development Bank.

Méndez, Publio. 1976. *Manual práctico sobre el seguro social.* Caracas: Editorial Vadell.

Mesa-Lago, C. 1989. Aspectos económicos y financieros de la seguridad social en América Latina y el Caribe. Pittsburgh, Penn. Mimeo.

Ministry of Labor. 1980-89. *Memoria y cuenta*. Caracas: MT.

Oficina Central de Estadística y Censos de Venezuela (OCEI). 1936-91. *Censo nacional de población y vivienda*. Caracas: OCEI.

Ramírez, J. 1970. *Consideraciones en relación al concepto de seguridad social*. Caracas: Universidad Central de Venezuela.

United Nations. 1992. *Demographic Yearbook, 1990*. New York: United Nations.

APPENDIX

Table 5A.1. Population Projection by Sex and Age Group, 1985–2030
(Thousands of individuals and percentages)

	1985		1990		1995		2000		2005
TOTAL	17,318	2.66%	19,751	2.31%	22,142	1.97%	24,412	1.66%	26,513
MEN									
0–4	1,306	1.33%	1,395	0.20%	1,409	–0.39%	1,382	–0.57%	1,343
5–9	1,159	2.35%	1,302	1.33%	1,391	0.21%	1,406	–0.39%	1,379
10–14	1,022	2.53%	1,158	2.36%	1,301	1.32%	1,389	0.22%	1,404
15–19	951	1.43%	1,021	2.50%	1,155	2.36%	1,298	1.32%	1,386
20–24	852	2.22%	951	1.37%	1,018	2.49%	1,151	2.34%	1,292
25–29	727	3.25%	853	2.13%	948	1.36%	1,014	2.46%	1,145
30–34	630	2.93%	728	3.15%	850	2.12%	944	1.32%	1,008
35–39	516	4.04%	629	2.85%	724	3.14%	845	2.09%	937
40–44	383	5.98%	512	3.97%	622	2.85%	716	3.12%	835
45–49	302	4.54%	377	5.94%	503	3.97%	611	2.84%	703
50–54	258	2.51%	292	4.51%	364	5.95%	486	4.02%	592
55–59	214	2.57%	243	2.58%	276	4.50%	344	6.03%	461
60–64	160	4.04%	195	2.63%	222	2.57%	252	4.63%	316
65–69	113	4.08%	138	4.14%	169	2.69%	193	2.65%	220
70–74	75	3.71%	90	4.10%	110	4.33%	136	2.78%	156
75 and +	81	1.67%	88	3.00%	102	3.82%	123	4.32%	152
Total	8,749	2.65%	9,972	2.28%	11,164	1.94%	12,290	1.64%	13,329
WOMEN									
0–4	1,254	1.34%	1,340	0.18%	1,352	–0.40%	1,325	–0.60%	1,286
5–9	1,115	2.34%	1,252	1.34%	1,338	0.19%	1,351	–0.40%	1,324
10–14	985	2.51%	1,115	2.34%	1,252	1.34%	1,338	0.18%	1,350
15–19	920	1.37%	985	2.51%	1,115	2.34%	1,252	1.32%	1,337
20–24	827	2.20%	922	1.35%	986	2.49%	1,115	2.33%	1,251
25–29	709	3.18%	829	2.17%	923	1.35%	987	2.45%	1,114
30–34	615	2.91%	710	3.17%	830	2.15%	923	1.31%	985
35–39	502	4.11%	614	2.92%	709	3.15%	828	2.13%	920
40–44	377	5.81%	500	4.09%	611	2.90%	705	3.14%	823
45–49	302	4.31%	373	5.82%	495	4.13%	606	2.90%	699
50–54	259	2.78%	297	4.32%	367	5.82%	487	4.16%	597
55–59	216	3.13%	252	2.78%	289	4.38%	358	5.86%	476
60–64	167	4.29%	206	3.19%	241	2.82%	277	4.43%	344
65–69	124	4.43%	154	4.40%	191	3.24%	224	2.95%	259
70–74	88	3.99%	107	4.60%	134	4.50%	167	3.25%	196
75 and +	109	2.45%	123	3.35%	145	4.30%	179	4.49%	223
Total	8,569	2.68%	9,779	2.34%	10,978	2.00%	12,122	1.69%	13,184

Source: Bulatao, 1989.

	2010		2015		2020		2025		2030
1.39%	28,403	1.22%	30,182	1.21%	32,047	1.04%	33,746	0.87%	35,240
−0.85%	1,287	0.34%	1,309	0.77%	1,360	0.15%	1,370	−0.26%	1,352
−0.57%	1,340	−0.85%	1,284	0.34%	1,306	0.77%	1,357	0.16%	1,368
−0.39%	1,377	−0.57%	1,338	−0.84%	1,283	0.34%	1,305	0.75%	1,355
0.20%	1,400	−0.37%	1,374	−0.59%	1,334	−0.84%	1,279	0.36%	1,302
1.31%	1,379	0.20%	1,393	−0.38%	1,367	−0.56%	1,329	−0.84%	1,274
2.32%	1,284	1.32%	1,371	0.20%	1,385	−0.36%	1,360	−0.57%	1,322
2.44%	1,137	2.33%	1,276	1.31%	1,362	0.23%	1,378	−0.37%	1,353
1.31%	1,000	2.46%	1,129	2.33%	1,267	1.32%	1,353	0.24%	1,369
2.09%	926	1.33%	989	2.46%	1,117	2.36%	1,255	1.33%	1,341
3.15%	821	2.10%	911	1.33%	973	2.48%	1,100	2.38%	1,237
2.87%	682	3.14%	796	2.14%	885	1.38%	948	2.51%	1,073
4.00%	561	2.93%	648	3.21%	759	2.17%	845	1.43%	907
6.01%	423	4.10%	517	2.99%	599	3.28%	704	2.23%	786
4.72%	277	6.07%	372	4.20%	457	3.05%	531	3.35%	626
2.67%	178	4.80%	225	6.27%	305	4.27%	376	3.15%	439
3.55%	181	3.21%	212	4.33%	262	5.72%	346	4.97%	441
1.35%	14,253	1.22%	15,144	1.13%	16,021	1.00%	16,836	0.83%	17,545
−0.84%	1,233	0.35%	1,255	0.77%	1,304	0.15%	1,314	−0.26%	1,297
−0.61%	1,284	−0.82%	1,232	0.34%	1,253	0.77%	1,302	0.17%	1,313
−0.40%	1,323	−1.43%	1,231	0.00%	1,231	0.34%	1,252	0.79%	1,302
0.18%	1,349	−0.40%	1,322	−0.60%	1,283	−0.84%	1,230	0.36%	1,252
1.31%	1,335	0.18%	1,347	−0.40%	1,320	−0.60%	1,281	−0.83%	1,229
2.31%	1,249	1.31%	1,333	0.18%	1,345	−0.40%	1,318	−0.60%	1,279
2.46%	1,112	2.30%	1,246	1.31%	1,330	0.18%	1,342	−0.39%	1,316
1.31%	982	2.44%	1,108	2.31%	1,242	1.33%	1,327	0.18%	1,339
2.14%	915	1.32%	977	2.46%	1,103	2.32%	1,237	1.34%	1,322
3.14%	816	2.14%	907	1.33%	969	2.48%	1,095	2.34%	1,229
2.91%	689	3.16%	805	2.17%	896	1.35%	958	2.48%	1,083
4.14%	583	2.94%	674	3.17%	788	2.21%	879	1.35%	940
5.89%	458	4.18%	562	2.98%	651	3.23%	763	2.23%	852
4.45%	322	5.91%	429	4.24%	528	3.06%	614	3.27%	721
3.07%	228	4.56%	285	5.98%	381	4.38%	472	3.11%	550
4.05%	272	3.62%	325	4.34%	402	5.52%	526	4.99%	671
1.42%	14,150	1.22%	15,038	1.28%	16,026	1.08%	16,910	0.91%	17,695

Table 5A.2. Projection of the Active Population by Sex and Age Group, 1985–2030
(Thousands of individuals)

	1985	1990	1995	2000	2005	2010	2015	2020	2025	2030
TOTAL	6,441	7,571	8,781	10,096	11,475	12,838	14,106	15,204	16,095	16,811
MEN										
15–19	442	475	537	604	644	651	639	620	595	605
20–24	711	793	849	960	1,078	1,150	1,162	1,140	1,108	1,063
25–29	686	804	894	956	1,080	1,211	1,293	1,306	1,282	1,247
30–34	611	706	825	916	978	1,103	1,238	1,321	1,337	1,312
35–39	498	608	699	816	905	966	1,091	1,224	1,307	1,322
40–44	376	503	611	704	821	910	972	1,098	1,234	1,318
45–49	291	364	485	590	678	792	879	939	1,062	1,194
50–54	239	270	337	450	548	632	737	820	878	994
55–59	187	212	241	301	403	490	566	663	739	793
60–64	122	149	170	193	242	324	396	458	539	601
65–69	84	102	125	143	163	205	275	338	393	463
70–74	40	48	59	72	83	95	120	162	200	234
75 and +	24	26	30	36	44	53	62	76	101	128
Total	4,311	5,061	5,862	6,740	7,667	8,581	9,429	10,166	10,773	11,274
WOMEN										
15–19	182	195	221	248	265	267	262	254	244	248
20–24	308	344	368	416	467	498	502	492	478	458
25–29	353	413	460	492	555	622	664	670	656	637
30–34	357	413	482	536	572	646	724	773	780	765
35–39	299	366	423	493	548	585	660	740	791	798
40–44	198	262	320	369	431	479	512	578	648	693
45–49	148	183	243	298	343	401	445	476	538	603
50–54	116	133	164	218	267	308	360	401	428	484
55–59	69	81	92	115	152	187	216	252	281	301
60–64	50	61	72	82	102	136	167	193	227	253
65–69	28	35	44	51	59	73	98	120	140	164
70–74	16	19	24	30	35	41	51	69	85	99
75 and +	5	6	7	9	11	14	16	20	26	34
Total	2,130	2,510	2,919	3,357	3,808	4,257	4,677	5,038	5,322	5,537

Source: Author's estimates, based on data from the OCEI Household Survey, 2nd half of 1991.

Table 5A.3. Modern Private Sector Employees and Workers by Sex and Age Group, 1985–2030
(Thousands of individuals)

	1985	1990	1995	2000	2005	2010	2015	2020	2025	2030
TOTAL	2,324	2,708	3,108	3,539	3,988	4,427	4,804	5,091	5,301	5,452
MEN										
15–19	193	207	234	264	281	284	279	271	260	264
20–24	362	404	432	488	548	585	591	580	564	541
25–29	329	387	430	460	519	582	621	628	616	599
30–34	262	302	353	392	419	472	530	566	572	562
35–39	163	199	229	267	296	316	357	400	428	433
40–44	116	155	188	217	253	281	300	338	380	406
45–49	104	129	173	210	241	282	313	334	378	425
50–54	71	81	101	135	164	189	220	245	262	297
55–59	49	56	63	79	106	129	149	174	194	208
60–64	37	46	52	59	74	99	121	140	164	183
65–69	19	23	29	33	37	47	63	77	90	106
70–74	5	6	7	8	10	11	14	19	23	27
75 and +	6	7	8	9	11	14	16	20	26	33
Total	1,716	2,001	2,298	2,620	2,959	3,290	3,573	3,792	3,957	4,084
WOMEN										
15–19	58	62	70	79	84	85	83	81	77	79
20–24	149	167	178	201	226	241	243	238	231	222
25–29	101	118	131	140	158	177	189	191	187	181
30–34	120	139	162	180	192	217	243	260	262	257
35–39	78	95	110	128	142	152	171	192	205	207
40–44	34	46	56	64	75	84	89	101	113	121
45–49	32	39	52	63	73	85	95	101	114	128
50–54	12	14	17	23	28	33	38	43	45	51
55–59	5	6	7	9	11	14	16	19	21	23
60–64	11	14	16	18	23	30	37	43	51	57
65–69	7	9	11	13	15	19	25	31	36	42
70–74	0	0	0	0	0	0	0	0	0	0
75 and +	0	0	0	0	0	0	0	0	0	0
Total	607	707	810	919	1,029	1,137	1,231	1,299	1,344	1,368

Source: Author's estimates, based on data from the OCEI Household Survey, 2nd half of 1991.

Table 5A.4. Projection of Public Sector Employees and Workers by Sex and Age Group, 1985–2030
(Thousands of individuals)

	1985	1990	1995	2000	2005	2010	2015	2020	2025	2030
TOTAL	1,314	1,572	1,839	2,115	2,402	2,686	2,953	3,190	3,382	3,513
MEN										
15–19	21	22	25	28	30	31	30	29	28	28
20–24	83	93	99	112	126	134	136	133	129	124
25–29	118	138	153	164	185	208	222	224	220	214
30–34	110	127	148	165	176	198	223	238	240	236
35–39	102	125	144	168	186	198	224	251	268	272
40–44	104	139	169	194	227	251	268	303	340	364
45–49	53	66	87	106	122	143	158	169	191	215
50–54	43	49	61	82	100	115	134	149	159	180
55–59	18	21	24	29	39	48	55	65	72	77
60–64	18	22	25	28	35	47	57	66	78	87
65–69	6	7	9	10	11	14	19	23	27	32
70–74	2	2	2	3	3	4	5	7	8	10
75 and +	0	0	0	0	0	0	0	0	0	0
Total	677	810	946	1,089	1,240	1,391	1,531	1,657	1,763	1,839
WOMEN										
15–19	8	9	10	11	12	12	12	11	11	11
20–24	72	80	86	97	109	116	117	115	112	107
25–29	117	137	152	163	184	206	220	222	217	211
30–34	118	136	159	177	189	213	239	255	257	252
35–39	129	157	182	212	236	252	284	318	340	343
40–44	88	117	143	165	193	214	229	259	290	310
45–49	57	70	93	114	132	154	171	182	206	231
50–54	34	39	48	63	78	90	105	117	125	141
55–59	8	9	10	13	17	21	24	28	32	34
60–64	6	8	9	10	13	17	21	24	28	32
65–69	0	0	0	0	0	1	1	1	1	1
70–74	0	0	0	0	0	0	0	0	0	0
75 and +	0	0	0	0	0	0	0	0	0	0
Total	637	762	893	1,026	1,162	1,295	1,422	1,533	1,619	1,674

Source: Author's estimates, based on data from the OCEI Household Survey, 2nd half of 1991.

Table 5A.5. Projection of Contributors by Type of System, Sex and Age Group, and Income from Contributions, 1985–2030: Scenario 1

Scenario 1: Wage contribution limit is adjusted every 10 years

	Contributors		Contribution wage		General system		Partial system		Government contribution	Revenue per contributor
	General system	Partial system	Private	Public	Revenue per contributor	Annual total	Revenue per contributor	Annual total	Annual total	
	(Thousands of individuals)		(Bs contributed/year)		(Bs)	(Millions of Bs)	(Bs)	(Millions of Bs)	(Millions of Bs)	(Millions of Bs)
1985	1,482	535	1,681	522	202	3,587	22	143	682	4,412
1986	1,528	555	1,917	455	230	4,218	19	129	795	5,141
1987	1,575	575	2,391	1,394	287	5,424	59	409	1,067	6,900
1988	1,624	596	2,913	4,431	350	6,812	128	912	1,413	9,136
1989	1,675	618	2,957	1,745	355	7,133	74	550	1,405	9,088
1990	1,727	640	6,406	3,081	897	18,592	193	1,480	3,671	23,743
1991	1,775	661	8,425	4,051	1,179	25,125	243	1,927	4,948	32,000
1992	1,825	682	11,078	5,327	1,551	33,958	320	2,614	6,689	43,262
1993	1,876	703	14,568	7,005	2,040	45,903	420	3,547	9,044	58,495
1994	1,928	726	19,157	9,212	2,100	48,592	553	4,814	9,768	63,174
1995	1,983	749	25,191	12,113	2,100	49,963	727	6,534	10,333	66,830
1996	2,034	770	31,867	15,323	2,100	51,268	900	8,319	10,899	70,486
1997	2,088	792	40,312	19,384	2,100	52,613	900	8,555	11,188	72,355
1998	2,143	815	50,994	24,521	2,100	53,998	900	8,798	11,485	74,281
1999	2,199	838	64,508	31,019	2,100	55,425	900	9,049	11,792	76,267
2000	2,258	862	81,602	39,238	2,100	56,896	900	9,309	12,109	78,313
2001	2,312	884	99,147	47,675	6,409	177,795	2,747	29,134	37,847	244,776
2002	2,368	907	120,463	57,925	6,409	182,074	2,747	29,881	38,767	250,722
2003	2,425	930	146,363	70,379	6,409	186,474	2,747	30,650	39,712	256,836
2004	2,484	954	177,831	85,510	6,409	190,997	2,747	31,441	40,684	263,122
2005	2,544	979	216,064	103,895	6,409	195,648	2,747	32,256	41,683	269,587
2006	2,597	1,001	251,715	121,037	6,409	199,726	2,747	32,980	42,562	275,267
2007	2,652	1,023	293,248	141,009	6,409	203,913	2,747	33,723	43,464	281,099

Year										
2008	2,707	1,046	341,634	164,275	6,409	208,212	2,747	34,485	44,389	287,087
2009	2,765	1,070	398,003	191,380	6,409	212,628	2,747	35,267	45,340	293,236
2010	2,824	1,094	463,674	222,958	6,409	217,164	2,747	36,070	46,317	299,551
2011	2,870	1,115	516,996	248,598	12,890	443,864	5,524	73,926	94,704	612,494
2012	2,916	1,136	576,451	277,187	12,890	451,116	5,524	75,334	96,288	622,738
2013	2,965	1,158	642,743	309,064	12,890	458,558	5,524	76,776	97,913	633,247
2014	3,014	1,180	716,658	344,606	12,890	466,194	5,524	78,252	99,579	644,026
2015	3,065	1,203	799,074	384,236	12,890	474,032	5,524	79,764	101,289	655,085
2016	3,099	1,222	851,014	409,211	12,890	479,409	5,524	80,986	102,496	662,891
2017	3,135	1,240	906,329	435,810	12,890	484,927	5,524	82,236	103,734	670,897
2018	3,172	1,260	965,241	464,137	12,890	490,590	5,524	83,514	105,004	679,107
2019	3,209	1,280	1,027,982	494,306	12,890	496,400	5,524	84,821	106,305	687,527
2020	3,248	1,300	1,094,800	526,436	12,890	502,364	5,524	86,159	107,641	696,163
2021	3,273	1,315	1,165,962	560,655	16,451	646,125	7,051	111,225	138,519	895,869
2022	3,299	1,330	1,241,750	597,097	16,451	651,246	7,051	112,517	139,692	903,455
2023	3,326	1,345	1,322,464	635,908	16,451	656,526	7,051	113,839	140,900	911,264
2024	3,353	1,361	1,408,424	677,242	16,451	661,967	7,051	115,193	142,142	919,302
2025	3,382	1,378	1,499,971	721,263	16,451	667,574	7,051	116,579	143,421	927,574
2026	3,400	1,388	1,597,469	768,145	16,451	671,123	7,051	117,436	144,227	932,786
2027	3,418	1,398	1,701,305	818,075	16,451	674,802	7,051	118,315	145,061	938,179
2028	3,437	1,409	1,811,890	871,250	16,451	678,615	7,051	119,218	145,924	943,757
2029	3,457	1,420	1,929,663	927,881	16,451	682,564	7,051	120,145	146,816	949,525
2030	3,478	1,431	2,055,091	988,193	16,451	686,652	7,051	121,097	147,737	955,486

Projection hypothesis	1991–95	1996–2000	2001–05	2006–10	2011–15	2016–20	2021–25	2026–30
Inflation	30.00%	25.00%	20.00%	15.00%	10.00%	5.00%	5.00%	5.00%
Real wage growth	1.50%	1.50%	1.50%	1.50%	1.50%	1.50%	1.50%	1.50%
% contribution								
general	14.00	14.00	14.00	14.00	14.00	14.00	14.00	14.00
partial	6.00	6.00	6.00	6.00	6.00	6.00	6.00	6.00
Contribution limit	15,000	15,000	45,776	45,776	92,073	92,073	117,511	117,511

Table 5A.6. Projection of Contributors by Type of System, Sex and Age Group, and Income from Contributions, 1985–2030: Scenario 2

Scenario 2: Wage contribution limit is eliminated

	Contributors		Contribution system		General system		Partial system		Government contribution	Income per contributor
	General system	Partial system	Private	Public	Revenue per contributor	Annual total	Revenue per contributor	Annual total	Annual total	
	(Thousands of individuals)		(Bs contributed/year)		(Bs)	(Millions of Bs)	(Bs)	(Millions of Bs)	(Millions of Bs)	(Millions of Bs)
1985	1,482	535	1,681	522	202	3,587	22	143	682	4,412
1986	1,528	555	1,917	455	230	4,218	19	129	795	5,141
1987	1,575	575	2,391	1,394	287	5,424	59	409	1,067	6,900
1988	1,624	596	2,913	4,431	350	6,812	128	912	1,413	9,136
1989	1,675	618	2,957	1,745	355	7,133	74	550	1,405	9,088
1990	1,727	640	6,406	3,081	897	18,592	193	1,480	3,671	23,743
1991	1,775	661	8,425	4,051	1,179	25,125	243	1,927	4,948	32,000
1992	1,825	682	11,078	5,327	1,551	33,958	320	2,614	6,689	43,262
1993	1,876	703	14,568	7,005	2,040	45,903	420	3,547	9,044	58,495
1994	1,928	726	19,157	9,212	2,682	62,057	553	4,814	12,231	79,102
1995	1,983	749	25,191	12,113	3,527	83,908	727	6,534	16,542	106,984
1996	2,034	770	31,867	15,323	4,461	108,917	919	8,499	21,475	138,891
1997	2,088	792	40,312	19,384	5,644	141,394	1,163	11,055	27,883	180,332
1998	2,143	815	50,994	24,521	7,139	183,572	1,471	14,382	36,206	234,160
1999	2,199	838	64,508	31,019	9,031	238,356	1,861	18,713	47,018	304,086
2000	2,258	862	81,602	39,238	11,424	309,520	2,354	24,350	61,065	394,935
2001	2,312	884	99,147	47,675	13,881	385,084	2,860	30,342	75,982	491,408
2002	2,368	907	120,463	57,925	16,865	479,139	3,475	37,811	94,550	611,501
2003	2,425	930	146,363	70,379	20,491	596,220	4,223	47,123	117,667	761,010
2004	2,484	954	177,831	85,510	24,896	741,978	5,131	58,732	146,290	947,161
2005	2,544	979	216,064	103,895	30,249	923,455	6,234	73,208	182,240	1,178,953
2006	2,597	1,001	251,715	121,037	35,240	1,098,250	7,262	87,202	216,819	1,402,271
2007	2,652	1,023	293,248	141,009	41,055	1,306,285	8,461	103,878	257,919	1,668,082

Year										
2008	2,707	1,046	341,634	164,275	47,829	1,553,911	9,857	123,754	306,845	1,984,510
2009	2,765	1,070	398,003	191,380	55,720	1,848,700	11,483	147,445	365,095	2,361,239
2010	2,824	1,094	463,674	222,958	64,914	2,199,680	13,377	175,685	434,454	2,809,818
2011	2,870	1,115	516,996	248,598	72,379	2,492,337	14,916	199,602	492,356	3,184,294
2012	2,916	1,136	576,451	277,187	80,703	2,824,362	16,631	226,796	558,057	3,609,215
2013	2,965	1,158	642,743	309,064	89,984	3,201,112	18,544	257,717	632,620	4,091,449
2014	3,014	1,180	716,658	344,606	100,332	3,628,679	20,676	292,881	717,253	4,638,813
2015	3,065	1,203	799,074	384,236	111,870	4,113,996	23,054	332,871	813,332	5,260,199
2016	3,099	1,222	851,014	409,211	119,142	4,431,108	24,553	359,937	876,282	5,667,327
2017	3,135	1,240	906,329	435,810	126,886	4,773,447	26,149	389,248	944,257	6,106,951
2018	3,172	1,260	965,241	464,137	135,134	5,143,083	27,848	420,992	1,017,669	6,581,744
2019	3,209	1,280	1,027,982	494,306	143,917	5,542,260	29,658	455,376	1,096,968	7,094,605
2020	3,248	1,300	1,094,800	526,436	153,272	5,973,414	31,586	492,624	1,182,638	7,648,676
2021	3,273	1,315	1,165,962	560,655	163,235	6,410,973	33,639	530,665	1,269,626	8,211,264
2022	3,299	1,330	1,241,750	597,097	173,845	6,881,805	35,826	571,722	1,363,250	8,816,777
2023	3,326	1,345	1,322,464	635,908	185,145	7,388,535	38,155	616,040	1,464,037	9,468,612
2024	3,353	1,361	1,408,424	677,242	197,179	7,934,003	40,635	663,885	1,572,554	10,170,443
2025	3,382	1,378	1,499,971	721,263	209,996	8,521,284	43,276	715,544	1,689,416	10,926,245
2026	3,400	1,388	1,597,469	768,145	223,646	9,123,419	46,089	767,655	1,809,077	11,700,152
2027	3,418	1,398	1,701,305	818,075	238,183	9,769,713	49,084	823,677	1,937,531	12,530,922
2028	3,437	1,409	1,811,890	871,250	253,665	10,463,532	52,275	883,912	2,075,448	13,422,892
2029	3,457	1,420	1,929,663	927,881	270,153	11,208,507	55,673	948,686	2,223,551	14,380,744
2030	3,478	1,431	2,055,091	988,193	287,713	12,008,556	59,292	1,018,351	2,382,621	15,409,528

Projection hypothesis	1991–95	1996–2000	2001–05	2006–10	2011–15	2016–20	2021–25	2026–30
Inflation	30.00%	25.00%	20.00%	15.00%	10.00%	5.00%	5.00%	5.00%
Real wage growth	1.50%	1.50%	1.50%	1.50%	1.50%	1.50%	1.50%	1.50%
% contribution								
general	14.00	14.00	14.00	14.00	14.00	14.00	14.00	14.00
partial	6.00	6.00	6.00	6.00	6.00	6.00	6.00	6.00
Contribution limit	—	—	—	—	—	—	—	—

Table 5A.7. Projection of IVSS Expenditures on Retirements, 1985–2030: Scenario 3

Scenario 3: Monthly retirement payment equals one-third of the minimum wage

	Number of retirees (Thousands of individuals)	Total (Millions of Bs)	Total retirements Monthly payment/retiree	
			nominal	1992=100
1985	80.36	879	911.9	7,697.6
1986	91.63	1,019	926.9	7,013.8
1987	99.59	1,151	963.4	5,689.6
1988	108.21	1,455	1,120.7	5,111.9
1989	118.97	1,527	1,069.4	2,644.5
1990	131.80	2,865	1,811.8	3,185.3
1991	144.26	3,998	2,309.6	3,025.6
1992	157.22	5,448	2,887.6	2,887.6
1993	170.70	8,108	3,958.50	3,045.0
1994	184.54	11,567	5,223.24	3,090.7
1995	199.78	16,523	6,892.07	3,137.0
1996	216.23	22,689	8,744.31	3,184.1
1997	234.58	31,231	11,094.34	3,231.9
1998	255.00	43,073	14,075.95	3,280.3
1999	276.46	59,246	17,858.86	3,329.5
2000	300.29	81,648	22,658.42	3,379.5
2001	326.34	108,077	27,597.96	3,430.2
2002	355.17	143,267	33,614.32	3,481.6
2003	386.98	190,128	40,942.24	3,533.8
2004	418.19	250,252	49,867.65	3,586.9
2005	452.64	329,913	60,738.79	3,640.7
2006	490.20	417,045	70,897.36	3,695.3
2007	530.68	526,993	82,754.94	3,750.7
2008	574.23	665,621	96,595.70	3,807.0
2009	619.48	838,161	112,751.33	3,864.1
2010	666.47	1,052,561	131,608.99	3,922.0
2011	711.56	1,254,688	146,941.44	3,980.9
2012	757.60	1,491,507	164,060.12	4,040.6
2013	804.62	1,768,623	183,173.12	4,101.2
2014	852.64	2,092,512	204,512.79	4,162.7
2015	901.45	2,470,021	228,338.53	4,225.1
2016	951.03	2,777,211	243,351.79	4,288.5
2017	1,001.10	3,115,659	259,352.17	4,352.8
2018	1,051.64	3,488,138	276,404.58	4,418.1
2019	1,102.27	3,896,446	294,578.18	4,484.4
2020	1,152.64	4,342,406	313,946.69	4,551.7
2021	1,202.63	4,828,645	334,588.69	4,619.9
2022	1,251.22	5,354,027	356,587.89	4,689.2
2023	1,298.19	5,920,248	380,033.55	4,759.6
2024	1,343.31	6,528,821	405,020.75	4,831.0
2025	1,386.92	7,183,964	431,650.87	4,903.4
2026	1,428.83	7,887,695	460,031.91	4,977.0
2027	1,470.01	8,648,585	490,279.01	5,051.6
2028	1,510.37	9,470,295	522,514.86	5,127.4
2029	1,549.82	10,356,597	556,870.21	5,204.3
2030	1,588.65	11,314,073	593,484.42	5,282.39

Source: Author's calculations.

Table 5A.8. Projection of IVSS Expenditures on Retirements, 1985–2030: Scenario 4

Scenario 4: Monthly retirement payment equals the minimum wage

	Number of retirees (Thousands of individuals)	Total (Millions of Bs)	Total retirements Monthly payment/retiree	
			nominal	1992=100
1985	80.36	879	911.9	7,697.6
1986	91.63	1,019	926.9	7,013.8
1987	99.59	1,151	963.4	5,689.6
1988	108.21	1,455	1,120.7	5,111.9
1989	118.97	1,527	1,069.4	2,644.5
1990	131.80	2,865	1,811.8	3,185.3
1991	144.26	3,998	2,309.6	3,025.6
1992	157.22	5,448	2,887.6	2,887.6
1993	170.70	24,325	11,875.50	9,135.0
1994	184.54	34,701	15,669.72	9,272.0
1995	199.78	49,569	20,676.20	9,411.1
1996	216.23	68,067	26,232.93	9,552.3
1997	234.58	93,692	33,283.03	9,695.6
1998	255.00	129,219	42,227.84	9,841.0
1999	276.46	177,739	53,576.57	9,988.6
2000	300.29	244,945	67,975.27	10,138.4
2001	326.34	324,231	82,793.88	10,290.5
2002	355.17	429,802	100,842.95	10,444.9
2003	386.98	570,385	122,826.71	10,601.5
2004	418.19	750,757	149,602.94	10,760.6
2005	452.64	989,738	182,216.38	10,922.0
2006	490.20	1,251,134	212,692.07	11,085.8
2007	530.68	1,580,979	248,264.82	11,252.1
2008	574.23	1,996,863	289,787.11	11,420.9
2009	619.48	2,514,484	338,254.00	11,592.2
2010	666.47	3,157,683	394,826.98	11,766.1
2011	711.56	3,764,064	440,824.33	11,942.6
2012	757.60	4,474,520	492,180.36	12,121.7
2013	804.62	5,305,868	549,519.37	12,303.5
2014	852.64	6,277,535	613,538.38	12,488.1
2015	901.45	7,410,064	685,015.60	12,675.4
2016	951.03	8,331,633	730,055.37	12,865.5
2017	1,001.10	9,346,977	778,056.51	13,058.5
2018	1,051.64	10,464,414	829,213.73	13,254.4
2019	1,102.27	11,689,338	883,734.53	13,453.2
2020	1,152.64	13,027,219	941,840.08	13,655.0
2021	1,202.63	14,485,936	1,003,766.06	13,859.8
2022	1,251.22	16,062,081	1,069,763.68	14,067.7
2023	1,298.19	17,760,743	1,140,100.65	14,278.7
2024	1,343.31	19,586,462	1,215,062.26	14,492.9
2025	1,386.92	21,551,893	1,294,952.61	14,710.3
2026	1,428.83	23,663,085	1,380,095.74	14,931.0
2027	1,470.01	25,945,756	1,470,837.04	15,154.9
2028	1,510.37	28,410,884	1,567,544.57	15,382.3
2029	1,549.82	31,069,792	1,670,610.63	15,613.0
2030	1,588.65	33,942,219	1,780,453.27	15,847.18

Source: Author's calculations.

Table 5A.9. Projection of Expenditures on Medical Care, 1985–2030

	Beneficiaries			Expenditures				
				Per beneficiary			Total	
	Contributors	Dependents	Total	Hospitali-zations	Medical care	Total	Hospitali-zations	Medical care
	(Thousands of individuals)			(Thousands of current Bs)		(1992 Bs)	(Millions of current Bs)	
1985	1,482.3	3,705.7	5,188.0	0.0	0.4	3.7	230.4	2,303.7
1986	1,528.0	3,820.0	5,348.0	0.1	0.6	4.7	333.9	3,339.4
1987	1,575.3	3,938.3	5,513.6	0.1	0.7	4.2	388.5	3,885.2
1988	1,624.3	4,060.7	5,684.9	0.1	0.9	4.1	513.0	5,130.1
1989	1,675.0	4,187.4	5,862.3	0.1	1.5	3.6	856.5	8,565.0
1990	1,727.4	4,318.6	6,046.0	0.2	2.5	4.3	1,488.5	14,885.0
1991	1,775.2	4,438.1	6,213.3	0.3	3.4	4.5	2,134.3	21,343.5
1992	1,824.6	4,561.5	6,386.1	0.5	4.5	4.5	2,873.7	28,737.4
1993	1,875.6	4,688.9	6,564.5	0.6	5.9	4.5	3,840.2	38,402.5
1994	1,928.2	4,820.6	6,748.8	0.8	7.6	4.5	5,132.5	51,325.0
1995	1,982.7	4,956.6	6,939.3	1.0	9.9	4.5	6,860.5	68,605.2
1996	2,034.5	5,086.1	7,120.6	1.2	12.4	4.5	8,799.7	87,997.0
1997	2,087.8	5,219.5	7,307.3	1.5	15.4	4.5	11,288.1	112,881.1
1998	2,142.8	5,356.9	7,499.7	1.9	19.3	4.5	14,481.6	144,816.1
1999	2,199.4	5,498.5	7,697.9	2.4	24.1	4.5	18,580.4	185,804.3
2000	2,257.8	5,644.4	7,902.2	3.0	30.2	4.5	23,841.8	238,417.6
2001	2,311.9	5,779.7	8,091.6	3.6	36.2	4.5	29,296.2	292,961.6
2002	2,367.5	5,918.9	8,286.4	4.3	43.4	4.5	36,001.6	360,015.7
2003	2,424.8	6,061.9	8,486.6	5.2	52.1	4.5	44,245.7	442,457.4
2004	2,483.6	6,208.9	8,692.5	6.3	62.6	4.5	54,382.7	543,827.2
2005	2,544.0	6,360.1	8,904.1	7.5	75.1	4.5	66,848.3	668,483.4
2006	2,597.1	6,492.7	9,089.7	8.6	86.3	4.5	78,478.0	784,780.0
2007	2,651.5	6,628.8	9,280.3	9.9	99.3	4.5	92,141.7	921,417.4
2008	2,707.4	6,768.6	9,476.0	11.4	114.2	4.5	108,197.3	1,081,973.2
2009	2,764.8	6,912.1	9,677.0	13.1	131.3	4.5	127,065.8	1,270,658.3
2010	2,823.8	7,059.6	9,883.4	15.1	151.0	4.5	149,242.9	1,492,429.2
2011	2,869.5	7,173.8	10,043.3	16.6	166.1	4.5	166,824.1	1,668,241.0
2012	2,916.4	7,291.0	10,207.4	18.3	182.7	4.5	186,504.9	1,865,049.1
2013	2,964.5	7,411.3	10,375.8	20.1	201.0	4.5	208,539.6	2,085,396.3
2014	3,013.9	7,534.7	10,548.6	22.1	221.1	4.5	233,213.7	2,332,137.3
2015	3,064.6	7,661.4	10,725.9	24.3	243.2	4.5	260,847.8	2,608,478.2
2016	3,099.3	7,748.3	10,847.6	25.5	255.4	4.5	276,997.2	2,769,972.0
2017	3,135.0	7,837.5	10,972.5	26.8	268.1	4.5	294,194.7	2,941,947.1
2018	3,171.6	7,929.0	11,100.6	28.2	281.5	4.5	312,511.5	3,125,114.9
2019	3,209.2	8,022.9	11,232.1	29.6	295.6	4.5	332,023.7	3,320,236.9
2020	3,247.7	8,119.3	11,367.0	31.0	310.4	4.5	352,812.9	3,528,128.7
2021	3,272.9	8,182.2	11,455.1	32.6	325.9	4.5	373,323.6	3,733,236.4
2022	3,298.8	8,247.1	11,545.9	34.2	342.2	4.5	395,096.9	3,950,968.7
2023	3,325.6	8,313.9	11,639.5	35.9	359.3	4.5	418,214.6	4,182,146.5
2024	3,353.1	8,382.8	11,735.9	37.7	377.3	4.5	442,764.7	4,427,646.9
2025	3,381.5	8,453.8	11,835.3	39.6	396.1	4.5	468,840.7	4,688,407.3
2026	3,399.5	8,498.8	11,898.3	41.6	415.9	4.5	494,900.1	4,949,001.5
2027	3,418.1	8,545.4	11,963.5	43.7	436.7	4.5	522,494.2	5,224,942.1
2028	3,437.5	8,593.6	12,031.1	45.9	458.6	4.5	551,718.7	5,517,186.6
2029	3,457.5	8,643.6	12,101.1	48.2	481.5	4.5	582,675.6	5,826,755.8
2030	3,478.2	8,695.4	12,173.6	50.6	505.6	4.5	615,473.7	6,154,737.4

Source: Author's calculations.

Table 5A.10. IVSS: Projection of Expenditures on Daily Allowances, 1985–2030

	Scenario 1			Scenario 2		
	Allowances per contributor (Curr. Bs x 1,000)	(1992 Bs x 1,000)	Total expenditure (Millions of Bs)	Allowances per contributor (Curr. Bs x 1,000)	(1992 Bs x 1,000)	Total expenditure (Millions of Bs)
1985	0.14	1.21	213.3	0.14	1.21	213.3
1986	0.15	1.11	224.8	0.15	1.11	224.8
1987	0.16	0.93	249.4	0.16	0.93	249.4
1988	0.17	0.78	279.5	0.17	0.78	279.5
1989	0.14	0.34	229.0	0.14	0.34	229.0
1990	0.26	0.45	447.0	0.26	0.45	447.0
1991	0.74	0.97	1,316.0	0.74	0.97	1,316.0
1992	0.99	0.99	1,810.0	0.99	0.99	1,810.0
1993	1.10	0.85	2,065.6	1.10	0.85	2,065.6
1994	1.13	0.67	2,186.6	1.45	0.86	2,792.6
1995	1.13	0.52	2,248.3	1.90	0.87	3,775.9
1996	1.13	0.41	2,307.1	2.41	0.88	4,901.3
1997	1.13	0.33	2,367.6	3.05	0.89	6,362.7
1998	1.13	0.26	2,429.9	3.86	0.90	8,260.7
1999	1.13	0.21	2,494.1	4.88	0.91	10,726.0
2000	1.13	0.17	2,560.3	6.17	0.92	13,928.4
2001	3.46	0.43	8,000.8	7.50	0.93	17,328.8
2002	3.46	0.36	8,193.3	9.11	0.94	21,561.3
2003	3.46	0.30	8,391.3	11.07	0.96	26,829.9
2004	3.46	0.25	8,594.9	13.44	0.97	33,389.0
2005	3.46	0.21	8,804.1	16.33	0.98	41,555.5
2006	3.46	0.18	8,987.7	19.03	0.99	49,421.3
2007	3.46	0.16	9,176.1	22.17	1.00	58,782.8
2008	3.46	0.14	9,369.6	30.09	1.03	83,191.5
2010	3.46	0.10	9,772.4	35.05	1.04	98,985.6
2011	6.96	0.19	19,973.9	39.08	1.06	112,155.1
2012	6.96	0.17	20,300.2	43.58	1.07	127,096.3
2013	6.96	0.16	20,635.1	48.59	1.09	144,050.0
2014	6.96	0.14	20,978.7	54.18	1.10	163,290.6
2015	6.96	0.13	21,331.4	60.41	1.12	185,129.8
2016	6.96	0.12	21,573.4	64.34	1.13	199,399.9
2017	6.96	0.12	21,821.7	68.52	1.15	214,805.1
2018	6.96	0.11	22,076.5	72.97	1.17	231,438.7
2019	6.96	0.11	22,338.0	77.72	1.18	249,401.7
2020	6.96	0.10	22,606.4	82.77	1.20	268,803.6
2021	8.88	0.12	29,075.6	88.15	1.22	288,493.8
2022	8.88	0.12	29,306.1	93.88	1.23	309,681.2
2023	8.88	0.11	29,543.6	99.98	1.25	332,484.1
2024	8.88	0.11	29,788.5	106.48	1.27	357,030.2
2025	8.88	0.10	30,040.8	113.40	1.29	383,457.8
2026	8.88	0.10	30,200.5	120.77	1.31	410,553.8
2027	8.88	0.09	30,366.1	128.62	1.33	439,637.1
2028	8.88	0.09	30,537.7	136.98	1.34	470,858.9
2029	8.88	0.08	30,715.4	145.88	1.36	504,382.8
2030	8.88	0.08	30,899.3	155.36	1.38	540,385.0

Table 5A.11. IVSS: Projection of General Administrative Expenditures, 1985–2030

	Expenditures per contributor		Total
	(Curr Bs x 1,000)	(1992 Bs x 1,000)	(Millions of Bs)
1985	0.19	1.64	391.9
1986	0.24	1.83	504.3
1987	0.27	1.58	574.5
1988	0.36	1.63	790.9
1989	0.69	1.70	1,576.1
1990	0.97	1.70	2,289.6
1991	1.30	1.70	3,161.1
1992	1.70	1.70	4,260.6
1993	2.21	1.70	5,699.4
1994	2.87	1.70	7,625.2
1995	3.73	1.70	10,203.2
1996	4.67	1.70	13,094.4
1997	5.84	1.70	16,806.6
1998	7.29	1.70	21,573.5
1999	9.12	1.70	27,695.3
2000	11.40	1.70	35,558.1
2001	13.68	1.70	43,711.5
2002	16.41	1.70	53,739.3
2003	19.70	1.70	66,073.3
2004	23.63	1.70	81,245.4
2005	28.36	1.70	99,910.5
2006	32.62	1.70	117,343.1
2007	37.51	1.70	137,832.2
2008	43.13	1.70	161,916.4
2009	49.61	1.70	190,229.8
2010	57.05	1.70	223,518.9
2011	62.75	1.70	250,040.5
2012	69.03	1.70	279,747.2
2013	75.93	1.70	313,026.2
2014	83.52	1.70	350,312.2
2015	91.87	1.70	392,093.7
2016	96.47	1.70	416,829.6
2017	101.29	1.70	443,193.6
2018	106.35	1.70	471,297.3
2019	111.67	1.70	501,259.9
2020	117.26	1.70	533,209.2
2021	123.12	1.70	564,803.8
2022	129.27	1.70	598,371.4
2023	135.74	1.70	634,041.4
2024	142.53	1.70	671,952.2
2025	149.65	1.70	712,251.5
2026	157.13	1.70	752,280.4
2027	164.99	1.70	794,685.1
2028	173.24	1.70	839,614.3
2029	181.90	1.70	887,226.6
2030	191.00	1.70	937,690.7

Table 5A.12.   Projection of Revenue, Expenditures and Total of the Legal Reserve Funds of the Venezuelan Social Insurance Institute, 1985–2030: Scenario 1-A
(Millions of current Bs)

Scenario 1-A: Wage contribution limit is adjusted every 10 years and the monthly retirement payment equals one-third of the minimum wage

	Medical Care Fund				Daily Allowance Fund			
	Revenue	Expenditures	Surplus	Total	Revenue	Expenditures	Surplus	Total
1985	1,601	2,304	(702)	(702)	256	213	43	43
1986	1,883	3,339	(1,457)	(2,159)	301	225	76	119
1987	2,421	3,885	(1,464)	(3,623)	387	249	138	257
1988	3,041	5,130	(2,089)	(5,712)	487	280	207	465
1989	3,184	8,565	(5,381)	(6,830)	509	229	280	1,895
1990	8,300	14,885	(6,585)	(13,415)	1,328	447	881	2,776
1991	11,217	21,343	(10,127)	(23,542)	1,795	1,316	479	3,255
1992	15,160	28,737	(13,577)	(37,119)	2,426	1,810	616	3,870
1993	20,492	38,402	(17,910)	(55,029)	3,279	2,066	1,213	5,083
1994	21,693	51,325	(29,632)	(84,661)	3,471	2,187	1,284	6,368
1995	22,305	68,605	(46,300)	(130,962)	3,569	2,248	1,320	7,688
1996	22,888	87,997	(65,109)	(196,071)	3,662	2,307	1,355	9,043
1997	23,488	112,881	(89,393)	(285,464)	3,758	2,368	1,390	10,433
1998	24,106	144,816	(120,710)	(406,174)	3,857	2,430	1,427	11,861
1999	24,743	185,804	(161,061)	(567,235)	3,959	2,494	1,465	13,325
2000	25,400	238,418	(213,018)	(780,253)	4,064	2,560	1,504	14,829
2001	79,373	292,962	(213,589)	(993,842)	12,700	8,001	4,699	19,528
2002	81,283	360,016	(278,733)	(1,272,575)	13,005	8,193	4,812	24,340
2003	83,247	442,457	(359,210)	(1,631,785)	13,320	8,391	4,928	29,268
2004	85,266	543,827	(458,561)	(2,090,346)	13,643	8,595	5,048	34,316
2005	87,343	668,483	(581,141)	(2,671,486)	13,975	8,804	5,171	39,486
2006	89,163	784,780	(695,617)	(3,367,103)	14,266	8,988	5,278	44,765
2007	91,032	921,417	(830,385)	(4,197,488)	14,565	9,176	5,389	50,154
2008	92,952	1,081,973	(989,021)	(5,186,509)	14,872	9,370	5,503	55,657
2009	94,923	1,270,658	(1,175,735)	(6,362,244)	15,188	9,568	5,619	61,276
2010	96,948	1,492,429	(1,395,481)	(7,757,725)	15,512	9,772	5,739	67,016
2011	198,154	1,668,241	(1,470,087)	(9,227,813)	31,705	19,974	11,731	78,746
2012	201,391	1,865,049	(1,663,658)	(10,891,471)	32,223	20,300	11,922	90,669
2013	204,713	2,085,396	(1,880,683)	(12,772,153)	32,754	20,635	12,119	102,788
2014	208,123	2,332,137	(2,124,015)	(14,896,168)	33,300	20,979	12,321	115,109
2015	211,621	2,608,478	(2,396,857)	(17,293,025)	33,859	21,331	12,528	127,637
2016	214,022	2,769,972	(2,555,950)	(19,848,975)	34,244	21,573	12,670	140,307
2017	216,485	2,941,947	(2,725,462)	(22,574,437)	34,638	21,822	12,816	153,123
2018	219,013	3,125,115	(2,906,102)	(25,480,539)	35,042	22,077	12,966	166,088
2019	221,607	3,320,237	(3,098,630)	(28,579,168)	35,457	22,338	13,119	179,207
2020	224,269	3,528,129	(3,303,859)	(31,883,027)	35,883	22,606	13,277	192,484
2021	288,449	3,733,236	(3,444,788)	(35,327,815)	46,152	29,076	17,076	209,560
2022	290,735	3,950,969	(3,660,234)	(38,988,049)	46,518	29,306	17,212	226,772
2023	293,092	4,182,146	(3,889,055)	(42,877,104)	46,895	29,544	17,351	244,123
2024	295,521	4,427,647	(4,132,126)	(47,009,230)	47,283	29,788	17,495	261,618
2025	298,024	4,688,407	(4,390,383)	(51,399,613)	47,684	30,041	17,643	279,261
2026	299,608	4,949,001	(4,649,393)	(56,049,006)	47,937	30,201	17,737	296,997
2027	301,251	5,224,942	(4,923,691)	(60,972,697)	48,200	30,366	17,834	314,832
2028	302,953	5,517,187	(5,214,233)	(66,186,931)	48,473	30,538	17,935	332,766
2029	304,716	5,826,756	(5,522,040)	(71,708,970)	48,755	30,715	18,039	350,806
2030	306,541	6,154,737	(5,848,196)	(77,557,167)	49,047	30,899	18,147	368,953

Pension Fund				Administration Fund			
Revenue	Expenditures	Surplus	Total	Revenue	Expenditures	Surplus	Total
1,872	1,319	553	553	682	622	60	60
2,162	1,529	633	1,186	795	838	(43)	17
3,024	1,727	1,297	2,483	1,067	963	104	120
4,196	2,183	2,013	4,497	1,413	1,304	109	229
3,989	2,290	1,699	22,762	1,405	2,433	(1,027)	614
10,444	4,298	6,146	34,624	3,671	3,778	(107)	507
14,041	5,997	8,043	50,259	4,948	5,295	(348)	159
18,987	8,172	10,815	70,415	6,689	7,134	(445)	(286)
25,679	12,163	13,516	95,364	9,044	9,540	(495)	(781)
28,242	17,350	10,892	120,094	9,768	12,758	(2,990)	(3,771)
30,623	24,785	5,839	137,722	10,333	17,064	(6,730)	(10,502)
33,038	34,033	(995)	137,752	10,899	21,894	(10,996)	(21,497)
33,922	46,846	(12,924)	124,828	11,188	28,095	(16,907)	(38,404)
34,833	64,610	(29,777)	95,051	11,485	36,055	(24,570)	(62,974)
35,772	88,870	(53,098)	41,953	11,792	46,276	(34,483)	(97,457)
36,740	122,472	(85,732)	(43,779)	12,109	59,400	(47,291)	(144,748)
114,857	162,116	(47,259)	(91,038)	37,847	73,008	(35,160)	(179,909)
117,667	214,901	(97,234)	(188,272)	38,767	89,741	(50,974)	(230,883)
120,557	285,193	(164,636)	(352,908)	39,712	110,319	(70,607)	(301,490)
123,529	375,378	(251,849)	(604,757)	40,684	135,628	(94,944)	(396,434)
126,586	494,869	(368,283)	(973,040)	41,683	166,759	(125,075)	(521,510)
129,276	625,567	(496,291)	(1,469,331)	42,562	195,821	(153,259)	(674,769)
132,038	790,489	(658,452)	(2,127,783)	43,464	229,974	(186,510)	(861,279)
134,873	998,432	(863,559)	(2,991,341)	44,389	270,114	(225,724)	(1,087,004)
137,785	1,257,242	(1,119,458)	(4,110,799)	45,340	317,296	(271,955)	(1,358,959)
140,775	1,578,842	(1,438,067)	(5,548,866)	46,317	372,762	(326,445)	(1,685,404)
287,932	1,882,032	(1,594,100)	(7,142,966)	94,704	416,865	(322,161)	(2,007,565)
292,837	2,237,260	(1,944,423)	(9,087,390)	96,288	466,252	(369,964)	(2,377,529)
297,867	2,652,934	(2,355,067)	(11,442,457)	97,913	521,566	(423,653)	(2,801,183)
303,025	3,138,767	(2,835,743)	(14,278,199)	99,579	583,526	(483,947)	(3,285,129)
308,315	3,705,032	(3,396,717)	(17,674,916)	101,289	652,942	(551,652)	(3,836,781)
312,130	4,165,817	(3,853,687)	(21,528,603)	102,496	693,827	(591,330)	(4,428,112)
316,040	4,673,489	(4,357,449)	(25,886,052)	103,734	737,388	(633,654)	(5,061,766)
320,048	5,232,207	(4,912,159)	(30,798,211)	105,004	783,809	(678,805)	(5,740,571)
324,157	5,844,669	(5,520,512)	(36,318,723)	106,305	833,284	(726,978)	(6,467,549)
328,370	6,513,610	(6,185,240)	(42,503,963)	107,641	886,022	(778,381)	(7,245,931)
422,749	7,242,968	(6,820,218)	(49,324,181)	138,519	938,127	(799,608)	(8,045,539)
426,510	8,031,041	(7,604,530)	(56,928,711)	139,692	993,468	(853,776)	(8,899,315)
430,378	8,880,372	(8,449,994)	(65,378,705)	140,900	1,052,256	(911,356)	(9,810,671)
434,355	9,793,231	(9,358,876)	(74,737,580)	142,142	1,114,717	(972,574)	(10,783,246)
438,445	10,775,946	(10,337,502)	(85,075,082)	143,421	1,181,092	(1,037,671)	(11,820,917)
441,013	11,831,543	(11,390,530)	(96,465,612)	144,227	1,247,181	(1,102,953)	(12,923,870)
443,667	12,972,878	(12,529,211)	(108,994,823)	145,061	1,317,179	(1,172,118)	(14,095,988)
446,408	14,205,442	(13,759,034)	(122,753,857)	145,924	1,391,333	(1,245,409)	(15,341,397)
449,239	15,534,896	(15,085,657)	(137,839,514)	146,816	1,469,902	(1,323,087)	(16,664,484)
452,161	16,971,110	(16,518,948)	(154,358,463)	147,737	1,553,164	(1,405,427)	(18,069,911)

Table 5A.13. Projection of Revenue, Expenditures and Total of the Legal Reserve Funds of the Venezuelan Social Insurance Institute, 1985–2030: Scenario 1-B
(Millions of current Bs)

Scenario 1-B: Wage contribution limit is adjusted every 10 years and the monthly retirement payment equals the minimum wage

	Medical Care Fund				Daily Allowance Fund			
	Revenue	Expenditures	Surplus	Total	Revenue	Expenditures	Surplus	Total
1985	1,601	2,304	(702)	(702)	256	213	43	43
1986	1,883	3,339	(1,457)	(2,159)	301	225	76	119
1987	2,421	3,885	(1,464)	(3,623)	387	249	138	257
1988	3,041	5,130	(2,089)	(5,712)	487	280	207	465
1989	3,184	8,565	(5,381)	(6,830)	509	229	280	1,895
1990	8,300	14,885	(6,585)	(13,415)	1,328	447	881	2,776
1991	11,217	21,343	(10,127)	(23,542)	1,795	1,316	479	3,255
1992	15,160	28,737	(13,577)	(37,119)	2,426	1,810	616	3,870
1993	20,492	38,402	(17,910)	(55,029)	3,279	2,066	1,213	5,083
1994	21,693	51,325	(29,632)	(84,661)	3,471	2,187	1,284	6,368
1995	22,305	68,605	(46,300)	(130,962)	3,569	2,248	1,320	7,688
1996	22,888	87,997	(65,109)	(196,071)	3,662	2,307	1,355	9,043
1997	23,488	112,881	(89,393)	(285,464)	3,758	2,368	1,390	10,433
1998	24,106	144,816	(120,710)	(406,174)	3,857	2,430	1,427	11,861
1999	24,743	185,804	(161,061)	(567,235)	3,959	2,494	1,465	13,325
2000	25,400	238,418	(213,018)	(780,253)	4,064	2,560	1,504	14,829
2001	79,373	292,962	(213,589)	(993,842)	12,700	8,001	4,699	19,528
2002	81,283	360,016	(278,733)	(1,272,575)	13,005	8,193	4,812	24,340
2003	83,247	442,457	(359,210)	(1,631,785)	13,320	8,391	4,928	29,268
2004	85,266	543,827	(458,561)	(2,090,346)	13,643	8,595	5,048	34,316
2005	87,343	668,483	(581,141)	(2,671,486)	13,975	8,804	5,171	39,486
2006	89,163	784,780	(695,617)	(3,367,103)	14,266	8,988	5,278	44,765
2007	91,032	921,417	(830,385)	(4,197,488)	14,565	9,176	5,389	50,154
2008	92,952	1,081,973	(989,021)	(5,186,509)	14,872	9,370	5,503	55,657
2009	94,923	1,270,658	(1,175,735)	(6,362,244)	15,188	9,568	5,619	61,276
2010	96,948	1,492,429	(1,395,481)	(7,757,725)	15,512	9,772	5,739	67,016
2011	198,154	1,668,241	(1,470,087)	(9,227,813)	31,705	19,974	11,731	78,746
2012	201,391	1,865,049	(1,663,658)	(10,891,471)	32,223	20,300	11,922	90,669
2013	204,713	2,085,396	(1,880,683)	(12,772,153)	32,754	20,635	12,119	102,788
2014	208,123	2,332,137	(2,124,015)	(14,896,168)	33,300	20,979	12,321	115,109
2015	211,621	2,608,478	(2,396,857)	(17,293,025)	33,859	21,331	12,528	127,637
2016	214,022	2,769,972	(2,555,950)	(19,848,975)	34,244	21,573	12,670	140,307
2017	216,485	2,941,947	(2,725,462)	(22,574,437)	34,638	21,822	12,816	153,123
2018	219,013	3,125,115	(2,906,102)	(25,480,539)	35,042	22,077	12,966	166,088
2019	221,607	3,320,237	(3,098,630)	(28,579,168)	35,457	22,338	13,119	179,207
2020	224,269	3,528,129	(3,303,859)	(31,883,027)	35,883	22,606	13,277	192,484
2021	288,449	3,733,236	(3,444,788)	(35,327,815)	46,152	29,076	17,076	209,560
2022	290,735	3,950,969	(3,660,234)	(38,988,049)	46,518	29,306	17,212	226,772
2023	293,092	4,182,146	(3,889,055)	(42,877,104)	46,895	29,544	17,351	244,123
2024	295,521	4,427,647	(4,132,126)	(47,009,230)	47,283	29,788	17,495	261,618
2025	298,024	4,688,407	(4,390,383)	(51,399,613)	47,684	30,041	17,643	279,261
2026	299,608	4,949,001	(4,649,393)	(56,049,006)	47,937	30,201	17,737	296,997
2027	301,251	5,224,942	(4,923,691)	(60,972,697)	48,200	30,366	17,834	314,832
2028	302,953	5,517,187	(5,214,233)	(66,186,931)	48,473	30,538	17,935	332,766
2029	304,716	5,826,756	(5,522,040)	(71,708,970)	48,755	30,715	18,039	350,806
2030	306,541	6,154,737	(5,848,196)	(77,557,167)	49,047	30,899	18,147	368,953

	Pension Fund				Administration Fund		
Revenue	Expenditures	Surplus	Total	Revenue	Expenditures	Surplus	Total
1,872	1,319	553	553	682	622	60	60
2,162	1,529	633	1,186	795	838	(43)	17
3,024	1,727	1,297	2,483	1,067	963	104	120
4,196	2,183	2,013	4,497	1,413	1,304	109	229
3,989	2,290	1,699	22,761	1,405	2,433	(1,027)	614
10,444	4,298	6,146	34,623	3,671	3,778	(107)	507
14,041	5,997	8,043	50,258	4,948	5,295	(348)	159
18,987	8,172	10,815	70,414	6,689	7,134	(445)	(286)
25,679	36,488	(10,809)	71,037	9,044	9,540	(495)	(781)
28,242	52,051	(23,809)	53,525	9,768	12,758	(2,990)	(3,771)
30,623	74,354	(43,731)	9,794	10,333	17,064	(6,730)	(10,502)
33,038	102,100	(69,062)	(59,268)	10,899	21,894	(10,996)	(21,497)
33,922	140,538	(106,617)	(165,885)	11,188	28,095	(16,907)	(38,404)
34,833	193,829	(158,996)	(324,881)	11,485	36,055	(24,570)	(62,974)
35,772	266,609	(230,837)	(555,718)	11,792	46,276	(34,483)	(97,457)
36,740	367,417	(330,677)	(886,395)	12,109	59,400	(47,291)	(144,748)
114,857	486,347	(371,491)	(1,257,886)	37,847	73,008	(35,160)	(179,909)
117,667	644,703	(527,036)	(1,784,922)	38,767	89,741	(50,974)	(230,883)
120,557	855,578	(735,021)	(2,519,943)	39,712	110,319	(70,607)	(301,490)
123,529	1,126,135	(1,002,606)	(3,522,548)	40,684	135,628	(94,944)	(396,434)
126,586	1,484,607	(1,358,022)	(4,880,570)	41,683	166,759	(125,075)	(521,510)
129,276	1,876,700	(1,747,424)	(6,627,994)	42,562	195,821	(153,259)	(674,769)
132,038	2,371,468	(2,239,430)	(8,867,425)	43,464	229,974	(186,510)	(861,279)
134,873	2,995,295	(2,860,422)	(11,727,847)	44,389	270,114	(225,724)	(1,087,004)
137,785	3,771,727	(3,633,942)	(15,361,789)	45,340	317,296	(271,955)	(1,358,959)
140,775	4,736,525	(4,595,750)	(19,957,539)	46,317	372,762	(326,445)	(1,685,404)
287,932	5,646,095	(5,358,163)	(25,315,702)	94,704	416,865	(322,161)	(2,007,565)
292,837	6,711,781	(6,418,944)	(31,734,646)	96,288	466,252	(369,964)	(2,377,529)
297,867	7,958,801	(7,660,935)	(39,395,581)	97,913	521,566	(423,653)	(2,801,183)
303,025	9,416,302	(9,113,278)	(48,508,859)	99,579	583,526	(483,947)	(3,285,129)
308,315	11,115,097	(10,806,781)	(59,315,640)	101,289	652,942	(551,652)	(3,836,781)
312,130	12,497,450	(12,185,320)	(71,500,960)	102,496	693,827	(591,330)	(4,428,112)
316,040	14,020,466	(13,704,426)	(85,205,387)	103,734	737,388	(633,654)	(5,061,766)
320,048	15,696,621	(15,376,573)	(100,581,960)	105,004	783,809	(678,805)	(5,740,571)
324,157	17,534,007	(17,209,849)	(117,791,810)	106,305	833,284	(726,978)	(6,467,549)
328,370	19,540,829	(19,212,459)	(137,004,268)	107,641	886,022	(778,381)	(7,245,931)
422,749	21,728,903	(21,306,154)	(158,310,422)	138,519	938,127	(799,608)	(8,045,539)
426,510	24,093,122	(23,666,611)	(181,977,034)	139,692	993,468	(853,776)	(8,899,315)
430,378	26,641,115	(26,210,737)	(208,187,771)	140,900	1,052,256	(911,356)	(9,810,671)
434,355	29,379,693	(28,945,338)	(237,133,108)	142,142	1,114,717	(972,574)	(10,783,246)
438,445	32,327,839	(31,889,394)	(269,022,503)	143,421	1,181,092	(1,037,671)	(11,820,917)
441,013	35,494,628	(35,053,615)	(304,076,118)	144,227	1,247,181	(1,102,953)	(12,923,870)
443,667	38,918,633	(38,474,967)	(342,551,085)	145,061	1,317,179	(1,172,118)	(14,095,988)
446,408	42,616,327	(42,169,919)	(384,721,003)	145,924	1,391,333	(1,245,409)	(15,341,397)
449,239	46,604,688	(46,155,449)	(430,876,452)	146,816	1,469,902	(1,323,087)	(16,664,484)
452,161	50,913,329	(50,461,168)	(481,337,620)	147,737	1,553,164	(1,405,427)	(18,069,911)

Table 5A.14. Projection of Revenue, Expenditures and Total of the Legal Reserve Funds of the Venezuelan Social Insurance Institute, 1985–2030: Scenario 2-A
(Millions of current Bs)

Scenario 2-A: Wage contribution limit is eliminated and the monthly retirement payment equals one-third of the minimum wage

	Medical Care Fund				Daily Allowance Fund			
	Revenue	Expenditures	Surplus	Total	Revenue	Expenditures	Surplus	Total
1985	1,601	2,304	(702)	(924)	256	213	43	43
1986	1,883	3,339	(1,457)	(2,381)	301	225	76	119
1987	2,421	3,885	(1,464)	(3,844)	387	249	138	257
1988	3,041	5,130	(2,089)	(5,933)	487	280	207	465
1989	3,184	8,565	(5,381)	(6,830)	509	229	280	1,895
1990	8,300	14,885	(6,585)	(13,415)	1,328	447	881	2,776
1991	11,217	21,343	(10,127)	(23,542)	1,795	1,316	479	3,255
1992	15,160	28,737	(13,577)	(37,119)	2,426	1,810	616	3,870
1993	20,492	38,402	(17,910)	(55,029)	3,279	2,066	1,213	5,083
1994	27,704	51,325	(23,621)	(78,650)	4,433	2,793	1,640	6,723
1995	37,459	68,605	(31,146)	(109,796)	5,993	3,776	2,218	8,941
1996	48,624	87,997	(39,373)	(149,169)	7,780	4,901	2,879	11,820
1997	63,122	112,881	(49,759)	(198,928)	10,100	6,363	3,737	15,556
1998	81,952	144,816	(62,864)	(261,793)	13,112	8,261	4,852	20,408
1999	106,409	185,804	(79,396)	(341,188)	17,025	10,726	6,299	26,707
2000	138,179	238,418	(100,239)	(441,427)	22,109	13,928	8,180	34,887
2001	171,913	292,962	(121,049)	(562,476)	27,506	17,329	10,177	45,065
2002	213,901	360,016	(146,114)	(708,591)	34,224	21,561	12,663	57,728
2003	266,170	442,457	(176,288)	(884,878)	42,587	26,830	15,757	73,485
2004	331,240	543,827	(212,587)	(1,097,465)	52,998	33,389	19,609	93,094
2005	412,257	668,483	(256,227)	(1,353,692)	65,961	41,555	24,406	117,500
2006	490,290	784,780	(294,490)	(1,648,181)	78,446	49,421	29,025	146,525
2007	583,163	921,417	(338,255)	(1,986,436)	93,306	58,783	34,523	181,048
2008	693,710	1,081,973	(388,263)	(2,374,699)	110,994	69,926	41,068	222,116
2009	825,312	1,270,658	(445,346)	(2,820,045)	132,050	83,191	48,858	270,975
2010	982,000	1,492,429	(510,429)	(3,330,474)	157,120	98,986	58,134	329,109
2011	1,112,650	1,668,241	(555,591)	(3,886,065)	178,024	112,155	65,869	394,978
2012	1,260,876	1,865,049	(604,173)	(4,490,238)	201,740	127,096	74,644	469,622
2013	1,429,068	2,085,396	(656,328)	(5,146,567)	228,651	144,050	84,601	554,222
2014	1,619,946	2,332,137	(712,191)	(5,858,758)	259,191	163,291	95,901	650,123
2015	1,836,605	2,608,478	(771,873)	(6,630,631)	293,857	185,130	108,727	758,850
2016	1,978,173	2,769,972	(791,799)	(7,422,430)	316,508	199,400	117,108	875,958
2017	2,131,003	2,941,947	(810,944)	(8,233,374)	340,961	214,805	126,155	1,002,114
2018	2,296,019	3,125,115	(829,096)	(9,062,470)	367,363	231,439	135,924	1,138,038
2019	2,474,223	3,320,237	(846,013)	(9,908,483)	395,876	249,402	146,474	1,284,512
2020	2,666,703	3,528,129	(861,426)	(10,769,909)	426,672	268,804	157,869	1,442,381
2021	2,862,042	3,733,236	(871,195)	(11,641,104)	457,927	288,494	169,433	1,611,814
2022	3,072,234	3,950,969	(878,734)	(12,519,838)	491,558	309,681	181,876	1,793,690
2023	3,298,453	4,182,146	(883,693)	(13,403,532)	527,753	332,484	195,268	1,988,958
2024	3,541,966	4,427,647	(885,681)	(14,289,213)	566,715	357,030	209,684	2,198,643
2025	3,804,145	4,688,407	(884,263)	(15,173,475)	608,663	383,458	225,205	2,423,848
2026	4,072,955	4,949,001	(876,047)	(16,049,522)	651,673	410,554	241,119	2,664,967
2027	4,361,479	5,224,942	(863,463)	(16,912,985)	697,837	439,637	258,200	2,923,166
2028	4,671,220	5,517,187	(845,967)	(17,758,952)	747,395	470,859	276,536	3,199,703
2029	5,003,798	5,826,756	(822,958)	(18,581,910)	800,608	504,383	296,225	3,495,928
2030	5,360,962	6,154,737	(793,775)	(19,375,685)	857,754	540,385	317,369	3,813,296

Pension Fund				Administration Fund			
Revenue	Expenditures	Surplus	Total	Revenue	Expenditures	Surplus	Total
1,872	1,319	553	553	682	622	60	60
2,162	1,529	633	1,186	795	838	(43)	17
3,024	1,727	1,297	2,483	1,067	963	104	120
4,196	2,183	2,013	4,497	1,413	1,304	109	229
3,989	2,290	1,699	22,762	1,405	2,433	(1,027)	614
10,444	4,298	6,146	34,624	3,671	3,778	(107)	507
14,041	5,997	8,043	50,259	4,948	5,295	(348)	159
18,987	8,172	10,815	70,415	6,689	7,134	(445)	(286)
25,679	12,163	13,516	95,364	9,044	9,540	(495)	(781)
34,735	17,350	17,384	126,586	12,231	12,758	(527)	(1,308)
46,990	24,785	22,205	165,331	16,542	17,064	(522)	(1,830)
61,012	34,033	26,979	208,597	21,475	21,894	(419)	(2,249)
79,227	46,846	32,381	258,918	27,883	28,095	(212)	(2,461)
102,890	64,610	38,280	316,200	36,206	36,055	151	(2,310)
133,634	88,870	44,765	379,816	47,018	46,276	742	(1,568)
173,583	122,472	51,111	447,507	61,065	59,400	1,665	97
216,008	162,116	53,892	510,022	75,982	73,008	2,974	3,071
268,825	214,901	53,924	563,946	94,550	89,741	4,809	7,880
334,586	285,193	49,394	613,339	117,667	110,319	7,348	15,229
416,472	375,378	41,094	654,433	146,450	135,628	10,822	26,051
518,446	494,869	23,576	678,009	182,290	166,759	15,531	41,582
616,715	625,567	(8,852)	669,158	216,819	195,821	20,998	62,580
733,694	790,489	(56,795)	612,363	257,919	229,974	27,945	90,525
872,961	998,432	(125,471)	486,892	306,845	270,114	36,731	127,256
1,038,782	1,257,242	(218,460)	268,432	365,095	317,296	47,799	175,055
1,236,244	1,578,842	(342,597)	(74,166)	434,454	372,762	61,692	236,747
1,401,264	1,882,032	(480,767)	(554,933)	492,356	416,865	75,491	312,238
1,588,542	2,237,260	(648,718)	(1,203,652)	558,057	466,252	91,805	404,043
1,801,110	2,652,934	(851,823)	(2,055,475)	632,620	521,566	111,054	515,097
2,042,422	3,138,767	(1,096,345)	(3,151,820)	717,253	583,526	133,727	648,824
2,316,405	3,705,032	(1,388,627)	(4,540,448)	813,332	652,942	160,390	809,215
2,496,364	4,165,817	(1,669,453)	(6,209,900)	876,282	693,827	182,455	991,670
2,690,731	4,673,489	(1,982,758)	(8,192,658)	944,257	737,388	206,868	1,198,539
2,900,693	5,232,207	(2,331,514)	(10,524,172)	1,017,669	783,809	233,861	1,432,399
3,127,538	5,844,669	(2,717,131)	(13,241,303)	1,096,968	833,284	263,684	1,696,083
3,372,663	6,513,610	(3,140,947)	(16,382,250)	1,182,638	886,022	296,616	1,992,700
3,621,670	7,242,968	(3,621,298)	(20,003,548)	1,269,626	938,127	331,498	2,324,198
3,889,735	8,031,041	(4,141,305)	(24,144,854)	1,363,250	993,468	369,782	2,693,980
4,178,370	8,880,372	(4,702,002)	(28,846,856)	1,464,037	1,052,256	411,781	3,105,760
4,489,208	9,793,231	(5,304,023)	(34,150,878)	1,572,554	1,114,717	457,837	3,563,597
4,824,021	10,775,946	(5,951,926)	(40,102,804)	1,689,416	1,181,092	508,324	4,071,921
5,166,447	11,831,543	(6,665,096)	(46,767,900)	1,809,077	1,247,181	561,897	4,633,818
5,534,075	12,972,878	(7,438,803)	(54,206,703)	1,937,531	1,317,179	620,352	5,254,170
5,928,830	14,205,442	(8,276,613)	(62,483,316)	2,075,448	1,391,333	684,115	5,938,284
6,352,788	15,534,896	(9,182,108)	(71,665,424)	2,223,551	1,469,902	753,648	6,691,933
6,808,191	16,971,110	(10,162,919)	(81,828,343)	2,382,621	1,553,164	829,457	7,521,390

Table 5A.15. Projection of Revenue, Expenditures and Total of the Legal Reserve Funds of the Venezuelan Social Insurance Institute, 1985-2030: Scenario 2-B
(Millions of current Bs)

Scenario 2-B: Wage contribution limit is eliminated and the monthly retirement payment equals the minimum wage

	Medical Care Fund				Daily Allowance Fund			
	Revenue	Expenditures	Surplus	Total	Revenue	Expenditures	Surplus	Total
1985	1,601	2,304	(702)	(702)	256	213	43	43
1986	1,883	3,339	(1,457)	(2,159)	301	225	76	119
1987	2,421	3,885	(1,464)	(3,623)	387	249	138	257
1988	3,041	5,130	(2,089)	(5,712)	487	280	207	465
1989	3,184	8,565	(5,381)	(6,830)	509	229	280	1,895
1990	8,300	14,885	(6,585)	(13,415)	1,328	447	881	2,776
1991	11,217	21,343	(10,127)	(23,542)	1,795	1,316	479	3,255
1992	15,160	28,737	(13,577)	(37,119)	2,426	1,810	616	3,870
1993	20,492	38,402	(17,910)	(55,029)	3,279	2,066	1,213	5,083
1994	27,704	51,325	(23,621)	(78,650)	4,433	2,793	1,640	6,723
1995	37,459	68,605	(31,146)	(109,796)	5,993	3,776	2,218	8,941
1996	48,624	87,997	(39,373)	(149,169)	7,780	4,901	2,879	11,820
1997	63,122	112,881	(49,759)	(198,928)	10,100	6,363	3,737	15,556
1998	81,952	144,816	(62,864)	(261,793)	13,112	8,261	4,852	20,408
1999	106,409	185,804	(79,396)	(341,188)	17,025	10,726	6,299	26,707
2000	138,179	238,418	(100,239)	(441,427)	22,109	13,928	8,180	34,887
2001	171,913	292,962	(121,049)	(562,476)	27,506	17,329	10,177	45,065
2002	213,901	360,016	(146,114)	(708,591)	34,224	21,561	12,663	57,728
2003	266,170	442,457	(176,288)	(884,878)	42,587	26,830	15,757	73,485
2004	331,240	543,827	(212,587)	(1,097,465)	52,998	33,389	19,609	93,094
2005	412,257	668,483	(256,227)	(1,353,692)	65,961	41,555	24,406	117,500
2006	490,290	784,780	(294,490)	(1,648,181)	78,446	49,421	29,025	146,525
2007	583,163	921,417	(338,255)	(1,986,436)	93,306	58,783	34,523	181,048
2008	693,710	1,081,973	(388,263)	(2,374,699)	110,994	69,926	41,068	222,116
2009	825,312	1,270,658	(445,346)	(2,820,045)	132,050	83,191	48,858	270,975
2010	982,000	1,492,429	(510,429)	(3,330,474)	157,120	98,986	58,134	329,109
2011	1,112,650	1,668,241	(555,591)	(3,886,065)	178,024	112,155	65,869	394,978
2012	1,260,876	1,865,049	(604,173)	(4,490,238)	201,740	127,096	74,644	469,622
2013	1,429,068	2,085,396	(656,328)	(5,146,567)	228,651	144,050	84,601	554,222
2014	1,619,946	2,332,137	(712,191)	(5,858,758)	259,191	163,291	95,901	650,123
2015	1,836,605	2,608,478	(771,873)	(6,630,631)	293,857	185,130	108,727	758,850
2016	1,978,173	2,769,972	(791,799)	(7,422,430)	316,508	199,400	117,108	875,958
2017	2,131,003	2,941,947	(810,944)	(8,233,374)	340,961	214,805	126,155	1,002,114
2018	2,296,019	3,125,115	(829,096)	(9,062,470)	367,363	231,439	135,924	1,138,038
2019	2,474,223	3,320,237	(846,013)	(9,908,483)	395,876	249,402	146,474	1,284,512
2020	2,666,703	3,528,129	(861,426)	(10,769,909)	426,672	268,804	157,869	1,442,381
2021	2,862,042	3,733,236	(871,195)	(11,641,104)	457,927	288,494	169,433	1,611,814
2022	3,072,234	3,950,969	(878,734)	(12,519,838)	491,558	309,681	181,876	1,793,690
2023	3,298,453	4,182,146	(883,693)	(13,403,532)	527,753	332,484	195,268	1,988,958
2024	3,541,966	4,427,647	(885,681)	(14,289,213)	566,715	357,030	209,684	2,198,643
2025	3,804,145	4,688,407	(884,263)	(15,173,475)	608,663	383,458	225,205	2,423,848
2026	4,072,955	4,949,001	(876,047)	(16,049,522)	651,673	410,554	241,119	2,664,967
2027	4,361,479	5,224,942	(863,463)	(16,912,985)	697,837	439,637	258,200	2,923,166
2028	4,671,220	5,517,187	(845,967)	(17,758,952)	747,395	470,859	276,536	3,199,703
2029	5,003,798	5,826,756	(822,958)	(18,581,910)	800,608	504,383	296,225	3,495,928
2030	5,360,962	6,154,737	(793,775)	(19,375,685)	857,754	540,385	317,369	3,813,296

Pension Fund				Administration Fund			
Revenue	Expenditures	Surplus	Total	Revenue	Expenditures	Surplus	Total
1,730	1,319	410	410	656	622	34	34
2,033	1,529	505	915	771	838	(67)	(33)
2,615	1,727	888	1,803	992	963	29	(4)
3,284	2,183	1,102	2,905	1,246	1,304	(58)	(62)
3,439	2,290	1,149	22,762	1,405	2,433	(1,027)	614
8,964	4,298	4,666	33,144	3,671	3,778	(107)	507
12,114	5,997	6,117	46,394	4,948	5,295	(348)	159
16,373	8,172	8,201	62,737	6,689	7,134	(445)	(286)
22,132	36,488	(14,356)	57,434	9,044	9,540	(495)	(781)
29,921	52,051	(22,131)	37,382	12,231	12,758	(527)	(1,308)
40,456	74,354	(33,898)	3,484	16,542	17,064	(522)	(1,830)
52,514	102,100	(49,587)	(46,102)	21,475	21,894	(419)	(2,249)
68,172	140,538	(72,367)	(118,469)	27,883	28,095	(212)	(2,461)
88,508	193,829	(105,321)	(223,790)	36,206	36,055	151	(2,310)
114,921	266,609	(151,688)	(375,478)	47,018	46,276	742	(1,568)
149,233	367,417	(218,184)	(593,662)	61,065	59,400	1,665	97
185,666	486,347	(300,682)	(894,344)	75,982	73,008	2,974	3,071
231,014	644,703	(413,690)	(1,308,034)	94,550	89,741	4,809	7,880
287,463	855,578	(568,114)	(1,876,148)	117,667	110,319	7,348	15,229
357,740	1,126,135	(768,395)	(2,644,543)	146,450	135,628	10,822	26,051
445,237	1,484,607	(1,039,370)	(3,683,913)	182,290	166,759	15,531	41,582
529,514	1,876,700	(1,347,187)	(5,031,100)	216,819	195,821	20,998	62,580
629,816	2,371,468	(1,741,652)	(6,772,752)	257,919	229,974	27,945	90,525
749,207	2,995,295	(2,246,088)	(9,018,840)	306,845	270,114	36,731	127,256
891,337	3,771,727	(2,880,389)	(11,899,229)	365,095	317,296	47,799	175,055
1,060,560	4,736,525	(3,675,965)	(15,575,195)	434,454	372,762	61,692	236,747
1,201,662	5,646,095	(4,444,433)	(20,019,628)	492,356	416,865	75,491	312,238
1,361,746	6,711,781	(5,350,035)	(25,369,662)	558,057	466,252	91,805	404,043
1,543,393	7,958,801	(6,415,408)	(31,785,070)	632,620	521,566	111,054	515,097
1,749,542	9,416,302	(7,666,761)	(39,451,831)	717,253	583,526	133,727	648,824
1,983,534	11,115,097	(9,131,563)	(48,583,394)	813,332	652,942	160,390	809,215
2,136,427	12,497,450	(10,361,023)	(58,944,417)	876,282	693,827	182,455	991,670
2,301,483	14,020,466	(11,718,983)	(70,663,400)	944,257	737,388	206,868	1,198,539
2,479,701	15,696,621	(13,216,921)	(83,880,321)	1,017,669	783,809	233,861	1,432,399
2,672,161	17,534,007	(14,861,845)	(98,742,166)	1,096,968	833,284	263,684	1,696,083
2,880,039	19,540,829	(16,660,790)	(115,402,956)	1,182,638	886,022	296,616	1,992,700
3,091,005	21,728,903	(18,637,898)	(134,040,854)	1,269,626	938,127	331,498	2,324,198
3,318,013	24,093,122	(20,775,108)	(154,815,963)	1,363,250	993,468	369,782	2,693,980
3,562,329	26,641,115	(23,078,786)	(177,894,749)	1,464,037	1,052,256	411,781	3,105,760
3,825,323	29,379,693	(25,554,370)	(203,449,119)	1,572,554	1,114,717	457,837	3,563,597
4,108,476	32,327,839	(28,219,363)	(231,668,481)	1,689,416	1,181,092	508,324	4,071,921
4,398,791	35,494,628	(31,095,837)	(262,764,318)	1,809,077	1,247,181	561,897	4,633,818
4,710,397	38,918,633	(34,208,236)	(296,972,554)	1,937,531	1,317,179	620,352	5,254,170
5,044,917	42,616,327	(37,571,409)	(334,543,964)	2,075,448	1,391,333	684,115	5,938,284
5,404,102	46,604,688	(41,200,586)	(375,744,550)	2,223,551	1,469,902	753,648	6,691,933
5,789,839	50,913,329	(45,123,490)	(420,868,039)	2,382,621	1,553,164	829,457	7,521,390

INDEX